"This book contains sixteen sets of st[...] [...] derful tale *The Wizard of Oz*. Any one o. [...] sixteen reflections is worth the price of the book! Bill Bausch has done it again! He has provided here a lovely introduction to the spiritual journey in an easy-to-read format that will enrich the most travel-weary pilgrim who picks it up."

Bill Huebsch
Author, *A Spirituality of Wholeness: A New Look at Grace*

"Another storytelling book? Yes and no. Lots of stories, but this time Bill Bausch weaves them into our spiritual journey. Thus, this book becomes more of a map than a reference volume. Knowing very well that every story is our story and that stories aim at the heart, the author asks us to use them for reflection, meditation, and spiritual growth. He takes his outline from a classic American story, *The Wizard of Oz*. As always, his approach is creative and imaginative, his suggestions practical and reasonable. Walk *The Yellow Brick Road* with Bill Bausch. You will be delighted, charmed, and heartened."

Fr. Frank McNulty
St. Teresa of Avila Parish
Summit, New Jersey

"Fr. Bill Bausch is one of our most gifted storytellers and writers on things spiritual because he is so in touch with both the human heart and God's heart. Let *The Yellow Brick Road* guide you on your own faith journey."

Mitch Finley
Author, *Prayer for People Who Think Too Much:
A Guide to Everyday, Anywhere Prayer from the
World's Faith Traditions*

"*The Yellow Brick Road* is one of those books you'll want to read with a highlighter in hand. Even though it's the familiar Wizard of Oz that William Bausch treats as a modern parable, this book is not *Pilgrim's Progress* lite. Father Bausch uses those fanged flying monkeys, for example, as an unforgettable image of the seven deadly sins, then connects them in a network of enticing stories that will surely find their way into parish penance services.

"If you believe, as Bausch does, that the story begins where the storyteller ends, you'll allow yourself plenty of soaking-in time after each chapter. You might also suggest this as a resource for small faith-sharing groups. The Questions for Reflection make you wonder how Father Bausch can be so enchanting and provocative at the same time!"

Page McKean Zyromski
Author, *Echo Stories for Children:*
Celebrating Saints and Seasons in Word and Action

"Open William Bausch's *The Yellow Brick Road* (ala *The Wizard of Oz*) and you find an engaging collection of stories, tales, and fables; take the time to open any of those stories and you find your own story; dare to open your own story and you're sure to find the real you; risk opening yourself, and, wonder of wonders, you find the presence of God. What one then comes to realize with much delight is that they all look alike, each the image not only of the one before but also of the one who is the heart and center of life, our God."

Joseph J. Juknialis
Catholic priest and storyteller
Author, *A Whirlwind of Ash*

"Classical literature abounds in hero tales of quests, journeys, trials, and homecomings. Many fine books have been written about the spiritual journey and the blessings, losses, insights, and conversions along the way. *The Yellow Brick Road* skillfully combines the two and includes a third dimension. Father Bausch uses *The Wizard of Oz* as a familiar example for the classic quest. He sanctifies the search with his practiced pastoral insights to illuminate our faith walk, and then from his vast resources this master storyteller adds stories that make us stop, gasp, smile, and sigh as we see ourselves in the struggles and triumphs of other pilgrims. This is a book to read slowly, and read again, a thought-filled companion to keep close by as we sometimes shuffle and sometimes skip toward the eternal kingdom.

Diane Crehan
Storyteller and author of *I Remember Jesus:*
Stories to Tell and How to Tell them

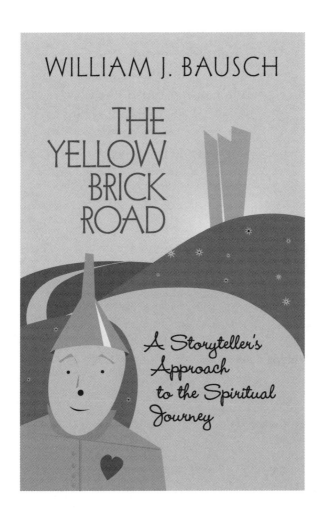

WILLIAM J. BAUSCH

THE
YELLOW
BRICK
ROAD

A Storyteller's
Approach
to the Spiritual
Journey

XXIII

TWENTY-THIRD PUBLICATIONS
Mystic, CT 06355

DEDICATION

To Candide Perdoni Nicorvo,
known to us as Aunt Kate,
on her ninety-ninth birthday:
the last of a remarkable clan.

Happy Birthday!

Fourth printing 2005

Twenty-Third Publications
A Division of Bayard
185 Willow Street
P.O. Box 180
Mystic, CT 06355
(860) 536-2611
(800) 321-0411
www.twentythirdpublications.com

ISBN:0-85622-991-2
Library of Congress Catalog Card Number: 99-71435
Printed in the U.S.A.

CREDITS

CONTENTS

INTRODUCTION

The title of this book, *The Yellow Brick Road*, automatically conjures up an image from the all-time favorite movie, *The Wizard of Oz*. As you shall read in the prologue to the first chapter, this title describes the motif—the pathway of a spiritual journey—which binds the chapters of this book together. The chapters are a series of reflections about the characters of Oz and what they might represent to us as we travel on our own spiritual journey.

Thus we begin in chapter one with the signposts of the journey, moving on to its detours in chapter two. Next, in chapter three, we meet Glinda, the Good Witch who bestows blessings—always a valuable person to have around when you need her! Chapter four gives us the Tin Man who is searching for a heart. He reveals the presence of wounded hearts among our fellow pilgrims, and perhaps even within ourselves. In chapter five, the Munchkins help us focus on imperfection. The Wizard dominates chapter six, posing four questions to test the authenticity of our journey.

The search for the witch's broom surfaces in chapter seven as a symbol of the search for the God who has already found us out. That old scold, Elmira Gulch, makes her nasty appearance in chapter eight. She, the one who would snatch Toto from Dorothy's arms, threatens our self-esteem to the point of almost making us give up on the journey. Scarecrow, in chapter nine, tells us of guilt: he is no good at all at what he is supposed to do; that is, scare off crows. And in chapter ten, that genial fraud Professor Marvel tells us something about loss.

In chapter eleven, the Cowardly Lion shows us our spiritual fears, while chapter twelve brings those malevolent flying monkeys who do mischief on our journey in the form of the capital sins. Chapter thirteen shows us a thing or two that Dorothy learned about what really matters as she nears her journey's end. Uncle Henry and Auntie Em, the senior citizens of the story who appear in chapter fourteen, must face the five challenges of old age before they finish their journey. In chapter fifteen, L. Frank Baum, author of *The Wizard of Oz*, appears to share with us the artist's way of seeing. Finally, in chapter sixteen, we meet the director of the movie, who will lead us through a consideration of spiritual ecology.

Thus, whimsically perhaps, we follow the story of the Wizard of Oz to learn how to understand our own spiritual journey. Special attention should be paid to the book's subtitle, *A Storyteller's Approach to the Spiritual Journey*. This describes the way a storyteller would unfold the journey. Like Chaucer's pilgrims in *The Canterbury Tales*, I use these stories to shorten the journey while evoking revelations along the way. I want to show that the larger story of the spiritual journey is explicated through individual stories which reveal and challenge. Thus there are many stories in this book—over sixty!

Yet I caution against the misuse of these stories. They are not for entertainment: they are for invitation and provocation. Invitation, because they invite you into them to recognize yourself there: the stories are you. Provocation, because they present you with a challenge as you make your spiritual journey. Therefore, respect must be paid to the stories on their own terms. They are best read thoughtfully and reflectively, then meditated on and reread. Many times, this will mean putting down the book, and simply thinking and praying and listening.

Many of these stories have appeared in my other books of homilies and story collections, such as *A World of Stories for Preachers and Teachers*. But such books were aimed at a specific and limited audience. It is my hope that these "twice-told tales," as used here in the context of a spiritual journey, will find a larger readership among the many faith-filled pilgrims in today's world.

Before I end this introduction I should say a word about L. Frank Baum, a nineteenth-century writer who collaborated with illustrator W.W. Denslow to produce the original children's book. Baum was born on May 15, 1856 in Chittennango, in upper New York State. When he grew up he took courses at Columbia, some in journalism. After college, he dabbled in journalism and started several newspapers and magazines. He became interested in the theater and wrote a musical play that was quite successful in its time.

Baum married Maud Gage in 1882, and they eventually had four sons. In 1888, Baum moved his family to South Dakota where he had taken a job as editor of a small newspaper. But soon, the building of the railroads put many of his customers—who were farmers—out of business. This caused his paper to go bankrupt and subsequently, the sheriff seized his assets. The family then moved to Chicago where Baum went to work as a reporter for *The Chicago Evening Post.*

It was at this time, around 1896, that Baum began to flirt with the idea of writing children's stories. He produced his first one in 1897 and another one in 1900 called *Father Goose,* which was a great success. But it was his next book that made him famous, a story called *The Wonderful Wizard of Oz.* He even went on to make a successful musical out of the book, which toured the country. In 1910, he finally moved to Hollywood where he continued to produce children's books, among them more Oz stories. He died there on May 5, 1919.

A final word. Honesty compels me to state forthrightly that both the style (a whimsical outline and the use of stories) as well as the contents of this book are ultimately light fare. They are introductory in nature, a palatable and painless way of arousing interest in and raising questions about the spiritual journey. I pretend no more than that. The very modest aim of this book, therefore, is to attempt a beginning, an awakening, a soft probing into the possibilities of the spiritual life. By introducing the reader to the perimeters of spirituality by way of a familiar storyline, I hope to whet the appetite for the true guides that fill our rich Christian tradition, past and present.

With that off my conscience, let us join the flawed foursome of the Wizard of Oz and begin our journey on the Yellow Brick Road.

ONE

THE YELLOW BRICK ROAD

Signposts

Prologue

Some six hundred years ago, Geoffrey Chaucer wrote a book about twenty-nine pilgrims, who set off for Canterbury on a pilgrimage to visit the shrine of the martyr Thomas à Becket. Along the way, these pilgrims used a time-honored way to make the long journey go by more quickly: they told stories. This diverse lot of storytellers included the bawdy wife of Bath, the gallant knight, the fastidious prioress, and the burly, drunken miller. The themes of the stories they told ranged from adultery, revenge, lechery, and avarice to courtly love and penitence.

This instinctive device—telling stories to pass the time—finds expression in every age. Here it pops up in Irish lore:

Once upon a time there was a Great Builder of Castles known as Goban. One day he was asked to build a castle for a king in a foreign country; to reach this place of work would require a long journey. Now Goban had one son who was nearing adulthood. He decided to bring his son along as company for the journey and also, so that they might get to know one another better. They set out on their long journey. After a while Goban said to his son, "Son, shorten the road for me." The son, thinking that the father was referring to the physical journey, pointed out some convenient shortcuts that avoided many of the twists and turns in the road. This approach did not please Goban, so he said they had better return home.

The next day they set out once more. After a while Goban again said to his son, "Son, shorten the road for me." This time the son thought that the father wished to be distracted from the journey as a way of easing the burden of travel. So he tried to get his father deeply involved in a description of the castle he was going to build. The father was again disappointed and said that they had better return home.

That night the son confided his troubles to his mother. He told her about the mysterious test that he was being subjected to by his father. He desperately wanted to make the journey with his father and win his love and respect, so the mother agreed to help him. She was a wise and compassionate woman and was anxious to make her son and her husband happy. So she told him the secret of shortening the road.

The next morning, father and son set out on their journey once more. After some time Goban asked his son to shorten the road for him. The son began to tell a story. In no time, they had completed the journey. The father and the son established a strong bond of love between them because of the nature of their journey together.

Why stories on a journey? Not only do they make the time pass quickly, but stories try to make sense out of the journey itself. Stories tease out meaning because life is a mystery in which both wonderful and terrible things happen. We have a need to explain the unexplainable—or at least to know that there is some impenetrable purpose behind the events of our journey. We need to know that the journey itself has a goal, a destination, and that we do not really ever travel alone but are accompanied by unseen presences.

Why stories on a journey? Their power—at least the power of a good story—is this: a story always says more than it says with words alone. It may appear simple and sometimes fantastic. But if you try to get beneath the figures of speech in the story and penetrate the metaphors, you will find a richer way to live life. You will also make your journey, if not easier, at least more purposeful. Stories have power because every story, in a sense, is our story.

Tanya and Ezidio, Buddhist monks, were heading home to the monastery after a long journey. The monsoons had just ended and the rivers were swollen. They came to a stream which was overflowing, and there was a lovely young lady, afraid to cross the stream. Tanya picked her up in his arms, carried her across, and set her down on the other side.

All was silent as the two monks continued their journey, till Ezidio could contain himself no longer. He said to Tanya, "Why did you do that? Why did you pick up that young lady? You know we monks are to avoid all contact with women, especially one so lovely." Tanya replied, "*I* put her down on the bank. Are *you* still carrying her?"

• ⬌

Once upon a time a fox said that he would provide worms for any bird that would share his feathers. One bird thought this was a good idea, so he pulled out a feather from one of his wings and gave it to the fox. In return, he received a worm. This was wonderful! The bird decided that this was a good way to get worms easily. But, after a while, the bird had plucked out so many feathers that it could not fly. And so the fox jumped on the bird and ate it. Moral: it's an awful thing to sell yourself like that, feather by feather, little by little.

These stories, like so many others, have a hook in them; they are commonly referred to as "myths." This kind of story catches you at a deeper level than simply the words themselves, for it carries a deeper truth. In that sense, myth says that although some stories are more factual than others, all stories are true; that is, all are truth-bearing. Take, for example, Jesus' story of the prodigal son. Is it factual? No. Jesus made it up. Is it true? Ah, yes, very much so. It is a "myth," if you will, for it tells us a truth about life, love, and compassion.

All of this is by way of preface, because the stories and reflections contained in this book concern the spiritual journey. These stories and reflections help to interpret the journey and give it meaning. Using stories, new or old, on the spiritual journey is actually quite universal. This technique appears in many, many forms in classical literature, not only in Chaucer's *Canterbury Tales* but in songs (*Song of Roland*), epics (*Beowulf*), poems (the "Iliad" and the "Odyssey"), myths (like the Arthurian legends), and admonitions (Bunyan's *Pilgrim's Progress*).

And so, our spiritual journey along the Yellow Brick Road will be a series of spiritual reflections laced with stories. As in the *Canterbury Tales*, many pilgrims will tell their stories along the way. But first, a word of advice: there are indeed many stories throughout this book, and the temptation will be to read them for their entertainment value. But I repeat the cautions stated in the introduction and suggest this: after each story, put the book down. Reflect on the story in light of the context and theme of each chapter. Let the message sink in, then go back and reread the chapter with a new awareness generated by the stories. Most of all, try to discover yourself within each of the stories.

The Wizard of Oz, the story which frames the reflections found in this book, is but a modern retelling of a very ancient myth. I could have chosen any one of thousands of classic stories that abound, but I know this one is familiar to all of you. Just about everyone has seen the fabulous movie—perhaps, like myself, seen it many times—or read the Oz books. What is remarkable about this story is that it is, indeed, not remarkable at all. The storyline of the Wizard is as old as the hills, one of the ancient hero-myths we all know. It is the story of one on a quest who journeys in search of a goal or a treasure or a lady love—or the Emerald City or "no place like home." In each, the hero meets opposition and returns from the journey wiser.

Each of these quests are metaphors for the search for God. Like all myths, the hero-adventurer myth encapsulates the traditional signposts of the human spiritual journey. The three phases of the journey—departure, struggle, return—describe what happens to us as well when we evolve from self-centeredness to an awareness of the spiritual self.

So let us go back to this favorite story and look at the familiar elements. We shall go behind the language and the metaphors to discover the spiritual message. Please note that what I am about to write describes the usual stages of the spiritual journey, a map which helps us to discern our own way.

First of all, the hero sagas start off with a state of discontent. Yes, things are fine as they are; things are comfortable. Still, nothing much is happening (in the spiritual life), and so there is an uneasiness. Dorothy was happy on her Kansas farm with Uncle Henry and Auntie Em and the three farmhands. Yet she was uneasy and wondered what was over the rainbow: were there, perhaps, bluebirds? For us, the question is similar: is there something more? Can I be something more? These questions, these enticements, set up the journey. This is what the spiritual writers call "holy discontent," and Dorothy was feeling it.

Where are you on your spiritual journey? Are you here?

The call

When one senses that holy unease inspired by the Spirit, one is set up for the second step: a call to find out, a call to adventure. In Dorothy's case, this call was a fearsome and hard-to-ignore tornado. And for some, the call may indeed be as dramatic as a tornado, like God's call to Moses from the burning bush; or Jesus knocking Saul off his horse on the way to Damascus; or Yahweh's threefold call to the yet-to-be prophet, the boy Samuel; or Virgil beckoning from the mist to Dante.

For many people, however, the call is not as dramatic or sudden; it is far more subtle. It may be that we suddenly experience a moment of intense friendship, a stunning sunset, or the total trust of a small child who falls asleep in one's lap. In such experiences a person is pulled out of the self and feels a sense of wholeness and harmony. Everything, for the moment, falls into place. Life is not absurd at all; there is meaning to it. It all makes marvelous, grand sense. There is a harmony, both without and within, that is quite compelling.

Some may pause in a momentary trance or in an extended time of ecstasy. (The word "ecstacy" literally means "to stand outside of oneself.") Reality—the ultimate reality of God—looms, not as a kind of overcast cloud or a static ghost-presence, but as One Who Approaches, One Who Calls. (Lest you raise an eyebrow, surveys show that such experiences are much more common than previously thought, cutting across all lines of sex, nationality, and creed. For obvious reasons, many people do not tell such stories openly or broadcast them, but such stories truly happen.)

Carlo Carretto, the spiritual writer, relates with poetic license the mystical experience of Francis of Assisi after his imprisonment and sickness at Perugia:

> Yes, now I saw the sun, the moon, the earth, the springs, the flowers. I had seen them before....But now they spoke to me, I felt them near, I loved them, they moved me. In fact, I did not cease to weep when I beheld a sunset, or the meadows covered with poppies and lilies. Everything seems new to me, ever itself into joy within my heart.
>
> I think my first real prayers were said at that time, although I had prayed with my mother so often before. In any case, I am sure my need to give thanks dates from that time.
> Thanks to the sky.
> Thanks to the earth.
> Thanks to life.
> Thanks to God.
> God! The "someone" that God was, so far away, whom I had known from my Umbrian childhood, was becoming very near and was beginning to speak to me with all the wonderful signs God placed in the sky and on the earth that we call creatures. I began to grasp that God was all around me, and had sent those marvelous messengers, creatures, before his face. I felt that he wished to speak to me. So I kept repeating, "What do you want me to do, Lord?"

Or try this more prosaic story:

> Several years ago a group of computer salesmen from Milwaukee went to a regional sales convention in Chicago. They assured their wives that they would be home in plenty of

time for dinner. But with one thing or another the meeting ran overtime so the men had to race to the station, tickets in hand. As they barraged through the terminal, one man (the one telling this story) inadvertently kicked over a table supporting a basket of apples. Without stopping they all reached the train and boarded it with a sigh of relief. All but the one.

This man paused, got in touch with his feelings, and experienced a twinge of compunction for the boy whose apple stand had been overturned. He waved goodbye to his companions and returned to the terminal. He was glad he did. The ten-year-old boy was blind. The salesman gathered up the apples and noticed that several of them were bruised. He reached into his wallet and said to the boy, "Here, please take this ten dollars for the damage we did. I hope it won't spoil your day." As he started to walk away the bewildered boy called after him, "Are you Jesus?" He stopped in his tracks. And he wondered.

And so it goes. Something calls, something—someone—makes a claim on us. Behind all of these examples is what theologians and psychologists call the human condition of being lost. This point very often occurs in the middle of our lives, in what is often described as a "midlife crisis." Then, many people discover that the attitudes and goals of the first half of their lives do not quite satisfy any longer, that things have not quite turned out as they planned. They realize mortality looms, and that no matter what external appearances may indicate, they are really not the masters of their homes or workplaces. It is precisely at such painful moments of confusion and doubt that a real spiritual journey is possible.

As the masters of the spiritual life instruct us, there is no other way to begin the journey. We certainly cannot begin from a position of success, adulation, confidence, pleasure, or any other means of self-elevation. As the wisdom of Alcoholics Anonymous puts it, you have to "hit bottom" to start the journey: you have to have the experience of being lost. Behind the lilting lyrics of "Somewhere Over the Rainbow" lies a deeper truth, that is, the human sense of being lost and of the search for happiness.

Are you here on the journey?

The challenge

Now begins the third step. It is a time of testing, the challenge to insight. The journey starts out quite in an exciting manner at first; but we soon find out this whole venture is not as easy as we thought, not as romantic. In *The Inferno*, as Dante began his journey he immediately ran into the three beasts: a leopard, a lion, and a wolf—the love of pleasure, fierce pride, and ravenous greed. So, too, would Dorothy meet her own inner demons—"lions and tigers and bears, oh my!"—and flying monkeys, not to mention the Wicked Witch of the West! These represent the sins that block the journey, the evils to be confronted in order to come to insight, to self-transformation.

Those "lions and tigers and bears," like our own inner demons—discouragement, depression, addiction, pride, and the many forces of evil and temptation—are ready to thwart Dorothy's journey. She soon comes to the realization that she cannot go it alone. She will need allies, friends, on this freely chosen adventure. She needs resources. And suddenly, as in all the hero-myth stories, they appear. They appear in keeping with the old Eastern adage: when the student is ready, the teacher appears. The teacher—friend, if you will—is usually a wise animal, often a turtle, as in the African myth stories or a fox, such as the fox in *The Little Prince*. It can also be an angel like Raphael, who in Scripture watched over Tobias as he made his way on his journey. Another example is Virgil, as he guides Dante through the Inferno:

> While I was rushing down that low place, my eyes made out a figure coming toward me of one grown faint, perhaps, from too much silence.

In our story, the friends turn out to be three: a scarecrow, a tin man, and a cowardly lion. Personality-wise, they are not the most stable group; but they are friends nevertheless, who will come through in a pinch. The subject of these first scenes in *The Wizard of Oz*—Dorothy's yearning for something more, her summons through a tornado, the meeting with friends—is part and parcel of the human condition. It illustrates the unease of existence, the yearning for something more, the hearts that are restless until they rest in God.

Responding to the spiritual journey is easy at first, until sin reminds us of the obstacles, until the wild beasts distract us, block our way. Dorothy is us. So are the lions, tigers and bears. Theologian Robert Barron expresses it this way:

> Christian theology begins, logically, with the awakening to crisis, with the sense that there is something dramatically wrong with us. Christianity is not a nature mysticism or system of contemplation; rather, it is a salvation religion which proposes a solution to a fundamental existential problem. Without a feel for the problem, Christianity's answer seems absurd...it is essential, as a first step, to wake up, to break out of self-complacency, to sense, with dramatic intensity, that all is not right.

Ugly trees and sweet apples

The first friend that Dorothy meets on the journey is Scarecrow. With her new-found companion at her side, she starts off again on the Yellow Brick Road. But Dorothy soon has another discovery to make. There is, you see, a creepy and scary forest to go through, with grotesque apple trees that frighteningly reach out and try to grab her. As Dorothy barely escapes their clutching branches, the Scarecrow taunts them into throwing their apples at him. Surprisingly, the apples turn out to be not as nasty as the trees; in fact, they are quite tasty, indeed. And here, behind the figure of these distorted trees, is a powerful metaphor that explicates a major theme of the spiritual journey.

The trees are grotesque and ugly, yet they give out wonderful apples: that is the point to remember. Belden Lane explains in his book, *The Solace of Fierce Landscapes*:

> Thomas Mann wasn't far wrong when he said that the grotesque is "the only guise in which the sublime may appear...." The grotesque reminds us of the *via negativa*, the discovery of God's presence in brokenness, weakness, renunci-

ation, and despair. It exposes our compulsive fears of being vulnerable in a society that values only competence. Our temptation is always to flee the monstrous terror of our own deformity, but by confronting it we discover a spirituality that exults in woundedness. This poses a radical challenge to our culture, however, and necessitates a rethinking of our twisted images of God, grace, and human nature. A spirituality of brokenness shows us how to live in the face of death and all the other threats of the grotesque. Yet it requires of us three acts which are extraordinarily difficult to do in our society.

First, it forces us to admit that grace rarely comes as a gentle invitation to change (remember the tornado!). More often than not it appears in the form of an assault, something we first are tempted to flee. Such was the prophetic experience of Jonah and Jeremiah. For them, receiving God's grace was more like being hit on the head with a book and called a warthog from hell, Ruby Turpin's disconcerting experience in Flannery O'Connor's story, "Revelation." God's grace comes sometimes like a kick in the teeth, leaving us broken, wholly unable any longer to deny our need.

The grotesque form is powerfully able to communicate this difficult truth, forcing on us the inescapable nature of our sin. It serves, therefore, a prophetic function, disturbing us into accepting our condition. It can't be "nice." Only in harshness can it heal....

The irony of the gospel is that it becomes truly "good news" only for those immersed in the bad news of their normal experience. It has to come as a shocking surprise, something so irregular that it may at first seem repulsive.

Like sweet apples from the grotesque trees, Lane is telling us of the discovery of grace in unlikely places, even in the deformities of our own lives: grace is not always gentle, but often times harsh. As Francis embraced the leper or Mother Teresa cradled the rotting bodies of Calcutta, we must beware of the temptation to flee our limitations and ugliness instead of confronting them, in order to discover the grace of broken places. This is a lesson which must be learned on all spiritual journeys.

Questions for reflection

1. Do I feel a holy discontent with my life? If so, can I recognize this as a sign that God is calling me to something deeper?

2. Am I convinced I can be more than I am right now?

3. What incidents in my life, both joyous and painful, have been summons to a deeper life in God?

4. What are my "lions and tigers and bears," the inner demons I must contend with?

5. Who are the companions on my journey? Do they hinder or speed the pace?

6. In what unlikely places have I discovered grace?

TWO

DETOURS ON THE ROAD

~ •

Forgetfulness

Let us recap the elements of the spiritual journey: the holy discontent, the call, the beginning of the venture, insight, and allies. As we might suspect, the journey will not be easy. Even with friends, there still awaits that most potent and most dangerous of all roadblocks on the spiritual journey. It is a temptation that very few heroes avoid, the temptation, I must say, that almost always works. It is the seduction of forgetfulness. Even Jesus was not exempt from this temptation. In the desert, Satan told him to change stones to bread, to jump from the pinnacle of the temple, to own the whole world—in a word, to forget who he is in exchange for the role of a magician and self-serving tyrant.

The same scenario happens in *The Wizard of Oz*. In the movie, the Wicked Witch looks into her crystal ball and sees the foursome on their journey. She knows she has to stop them. So what does she think of? Poppies! Yes, poppies. They will make them—what? Forget! Dorothy and her allies are overcome by the field of poppies, narcotized into unconsciousness, forgetfulness. They stop their journey.

This is a very common theme. Remember the fox and his silly side-kick in the Disney movie, *Pinocchio*, another typical hero-adventurer story? Pinocchio is on a journey to become "real." Along the way, however, he is distracted and gets sent to Pleasure Island. There he forgets who he is—a puppet in the process of becoming a real boy—

and begins instead to become something different: a jackass!

Recall another Disney movie, *The Lion King*. The blurb on the back of the videocassette—a typical hero-myth resume, by the way—reads:

> Set amid the majestic beauty of the Serengeti, Disney's epic coming-of-age saga tells of the love between a proud lion ruler, Mufasa, and his son Simba—a naive and curious cub who "just can't wait to be king." Out from the shadows prowl Simba's envious Uncle Scar and his hyena henchmen. Their scheming for the throne leads to tragedy...and Simba's exile from the kingdom he should rightfully rule.
>
> Befriended by the warmhearted warthog, Pumbaa, and his manic meerkat companion, Timon, Simba forgets his regal responsibilities and adopts the carefree lifestyle of "hakuna matata." But can Rafiki, a wise mystic baboon, help Simba reclaim his true destiny in the "circle of life"?

We can readily see that Simba is but a variation on the prodigal son, who has been seduced into forgetfulness—"hakuna matata," a live-it-up attitude—by his fairweather friends; who, like Pinocchio, was on his way to becoming "real" until he forgot who he was.

In much of the early spiritual writings, the primary sin was forgetfulness. You forget who you are. You forget your mission. You forget where you came from. The very atmosphere of your surroundings makes you forget: the crowd, the language, the dress, the attitudes, the values. On an everyday level, parents say to a daughter caught in some disappointment, "I don't care what everyone else does. You are who you are!" Or, if we commit some blunder, we apologize, "I don't know what came over me. I'm sorry. I forgot myself for the moment."

In the movie *Moonstruck*, there is a character named Rose Castorini, played by Olympia Dukakis. She is the matriarch of an Italian-American family. In one scene, she is the victim of a clumsy attempt by a professor who has walked her home from a nearby restaurant.

"Can I come inside?" he says slyly.

"No," she responds.

"Why not?" he continues.

Her response is, "Because I'm a married woman. Because I know who I am."

When you forget who you are, you fall to a lower level of consciousness like the old Sufi story of the orphaned eagle who is raised as a chicken by chickens and can't hear the call of his mates soaring above trying to tell him who he really is. You can get lost forever in forgetfulness.

The breakthrough to this spiritual amnesia is whatever calls you back to your true identity: sickness, trauma, the loss of a friend, a personal crisis, an outside influence (like Rafiki, the mystic baboon in *The Lion King*, who functions as a Hebrew prophet), or the hunger of the prodigal for food, for home.

Are you here in your journey? Into forgetfulness? Sin?

Awareness

The holy discontent, the call, the allies, forgetfulness overcome—now we must pause. Now we come to the critical question. As we negotiate our spiritual journey, as we pause and take a look at the map, we must take inventory: how do we know we are progressing? How do we know whether we are getting anywhere or just going around in circles? How did Dorothy know when her journey had taken a turn for the better?

We know our spiritual journey is on the right track when we come to a new state of awareness. What have I learned? How am I different? What change has been made in me? In the movie, Glinda, the good witch, raises the awareness issue when she says the following to Dorothy—who is wondering how she will ever get back to Kansas now that the Wizard has accidentally taken off in the balloon:

"You've always had the power to go back to Kansas."

Dorothy responds, "I have?"

The Scarecrow asks, "Why didn't you tell her before?"

"Because she wouldn't have believed me. She had to learn it for herself."

The Scarecrow asks, "What did you learn, Dorothy?" (That is, "What is your new awareness?")

Dorothy thinks a minute and replies, "I think it wasn't enough just to want to see Uncle Henry and Auntie Em. And if I ever go looking for my heart's desire again, I won't look any farther than my own backyard. Because if it isn't there, I never lost it to begin with. Is that right?"

Dorothy has learned something. She sees differently. A new inner awareness has taken hold of her. That is how she knows she is on the right track and is now ready to take a major step in getting back to Kansas. Awareness is the engine of the rest of life's journey. Learning to see is the key, *for you see what you are.* The Talmud says: "We do not see things as they are. We see things as *we* are." Robert Barron puts it another way:

Christianity is, above all, a way of seeing. Everything else in Christian life flows from and circles around the transformation of vision. Christians see differently, and that is why their prayer, their worship, their action, their whole way of being in the world, has a distinctive accent and flavor. What unites figures as diverse as James Joyce, Caravaggio, John Milton, the architect of Chartres, Dorothy Day, Dietrich Bonhoffer, and the later Bob Dylan is a peculiar and distinctive take on things, a style, a way, which flows finally from Jesus of Nazareth.

Origen of Alexandria once remarked that holiness is seeing with the eyes of Christ. Teilhard de Chardin said with great passion that his mission as a Christian thinker was to help people see, and Thomas Aquinas said that the ultimate goal of the Christian life is a "beatific vision," an act of seeing.

As Rabbi Harold Kushner writes in his book, *Who Needs God*: "Religion is not primarily a set of beliefs, a collection of prayers or a series of rituals. Religion is first and foremost a way of seeing. It can't change the facts about the world we live in, but it can change the way we see those facts, and that in itself can often make a difference."

This inner awareness, then, is the beginning of spiritual transformation. Learning to see outside in the same way you see inside is the way the spiritual life works. The hidden avenues of grace are always there. You have to learn to be aware of them. As the Buddha says: "Just don't do something. Stand there!"

Notice. Be aware of God's presence and grace in your everyday life. In the movie, Dorothy says about her home in Kansas: "I never lost it to begin with, did I?" No, Dorothy never lost it. What she was seeking was there all the time; she was just unaware of it.

Remember the musical, *Man of La Mancha?* It is the story of the ridiculed Don Quixote who lives with the illusion of being a knight of old, battling windmills that he imagines are dragons. Near the end of the musical, Don Quixote is dying. At his side is Aldonza, a worthless slut he has idealized by calling her Dulcinea—Sweet One—much to the howling laughter of the townsfolk. But Don Quixote has loved her in a way unlike anything she has ever experienced. When Don Quixote breathes his last, Aldonza begins to sing "The Impossible Dream." As the last echo of the song dies away, someone shouts to her, "Aldonza!" But she pulls herself up proudly and responds: "My name is Dulcinea."

What a gospel moment! What a replay of the way God loves us with all our sluttiness, as it were. The crazy knight's love had transformed Aldonza, giving her a new awareness of herself as Dulcinea. With her awareness, why would she ever return to sin? She is like the woman in the Gospel who was caught in adultery. Jesus told her: "Go; sin no more." That is, you can become more than you were. Remember Francis's new awareness: "Yes, now I saw the sun, the moon, the earth, the springs, the flowers, I had seen them before....But now they spoke to me...."

Awareness is the key to the spiritual life. It makes all the difference in how we live and love, how we act. Our challenge and task is to become more aware of what is going on around us; doing so is a sign that the journey is moving in the right direction.

In his book, *The Seven Habits of Highly Successful People*, Steve Covey gives us a simple example of a change of awareness. He writes:

I remember one Sunday morning on a subway in New York. People were sitting quietly—some reading newspapers, some lost in thought, some resting with their eyes closed. It was a calm, peaceful scene.

A man and his children entered the car. The children were soon yelling back and forth, throwing things, even grabbing people's papers. It was very disturbing and yet, the father, sitting next to me, did nothing.

It was not difficult to feel irritated. I could not believe he could be so insensitive as to let his children run wild and do nothing about it. It was easy to see that everyone else on the subway felt irritated too. So finally, with what I felt was unusual patience and restraint, I said, "Sir, your children are really disturbing a lot of people. I wonder if you couldn't control them a little more?"

The man lifted his gaze as if coming to a consciousness of the situation for the first time and said softly, "Oh, you're right. I guess I should do something about it. We just came from the hospital where their mother died about an hour ago. I don't know what to think and I guess they don't know how to handle it, either."

Can you imagine what I felt at that moment? Suddenly, I saw things differently. I felt differently. I behaved differently. My irritation vanished. I didn't have to worry about controlling my attitude or my behavior; my heart was filled with this man's pain. Feelings of sympathy and compassion flowed freely. "Your wife just died? Oh, I'm so sorry! Can you tell me about it? What can I do to help?"

Everything had changed in that instant of a new awareness.

Remember that wonderful book, Norton Juster's *The Phantom Tollbooth?* In it, the boy, Milo, travels to the Kingdom of Knowledge. Everywhere he goes Milo learns life-lessons. Here is a lesson from a character named Alec Bings at the "Point of View" Station:

"From here that looks like a bucket of water," Alec said, pointing to a bucket of water, "but from an ant's point of view it's a vast ocean, from an elephant's, just a cool drink, and to a fish, of course, it's home. So, you see, the way you see things depends a great deal on where you look at them from."

Recall Shelley's couplet:

> Two men looked out their prison bars;
> the one saw mud, the other stars.

Or how about this scene from Dostoyevsky's *The Brothers Karamazov*, where Father Zosima's brother, who had left his faith, returns to it during his last illness. The novelist says of the brother:

> The first birds of spring were flitting in the branches, chirping and singing in the windows....Looking at them and admiring them, he began suddenly begging their forgiveness... "Birds of heaven, happy birds, forgive me, for I have sinned against you too."
>
> None of us could understand that at the time, but he shed tears of joy. "Yes," he said, "there was such glory of God all about me; birds, trees, meadows, sky, only I lived in shame and dishonored it all and did not notice the beauty and the glory."

Awareness is the stuff of endless movies and classic novels and epiphanies of all sorts. The awareness metaphor, often used in the gospels, is seeing. "Now I see. What a fool I have been!" Think of Helen Keller, locked in her own world, the day she discovered she was not alone, the day she associated the wet well water with the funny game Annie Sullivan played in her hand. On that day, she became aware of a whole new world. In Greek mythology, Oedipus suddenly comprehends his pride, not when he killed his father and married his mother, but when he made himself equal to the gods. His understanding of everything—everything—is utterly changed: he knows, he becomes aware, that he has been totally wrong about the gods, about himself, about everything. He sees it all clearly now.

In the play *Our Town*, little Emily comes back from the dead to experience just one ordinary day of her life and she cannot stand it, now that she understands what is really important. She asks the stage manager, "Do any human beings ever realize life while they live it?— every, every minute?" And he says, "No. The saints and poets, maybe—they do some." And, of course, Charles Dickens gives us the classic story of a "blind" man given sight, a man scared to death into a new awareness: Ebenezer Scrooge.

Scrooge verbalized his discontent with a loud "Bah, humbug!" His call to something more, a call quite as unsettling as Dorothy's experience with the tornado, came in the form of the fearsome ghost of Marley, who moaned and rattled chains and locks. Scrooge further encountered "lions and tigers and bears," that is, the dreadful presences of Christmas past, present, and future. While reviewing his past, Scrooge discovered that he did indeed have allies for his journey, but he had discarded them along the way: his sister, Fan; his true love, Belle; his nephew, Fred; his soulful employee, Bob Cratchit; and the life-giving Mr. Fezziwig. Ultimately, however, it was a child—"a little child shall lead them" (Is 11:6)—who lifted the scales from Scrooge's eyes and gave him a new spiritual awareness. (This tale, too, is a variation on the hero-myth.)

Awareness is the infallible sign of progress on the spiritual journey, even though there is a long way to go. This is found especially in the awareness of God, of God's unconditional love for you, of your own dignity as God's son or daughter, of God's nearness: all of these affect your life and your conduct. When you see who you are—my Beloved, in whom I am well pleased—a turning point has been reached. Henri Nouwen says it well:

> Once we have come to the deep inner knowledge, a knowledge more of the heart than of the mind, that we are born out of love, and will die into love, that every part of our being is deeply rooted in love, and that this love is our true father and mother, then all forms of evil (including illness and death) lose their final power over us.

Awareness is both the means and the goal. If we have not moved into a new awareness—a new sense of who we are, what we are, a new sense of possibilities, of God's presence—then we are stuck on the journey.

So what does *The Wizard of Oz*—all stories, for that matter—have to say to us? It tells us that there are well-worn markers, signposts, on the spiritual journey, and that all steps must be negotiated. Remember, it all starts with a divine nagging, if you will, at our troubled state of innocence. "I'm OK" gives way to, "But still, something is missing."

This, in turn, gives way to the call: you can be, ought to be, more than you are right now. God is calling you. You do not have to be stuck in your role, your reputation, your sin, your mistakes. The amazing grace which saves wretches like us is out there beckoning. There is, in other words, a restlessness rooted in Augustine's famous phrase: our hearts are restless until they rest in you.

First, we hear the call, feel the inner need, answer the inner compulsion to journey toward God. Inevitably, the testing comes, a challenge. Obstacles within and without threaten the journey: fears, guilt, mocking companions, and above all, the seduction of forgetfulness. Here we need allies, teachers, companions, "soul friends" to survive the testing. We need time apart, time spent with the saints and mystics: the day of recollection, the retreat, quiet time. Slowly, a new awareness—of God, of ourselves as Beloved, of others—signals that the journey, although it may still be fraught with difficulties and uncertainties, is on the right track. The Emerald City is not far away.

Map guidelines

Let me underscore four important points.

1. *There is an absolute need for self-denial, or purgation, to negotiate the spiritual journey, even to begin it.* We are as much defined by what we say "no" to as by what we say "yes" to. Self-denial is one way we learn to listen. It means discipline, the strength to pull back from our culture and its stories, which constantly tell us that we are merely self-measuring units of consumption.

We are immersed in a culture which, as Father William O'Malley puts it, gives us "a world in which anyone who doesn't sport Nikes, or drives a five-year-old car, or hasn't bid farewell to virginity by age eighteen is a loser." We are conditioned by a profit-driven media which speaks seriously of "filling the marketing niche for one-to-two year olds." Subconsciously exposed to several thousand commercials a day, we are so saturated with the secular media and its values that Catholics live, spend money, act, vote, and have the same values as everyone else on matters such as assisted suicide, abortion, materialism, and greed. Like Pinocchio, we are constantly seduced to Pleasure Island instead of Treasure Island: "Where your heart is, there also is your treasure."

Anyone who is seriously interested in traversing the Yellow Brick Road must, like Jesus, occasionally go apart from the culture in order to gain perspective, to study the map, to reflect on questions such as "Who am I? What am I becoming?" We need to take our children away from the television set, and read to them and give them books on the lives of the saints. We need to lead them by the hand through Harlem or encourage them to go to Appalachia or the local soup kitchen, and there encounter the stories of fall and redemption and everyday grace.

2. *We need allies, a faith-sharing community—people who think the spiritual life is real.* Our culture is highly restrictive of consciousness. If we try to rise to a new level of consciousness, we will be suspect. But we need supportive people who affirm our journey. We do live by more than bread alone. A culture which values only certain experiences and declares that these are the only valid ones makes it difficult for people to seek deeper levels. This is why so many spiritual stories tell of people trying to break out of the herd—Francis of Assisi, Thomas Merton, Dorothy Day, and the like.

3. *We need teachers.* If we want to play basketball, we've got to play with better players, not ones who are worse than ourselves. We have to hang around with people who are further along the spiritual path, who seem integrated. We need role models and mentors. The saints and mystics, with their example of living faith-filled lives, have to be our companions on the spiritual journey.

We need spiritual directors and guides. And here we can refer to Sam Keen's practical criteria for choosing one. First, we must ask: does this spiritual authority offer a universal blueprint for salvation or a ready-made map for the spiritual journey? If so, run for your life! Life just isn't that simple or neat. Next, ask this: does this leader demand that you place loyalty to him or her higher than loyalty to your spouse or family? If so, then say a quick good-bye. Finally, does your spiritual guide have any friends, a community of equals? Or does this guide have only disciples? Nobody can claim universal compassion or love if they cannot have or keep friends.

As we seek a spiritual mentor, our notion of someone "spiritual" can be distorted. We usually envision someone who is wan, ethereal, just barely tolerating this messy earthly existence of ours. Eyes rolled up toward heaven, they look ascetic, constipated, other-worldly. No lust for life here. This little parable is apropos:

> When the devil saw a seeker of truth enter the house of the Master, he was determined to do everything in his power to turn him back from his quest. So he subjected him to every form of temptation—wealth, lust, prestige—but the seeker was able to fight off these temptations quite easily.
>
> But that changed when he actually got to the Master's house. There he was somewhat taken aback to see the Master sitting in an upholstered chair with his disciples at his feet. "That man certainly lacks humility, the principal virtue of saints," he thought to himself. Then he observed other things about the Master he did not like. For one thing, the Master took little notice of him. "I suppose that's because I do not fawn over him like the others do," he said to himself. He also disliked the kind of clothes the Master wore and the somewhat conceited way that he spoke. And all this led him to the conclusion that he had come to the wrong place and must continue his quest elsewhere.
>
> As he walked out of the room the Master, who had seen the devil seated in the corner of the room, said, "You need not have worried, tempter. He was yours from the very first, you know."

No, our spiritual guide should be someone who has friends, who laughs easily, who loves life.

4. *Since the spiritual journey is a human one, there will be reverses and false starts.* Sometimes this means we will have to go back to square one and begin all over again. We may have to join the woman who prayed "O God of the Second Chance, here I am again!" But that is OK. We can never weary God.

So now, we are all off to see the Wizard, the wonderful Wizard of heaven and earth. How do we get there? The Munchkins' advice is still valid. Follow the Yellow Brick Road, pay attention to the sign-posts, and don't travel alone. If we're off on the Yellow Brick Road to see the Wizard, we must negotiate the stages of the map—or at least use them as a guide for self-examination.

Questions for reflection

1. "I know who I am," said Rose Castorini. Do I know who I am?

2. Who or what makes me forget my identity as beloved of God?

3. How does my awareness of myself, others, and God shape my actions and attitudes?

4. "We do not see things as they are but as *we* are." So how am I?

5. "Christianity is a way of seeing." How do I see?

THREE

GLINDA

Blessing

Poor Esau. He said to his near-blind father, Isaac, "Let my father sit up and eat of his son's game, so that you may bless me" (Gen 27:31)—only to find out with dismay that his double-dealing brother Jacob had already stolen the blessing. And poor old bewildered Isaac, in a fit of trembling, could only reply, "Your brother has come to me deceitfully and he has taken away your blessing."

Poor Esau. To travel life's spiritual journey unblessed, without the sustenance of either a heritage or a promise, is a cruel fate. A blessing is a powerful thing to give—or to withhold. Blessing. It makes the journey light, while its lack makes the journey heavy. The blessing of the good witch, Glinda, made Dorothy's journey light, while the Wicked Witch of the West made it heavy. In this reflection I would like to share with you the theme of blessing for the journey, and the stories that tell of it.

In his book, *Against an Infinite Horizon*, Ronald Rolheiser says that several years ago he preached a homily on the baptism of Jesus. He remarked that the words which God speaks over Jesus at his baptism—"this is my beloved child in whom I take delight"—are words that God daily speaks to us. Some hours later, his doorbell rang and he was approached by a young man who had heard the homily and was both moved and distraught by it. The man had not been to church for some time, but had gone on this particular Sunday because he had pled guilty to a crime and was awaiting sentence. He was soon to go to prison.

The homily had struck a painful chord inside him because, first of all, he had trouble believing that God or anyone else loved him. Yet he wanted to believe this. Second, and even more painfully, he believed that nobody had ever been pleased or delighted with him. "Father," he said, "I know that in my whole life, nobody has ever been pleased with me. I was never good enough! Nobody has ever taken delight in anything I've ever done!" This young man had never been blessed; small wonder that he was about to go to prison.

What does it mean to be blessed? Blessing means three things. It means to speak well, to see well, and to pass on well.

To speak well

The word "bless," as you Latin scholars know, comes from *benedicere*—*bene*, meaning "well," and *dicere*, meaning "to speak." Therefore, to bless someone is to speak well of him or her. When I left home at seventeen for the seminary my father and mother blessed me. They made me kneel on the old linoleum floor of our kitchen, placed their hands on my head, and said the ritual words of Christian blessing which meant, "You are our beloved child in whom we are well pleased." I suspect that, had the young man whom Rolheiser writes of been blessed the same way by his parents—or anyone else significant to him—he would not be on his way to prison.

To be unblessed is to be bleeding in a very deep place. So much of our hunger is hunger for a blessing. So much of our aching is the ache to be blessed. So much of our sadness comes from the fact that nobody has ever taken delight and pleasure in us in a nonexploitative way.

Let me give you a rather poignant and candid example of an unblessing from a well-known Trappist, Father Vince Dwyer. I remember once hearing him tell about his life and his dad. Dwyer was raised in a clamdigging and farm community in New England, as his accent betrays. He was an early high school dropout who joined the Navy when he was old enough. (Remnants of that experience are heard in his vocabulary, which can be a trifle salty at times!)

Dwyer had a troubled relationship with his dad. He was always being put down by his father, who constantly reminded him that his brothers were brighter and smarter than himself, and that he was always doing everything wrong. Dwyer relates:

> You know, the imagery came to me one day when I was walking alone. I was a grown man now, a priest, and I had come back home. I went up to the farm and up in the barn there was a trapdoor and that's where they stored all the manure. They would open the trapdoor and then shovel the manure into the wagons and spread it out into the fields.
>
> Suddenly it hit me. That was the perfect imagery. Every time I tried to do something, somebody would kick the door open and I would be standing under the manure as it came tumbling down on me. Every time I wanted to do something, you know, every time I thought I was right, somebody put me down. The manure came tumbling. Every time I wanted to try something, they said I couldn't do it. More manure. No wonder I grew up with a very poor self-image and could not believe that God loved me. And my father was always on my back and said to me all the time, "You'll never wind up being anything but a clamdigger."
>
> Well, now I was a priest. I had finally gotten out of the Navy. I had graduated from high school and I went to college. Not only did I go to college, but I was first in my class. And then when I became a priest, they sent me to Catholic University and I got highest honors in my degree in theology. And I had a degree in psychology.
>
> So, here I am, walking along with my dad along the beachfront in Massachusetts, feeling good about myself, and my dad walks along and he says, "Well, I never thought you'd amount to anything." The trapdoor. More manure. "But I guess you made it and you can thank your mother and me for that."
>
> I said, "Dad, what kind of language is that? What do you mean, thank you and Mom for that?"
>
> He said, "You can thank us because we motivated you."
>
> I said, "Motivated? You always told me I'd wind up doing

nothing but digging clams."

He said, "That's what I mean, Son. If I told you you were good, you'd get proud. You'd never try. I always had to keep on your back."

"Dad," I said, "in all those years, you mean to say, when you put me down all those years when you said I'd never amount to anything, you were motivating me?"

"That's right."

I said, "Why?"

He said, "You have to ask that, Son? Because I love you."

There was a deep silence. I said, "Dad, this is the first time in your life you told me that you loved me."

His father said, "Well, Vincent, what do you think? Every time we motivated you, every time we put you down, every time we tried to get you to move, and every time we paid for your college and all that—that was the way we loved you."

I said, "Dad, that wasn't enough. That wasn't enough, Dad. That wasn't enough at all. If only you had told me in different ways, more than one way, that you loved me, it would have been so much easier, Dad."

Well—some of us have stood beneath the trapdoor, haven't we? And for some, I suspect, it still pours down on us. And maybe we unwittingly dump on others: "You're not an honor student, so I can't be a proud parent." "You didn't make the soccer team; how will I face my friends?" "She wears all the wrong clothes; how can we invite her?"

To bless is to speak well. And, when it happens…well, listen to a woman named Mary Ann Bird as she tells her story:

I grew up knowing that I was different, and I hated it. I was born with a cleft palate, and when I started school, my classmates made it clear to me how I must look to others: a little girl with a misshapen lip, crooked nose, lopsided teeth and garbled speech. When my schoolmates would ask, "What happened to your lip?" I'd tell them I'd fallen and cut it on a piece of glass. Somehow it seemed more acceptable to have suffered an accident than to have been born different. I was convinced that no one outside my family could love me.

There was, however, a teacher in the second grade who we all adored—Mrs. Leonard by name. She was short, round, happy—a sparkling lady. Annually, we would have a hearing test. I was virtually deaf in one of my ears; but when I had taken the test in the past years, I discovered that if I did not press my hand as tightly upon my ears as I was instructed to do, I could pass the test. Mrs. Leonard gave the test to everyone in class, and finally it was my turn.

I knew from past years that as we stood against the door and covered one ear, the teacher sitting at her desk would whisper something and we would have to repeat it back...things like "the sky is blue" or "do you have new shoes?" I waited there for those words which God must have put into her mouth, those seven words which changed my life. Mrs. Leonard said in her whisper, "I wish you were my little girl."

A few holidays ago I picked up an album for Christmas, with songs by Cris Williamson. On the back of the album there was a little biography of Williamson. She described where she came from and talked a little bit about growing up on a place called Moonlight Ranch, 'way out in, I think, the wilds of Montana. And she told a marvelous story about one Christmas in her house. Williamson noted how precise her mother was when the Christmas tree was put up: tinsel had to be put on by hand, piece by piece, and the lights had to be put on just so. She continues her story and writes:

It was a great honor in our family to be chosen to place the Christmas angel at the very tip of the tree. Dad would hold the child high in the air and the angel would slip over the tip until she shone high above the room.

That Christmas, as the afternoon gave way to gradual darkness, Mom cut my hair. My long braids had been shorn to shoulder length and the hair was all around me on the floor. I remember feeling sort of small and naked as I sat there on my hard chair in the kitchen. Dad came in out of the frosty cold with an armload of stove wood. He put it in the wooden box beside the stove and looked over at me sitting so pensively on my chair like a lamb that had just been shaved.

He knelt down beside me and picked up all the newly shorn hair from my head. The next thing I knew, he was calling me to the front room where the Christmas tree stood in all its shining splendor. I watched him as he carefully placed bits of my brown hair on the tree beside the tinsel and the glittering glass balls. He turned and smiled at me and said, "This year we will have real angel hair on the tree."

Scenes such as these, which speak well and offer blessings for life's journey, stick with us and make a difference in our lives. Witness the fact that these storytellers still remember and still retell the time of their blessings.

To see well

But if to bless someone is to speak well of them, the implication is that first, we must see them. And that brings me to our second characteristic of blessing: to bless is to see well. In blessing it is important that we see, that we recognize others, for our seeing tells them they count.

A few years ago, a family came to me for help with a painful incident involving their thirteen-year-old daughter, who was caught shoplifting. As things turned out, she was stealing things that she neither needed nor wanted. Moreover, stealing these things was not, as is often the case among teens, something intended to impress her peers, a rite of passage necessary for acceptance into a group of friends. Without saying so, she was stealing to get her father's attention.

Her father, struggling in his relationship with her mother, was not around a great deal and did not give a lot of attention to his daughter. So she forced his hand. It was he that she demanded come to the police station to pick her up and settle things with the police. In doing so he had to give his daughter his attention. He had to look at her. Her shoplifting was a way of forcing her father to see her.

In the book *The Aladdin Factor*, there is a story by Jane Nelson that could help a great many mothers and fathers. Nelson once received a call from a frantic single mother who was caught in a real power struggle with her fourteen-year-old daughter. The mother had found a six-pack of beer in her daughter's closet, so when her daughter came home, she said, "Okay, Maria, what is this?"

"It looks like a six-pack of beer to me, Mom," her daughter answered.

"Don't get smart with me, young lady. You tell me about this," said the mother. "Well, I don't know what you're talking about," the girl replied.

"I found this six-pack in your closet young lady. You'd better explain," her mother continued.

Maria thought real fast and said, "Oh yeah, I was hiding that for a friend."

"You expect me to believe that?" asked her mother. Maria got mad, stomped off to her bedroom, and slammed the door. (Does any of this sound familiar to some of you?)

When the mother called for advice, Jane Nelson asked, "Why were you so concerned with finding a six-pack of beer in her closet?"

"Because I don't want her to get into trouble," said the mother.

"I understand that," Nelson replied, "but why is it you don't want her to get into trouble?"

The mother answered, "Well, because I don't want her to ruin her life."

"I understand that," Nelson replied, "but why is it that you don't want her to ruin her life?"

Finally the mother got it. "Well, because I love her," she said.

"Do you think she got that message?" Nelson asked.

The answer is, "Of course not!"

"What do you think would happen," Nelson asked, "if you started with that message? If you saw her as someone you loved and she saw you as someone who cared? If you were to start with, 'Honey, I love you so much that I got really scared when I found this six-pack of beer in your closet. Could we talk about this? Because I'm really worried you could get into trouble; could we talk about it?'"

With this approach, Nelson says, you start by being vulnerable instead of conducting an inquisition that inevitably leads to denial. Starting from the position of love and vulnerability evokes closeness and trust so that the child can then open up and work together with you on some kind of solution.

Here is one more story on seeing told by a woman:

A soft-spoken woman with a firm touch, Mrs. Lake taught sixth grade. She kept her long auburn hair up in a barrette, showing off the drop earrings she always wore. From my first moment in her class I loved her. Though I was a good student, I was shy about speaking up in front of my classmates and could easily be overlooked. Not with Mrs. Lake.

That year had been a hard one at home. My father's alcoholism had grown worse. At night when I lay in bed I listened with dread to the pop of beer cans opening or the clink of ice cubes in a glass as whiskey was poured. Then came the loud slurred voice from the kitchen, my mother's tears, the slamming of doors. Before falling asleep I prayed, "Dear God, help me make him stop." Dad was an attorney and meticulous about polishing his wingtips every morning before work. So for Christmas I took the babysitting money I had saved and bought the best shoeshine kit I could find. I was so excited on Christmas Eve when he opened the heavy box. But I watched in stunned silence while Dad in an incomprehensible rage threw it across the living room, breaking it into pieces. Somehow I thought I was to blame.

How much safer I felt in Mrs. Lake's class. This was my sanctuary, the place where I felt appreciated, my papers coming back with her distinctive scrawl, my tests decorated with stars and smiley faces. When I gave oral reports, standing in front of the class, my knees shaking, I looked in her encouraging blue eyes and my fears subsided.

At the end of the year came the day for parent-teacher conferences, each student meeting with her parents and Mrs. Lake for a final evaluation and progress report. On the blackboard was an alphabetical schedule with a twenty-minute slot for each family. I was puzzled that I had been put at the end of the list, even though my last name began with B. It didn't matter. My parents would not be coming. When I brought home papers with Mrs. Lake's glowing remarks, they ended up in the trash, unnoticed. Letters reminding them about the school conference were ignored.

All day I tried to stay busy with our assigned projects while the room mother escorted my classmates to the doorway at the back of the class. Every twenty minutes a different name was called, a student walked out, and through the closed door I could hear the muffled voices of parents asking questions while Mrs. Lake offered suggestions. I couldn't even imagine having parents like that.

Finally, after everyone's name had been called, Mrs. Lake opened the door and motioned for me to join her. Three folding chairs were set up in the hallway in front of a desk covered with files, class projects, and Mrs. Lake's grade book. I watched as she folded up two of the chairs. Then she gestured for me to sit down in the one remaining. Moving her chair next to mine, Mrs. Lake lifted my chin. "First of all," she said, "I want you to know how much I love you." I saw all the warmth and compassion in those beautiful blue eyes that I had observed all year long. "Secondly," she continued, "you need to know it is not your fault that your parents are not here today."

It was the first time someone had said such a thing to me. For a moment I was scared. She knows our secret. But then I realized she had understood all along. "You deserve a conference whether your parents are here or not," she said. "You deserve to know how well I think you're doing."

She took out a stack of my papers and congratulated me on the good grades, pointing out my strengths. She showed me my diagnostic test scores and explained how high I had ranked nationally. She had even saved a stack of my watercolors—those things my mother usually consigned to the trash. During that meeting my perception changed. Because she saw me, I was allowed to see myself objectively, and because I knew Mrs. Lake cared for me, I believed what she told me. My home situation was the same, but I was a different person.

For a long moment Mrs. Lake and I looked at each other in silence. Then she gave me a hug. Afterward she gathered her papers and we returned to class. None of my friends ever asked me what she said, and if they had I don't know what I would have told them. It was too precious, too private, too wonderful. The growing up years that followed were often difficult, but my teacher had given me an extraordinary gift. For the first time I knew I was worthy of being loved. I had been seen as worthy. That made all the difference.

There is a deep longing inside us to be seen by those to whom we look up—our parents, our elders, our leaders, our teachers, our coaches, our pastors, and our bosses. It is important to us, more than we generally imagine, that those who are above us look at us, see us, recognize us. Look at me; I count! Bless me with your notice! Here I am! I'm your spouse; notice me! I'm your friend; notice me! I'm your child; notice me! I'm your pupil; notice me!

Good leaders see their people. Good parents see their children, good teachers their students. Good pastors see their parishioners, good executives their employees. We are blessed by being seen, by being noticed. And we all need to be seen. We find this at its most elementary level on every playground on earth. The little child is playing, yet constantly on the lookout for the parent, saying, "Mommy, look at me! Daddy, watch me!"

To bless is to see.

To pass on blessing

To bless is to speak well of someone; to bless is to see someone; finally, to bless is to pass on blessing.

Several years ago, at a workshop in Los Angeles, John Shea shared a story that speaks of the effect of a deep blessing. It is the story of a woman whom he met while teaching in Ireland one summer. In his class, he had asked each person to recount an incident of blessing from his or her own life. One woman, very timidly, shared her story.

The incident she recounted took place when she was twelve years old. The woman came from a large family, and each Sunday morning, to get them ready for church, her mother would line up all of her children and then, one by one, wash each child's face and comb each one's hair. Each child would wait patiently in line for his or her turn and then go out to play while the mother finished the rest.

One Sunday she was second in line and anxious to get her turn over with because it would mean nearly a half hour of play time while the others were being washed and combed. Then, just before her turn, her mother noticed that the youngest sister, at the end of the line, was missing a shoelace and asked her to go into the bedroom and get one. Not wanting to lose her place in the line and given that her mother did not ask her a second time, she did not go. Her mother said nothing as she combed her hair. When she was finished she went out to play.

After playing for about ten minutes, however, she felt guilty and went back into the house to get the shoelace for her baby sister. When she entered the mother had just removed her own shoelace and was bent down, putting it into her baby sister's shoe. Feeling doubly guilty, she went into her parents' bedroom and got a shoelace and, as her mother was combing her baby sister's hair, she bent down and put the shoelace into her mother's shoe. While she was doing this, her mother said nothing but gently stroked her hair.

When she finished telling that story, somebody in the class asked her what it meant and, rather embarrassed, she said: "I don't know...but it has just stayed with me all these years!"

A day later, Shea, who during this two-week course had the habit of sitting under a particular tree every day during the afternoon break and smoking a cigar, had settled himself under that tree when he realized he had forgotten to bring a cigar. Out of nowhere, the woman appeared: "Where is your cigar today?" she asked shyly. "I forgot to bring one!" he answered. Immediately, she produced a cigar, gave it to him, and disappeared without a word.

The next day after his conference, Shea found her sitting by herself at the back of the room. He went to her and confronted her with these words: "The cigar is the shoelace, isn't it?" "Yes," she answered, "ever since that day that my mother stroked my hair, through all these years—and long after she has died—I have had this secret covenant with her. I go through life supplying what is missing!"

Blessing begets blessing. When we are treated gently, gentleness grows in us. We all make an unconscious secret covenant with those who have blessed us, who have stroked our hair gently.

Nobody can bless like a teacher nor do many have the opportunity to do so. To bless is to speak well, especially to those who seldom hear words of affirmation. To bless is to see well, especially those who are invisible. To bless is to pass on well, especially to those whose legacy is harsh and fractured.

Let me sum up this chapter's reflection with a final story, the story of two people: a young, frightened boy and a telephone operator. Although they never saw each other, they abundantly blessed the other.

When I was quite young, my family had one of the first telephones in our neighborhood. I remember well the polished oak case fastened to the wall on the lower stair landing. The shiny receiver hung on the side of the box. I even remember the number, 107. I was too little to reach the telephone, but used to listen with fascination when my mother talked into it. Once she lifted me up to speak to my father, who was away on business. Magic! Then I discovered that somewhere inside that wonderful device lived an amazing person: her name was "Information Please" and there was nothing she did not know. My mother could ask her for anybody's number; when our clock ran down, Information Please immediately supplied the correct time.

My first personal experience with this genie-in-the-receiver came one day while my mother was visiting a neighbor. Amusing myself at the toolbench in the basement, I whacked my finger with a hammer. The pain was terrible, but there didn't seem to be much use in crying because there was no one home to offer sympathy. I walked around the house sucking my throbbing finger, finally arriving at the stairway.

The telephone! Quickly I ran for the footstool in the parlor and dragged it to the landing. Climbing up, I unhooked the receiver and held it to my ear. "Information Please," I said into the mouthpiece just above my head. A click or two, and a small, clear voice spoke into my ear: "Information."

"I hurt my fingerrr—" I wailed into the phone. The tears came readily enough, now that I had an audience.

"Isn't your mother home?" came the question.

"Nobody's home but me," I blubbered.

"Are you bleeding?"

"No," I replied. "I hit it with the hammer and it hurts."

"Can you open your icebox?" she asked. I said I could.

"Then chip off a little piece of ice and hold it on your finger. That will stop the hurt. Be careful when you use the ice pick," she admonished. "And don't cry. You'll be all right."

After that, I called Information Please for everything. I asked for help with my geography and she told me where Philadelphia was and the Orinoco, the romantic river I was going to explore when I grew up. She helped me with my arithmetic, and she told me that a pet chipmunk I had caught in the park just the day before would eat fruit and nuts. And there was the time that Petey, our pet canary, died. I called Information Please and told her the sad story. She listened, then said the usual things grownups say to soothe a child. But I was unconsoled. Why was it that birds should sing so beautifully and bring joy to whole families, only to end as a heap of feathers, legs up, on the bottom of a cage? She must have sensed my deep concern, for she said quietly, "Paul, always remember that there are other worlds to sing in."

In moments of doubt and perplexity I would recall the serene sense of security I had when I knew that I could call Information Please and get the right answer. I appreciated how very patient, understanding, and kind she was to have wasted her time on a little boy.

A few years later, on my way west to college, my plane put down in Seattle. I had about half an hour between plane connections, and I spent fifteen minutes or so on the phone with my sister who lived there now, happily mellowed by marriage and motherhood. Then, really without thinking what I was doing, I dialed my hometown operator and said, "Information Please." Miraculously, I heard again the small, clear voice I knew so well: "Information." I hadn't planned this, but I heard myself saying, "Could you tell me, please, how to spell the word 'fix'?" There was a long pause. Then came the softly spoken answer.

"I guess," said Information Please, "that your finger must have healed by now."

I laughed. "So it's really still you. I wonder if you have any idea how much you meant to me during all that time."

"I wonder," she replied, "if you know how much you meant to me. I never had any children, and I used to look forward to your calls. Silly, wasn't it?" It didn't seem silly, but I didn't say so. Instead I told her how often I had thought of her over the years, and I asked if I could call her again when I came back to visit my sister after the first semester was over.

"Please do. Just ask for Sally."

"Good-bye, Sally." It sounded strange for Information Please to have a name. "If I run into any chipmunks, I'll tell them to eat fruit and nuts."

"Do that," she said. "And I expect one of these days you'll be off for the Orinoco. Well, good-bye."

Just three months later I was back again at the Seattle airport. A different voice answered, "Information," and I asked for Sally.

"Are you a friend?"

"Yes," I said. "An old friend."

"Then I'm sorry to have to tell you. Sally had only been working part-time in the last few years because she was ill. She died five weeks ago."

But before I could hang up, she said, "Wait a minute. Did you say your name was Villard?"

"Yes."

"Well, Sally left a message for you. She wrote it down."

"What was it?" I asked, almost knowing in advance what it would be. "Here it is. I'll read it: 'Tell him I still say there are other worlds to sing in. He'll know what I mean.'" I thanked her and hung up. I did know what Sally meant.

The life-journey is not only hard without a blessing, but impossible. A blessing denied is a curse. If you have been blessed, thank those who gave it. If you have not been blessed, forgive those who have withheld it. If you are not blessing, begin today with a word, a gesture, a note, a phone call, a compliment, an affirmation, a prayer.

Let us close this chapter with two blessings which most of us will recognize. The first prayer is the ancient blessing of Aaron, while the second is the blessing we give each other at the end of Mass.

> May the Lord bless you and keep you.
> May he let his face shine on you
> and be gracious to you;
> May the Lord look upon you kindly
> And give you peace.

> May the blessing of Almighty God,
> The Father, Son and Holy Spirit
> Be with you all
> and remain with you forever. Amen.

Questions for reflection

1. Who has blessed me? Who has denied me blessing?

2. To bless is to speak well of others. Who speaks well of me? Who has spoken harshly of me? Have I forgiven them? Of whom do I speak well?

3. To bless is to see well. Who sees me, has always seen me? Who has not? How careful am I to see—really see—other people

around me and in my life?

4. To bless is to pass on well. Who has passed on blessing to me? To whom I have passed on blessing?

5. What are the blessings God has given me? How do I share these with others?

FOUR

MUNCHKINLAND

＊　●

Imperfection

After her traumatic trip into the sky on the wings of a tornado, Dorothy lands in a strange place. She opens her black and white door and steps into technicolor Munchkinland. Hidden giggles finally reveal the Munchkins, the little people.

The actors in the film who play the Munchkins are dwarfs and midgets. Through some genetic fluke they have not grown to full height. Seen through images of bodily perfection put forth by the media, these Munchkins could be seen as "imperfect." Yet "imperfect" though they be, here they are in a major film, acting, dancing, singing, and bringing delight to countless generations. Using this theme of imperfection—and we are all, by our very nature, imperfect beings—we will travel with the Munchkins through this reflection.

Here let me introduce you to a man you most likely have never heard of, H. Jackson Brown. On his fifty-first birthday he decided to jot down some of the lessons he had learned up to that point in his life. He wrote down the phrase, "I've learned that…" twenty times, then proceeded to complete the sentence each time. So enjoyable was the exercise for him that Brown began asking his friends and acquaintances to do the same. Eventually, he enlisted the help of hundreds of other people, from kindergarten kids to senior citizens. The result is a fascinating little book called *Live and Learn and Pass It*

On, a compilation of what hundreds of individuals say they have learned from life. Here are a few examples:

> A twenty year old: "I've learned that trust is the single most important factor in both personal and professional relationships."
>
> An eighty-two year old: "I've learned that even when I have pains, I don't have to be a pain."
>
> A fifty-four-year-old man: "I've learned that you can't hug your kids too much."
>
> A fifty-two-year-old woman: "I've learned that you can tell a lot about a man by the way he handles these three things: a rainy holiday, lost luggage, and tangled Christmas tree lights."
>
> A seven year old: "I've learned that you can't hide a piece of broccoli in a glass of milk."

I'd like to add three things of my own which I've learned over the years. First, I've learned that no cupcake ever tastes as good as it looks. Second, I've learned that all dogs go to heaven. Third, I've learned that most people think that in order for them to be loved they must be perfect. Yes, that's perplexing, but it's true.

Where does this notion come from, that we have to be perfect for others to love us? In his book, *How Good Do We Have To Be?*, Rabbi Harold Kushner says that this notion comes from three sources. One is our childhood. For example, the school child assumes that his report card is evaluating him as a person, not just his spelling or math performance. So a bad grade means "I am bad."

A youngster overhears his parents saying, "She's so shy around other children," or "He's so much shorter than other boys his age," and feels a sense of shame for having disappointed his parents. He is not perfect and so, he thinks in his childish way, his parents don't love him. Or when they grow up, people let themselves be defined by their worst moments instead of their best ones. "What's wrong with me? Why did I have that dessert? Why can't I ever stick to a diet?" They soon dub themselves as people who never can get it right rather than capable people who make an occasional human mistake.

And the next step, Kushner says, is to make the too-easy transla-

tion from "I have done some wrong things" to "I am a person who
constantly does wrong things" to "Anyone who really gets to know me
will discover that I am bad and will reject me."

So what happens? People become preoccupied with being perfect,
can't stand criticism, pretend to be more than they are, and find it
hard to apologize. And, of course, all this perfectionism thrives on
comparisons. Yet nothing gets us down on ourselves faster than measuring our achievements against those of others. "Look at how clean
she keeps her house. And her kids are all doing so well. I'm so inadequate. What's the matter with me?"

The second source that drives our desire to be perfect is advertising. As a professional bachelor, I do my own food shopping and can
make Kushner's words my own:

> At the supermarket checkout counter, I notice five women's
> magazines offering diet advice on their covers. I see the woman
> waiting on line ahead of me contemplating those same covers,
> and I wonder what is going through her mind as she does so. Is
> she feeling bad because her figure doesn't qualify her to be a
> fashion model? Has she been brainwashed to feel inadequate as
> a person for not meeting society's expectations of attractive-
> ness? Or, I think, is she wise enough to remember that age and
> genetics play dirty tricks on all of us?
>
> If the woman on line in front of me is divorced, she may feel,
> not that her marriage failed, but that she failed by not being the
> perfect sexual partner she should have been, a feeling that
> women are responsible for the emotional health of a relationship.
>
> At worst, she may be driven to anorexia or bulimia, almost
> exclusively women's afflictions, out of a sense of shame that her
> body isn't as perfect as the bodies of the models and movie stars
> held up as prototypes for her. Psychologists suspect that anorex-
> ia—starving oneself to the point of illness and sometimes
> death—results from a sense of self-loathing, a disgust with one's
> body.
>
> Women hate their bodies, are ashamed of their bodies,
> because society has taught them that they are evaluated by their

appearance. Their looks define who they are. Gather a hundred women at random and ask them how they feel about their looks, their hair, their figures, and I would guess that between ninety-five and one hundred of them would express some dissatisfaction. I have known strikingly attractive women who would become depressed over a five-pound weight gain or a barely visible cosmetic blemish.

Entire industries—fashion, cosmetics, perfume, low-calorie foods, bestselling diet books, plastic surgery, weight loss clinics—have been built on the foundation of women feeling ashamed of their appearance, to the point where one could speculate that if all the women in America were to wake up one morning feeling good about themselves, the American economy would collapse.

And at the heart of all this shame is the notion that to be acceptable, to be lovable, a woman has to measure up to some unrealistic standard of perfection—when all the while, the sad truth is that women who like themselves and are comfortable with who they are are much more pleasant company than women who are constantly depriving themselves and trying to hide their feelings of disappointment in themselves.

(A must-read book on this same topic is *Venus Envy: A History of Cosmetic Surgery,* by Elizabeth Haiken.)

Is there a male equivalent of anorexia? What drives men to self-loathing and self-destructive behavior? If society teaches women to feel ashamed of themselves for being too fat or unattractive, it teaches men to feel ashamed for not making a lot of money—and measuring up to the male media models like Fabio and Brad Pitt. And it's so easy to unconsciously transfer all these feelings to God. We think: I must be perfect in order for God to love me. How can I can even begin to answer God's call the way I am?

This brings us to the third culprit in the drive toward perfection: religion. Religion has sometimes taught that simple, normal human feelings are sinful; but in truth, normal human feelings are neutral. They just are. There is no right or wrong with feelings until we act on them. Many of us were taught that normal sexual thoughts were sinful, that normal emotions like pride and anger and envy were to be counted among the seven deadly sins. The message was you had to be perfect in order for God to love you. That's why, I think, God is more at home in small group meetings like A.A., with their slogans such as, "I'm not OK and you're not OK, but that's OK."

So nurture, the media, and religion all conspire unwittingly to tell us not only that we are not perfect, but that we must be so for people to love us; and, more devastatingly, as I said before, for God to love us. And with poor self-image we spend an unconscionable amount of time not only trying to impress people, but ducking God. As Rabbi Kushner says,

> But the truth is that if our parents cannot handle our mistakes, if they have trouble loving us despite our imperfections, it may be because they need us to be perfect to reflect credit on them. If our mates continue to harp on our failures, it may be because they want us to improve and don't know a better way of making that happen. If friends are unforgiving and reject us for our mistakes, it may be because our mistakes touched them at a particularly vulnerable and sensitive place.
>
> But God doesn't need us to meet His needs, and His expectations of us are more realistic than are those of the people around us. God loves the overweight woman as much as the slender one, the stumbling youngster as much as the athletically gifted one, the frustrated salesman as much as his more successful rival.

In fact, God would seem to love our imperfection because it breaks through the armor of perfectionist pretense and opens our souls to God's presence. We are all imperfect, flawed. The liturgy is right when it tells us to cry out, "Lord, have mercy!" and confess our sins at the beginning of Mass. But we are at Mass not only to be told what we already know, that we have done some things wrong. We are there to be assured that our misdeeds have not separated us from the love of God.

Yes, our faith sets high standards; it takes us to task for disfiguring our Christ-likeness; it annually leads us through the penitential season of Lent. But our faith also wants us to be washed clean of our sins and of our disappointment in ourselves.

Three lessons about imperfection

No matter what messages our upbringing, or advertising, or unbalanced religious training have given us, the fact is that we don't have to be perfect for people to love us. We don't have to be perfect for God to love us nor do we forfeit God's love if we are imperfect. That is the first lesson we must learn about accepting our imperfections.

If the first lesson says that we think our imperfections disqualify us from God's love, the second lesson says that we use our imperfections to disqualify ourselves, to shun God's call, God's desire to come into our lives. There is an old folktale that well captures this attitude:

> Once upon a time an evil king was succeeded by his younger brother, who was a good and kind person. In order to begin his reign in a spirit of love for his subjects, he decided to make a profound and public act of reconciliation with his people. Since he could not visit each person individually, he asked his people to select the person whom they considered to be the lowliest in his kingdom as their representative. He would have supper in the home of this person as an expression of his wish to be close to his people in their humble situations. A poor widow who lived in a small cottage deep in the forest was selected. She was delighted with the honor but requested a little time in order to prepare for the coming of the king.
>
> Days, weeks, and months passed by and there was still no sign from the widow that she was ready to receive the king. After investigating the cause of the delay the king discovered that the widow had enlisted the help of most of the people in the kingdom and they were now laying the foundations of a gigantic castle. It was reported that when this castle was finished, the poor widow would be ready to receive the king.
>
> The king was hurt and frustrated by this response to his attempt at reconciliation. The king, although powerful in every other respect, was powerless to move closer to his people. He

wanted to meet his people in their littleness and vulnerability, but they wanted to meet the king and start their journey of reconciliation from a position of power, control, and an idealized but false understanding of who they were.

This fable illustrates that a false humility—"O Lord, I am not worthy"—gives us a secret excuse for not being a saint, a theme we shall explore more fully in chapter eleven. Surely, we claim, God calls the more noble, the sinless—not me. God would never want me with all my imperfections and sins. When my humble house is a castle I'll invite God in. Until then—well, God's better off knocking on someone else's door.

But, of course, that excuse won't do; it won't do at all. A God who came into the world in a stable is a God who will come into our own small hovel of a life, as well.

The third lesson we must learn is that, as a matter of fact, imperfection is a door by which God's Spirit enters. When we approach God from a position of power and conceit, we put God off. When we approach from weakness, vulnerability, and need, we invite God in. The story Jesus told of the Pharisee and the publican who went up to the temple to pray underscores this sentiment. An honest awareness and acceptance of our imperfection humbles an overblown pride, forces us to our knees, exposes our needs, and empties the soul of ego so that God can enter. Imperfection, therefore, is not a barrier to God but an opening, a wound through which God can enter.

Now, if any of this has resonated with you—and I suspect it has—how much more must it resonate with our children?

The children. Who among them does not need a heavy dose of affirmation and acceptance because every day an incessant media duns them with messages of physical and social inadequacy unless they endlessly consume the fantasy products that will make them handsome and acceptable? The children, whose homes are often fractured, some of whose religious lives are piecemeal at best. Latchkeyed by single parents, subcontracted out to paid strangers by career parents, commodified by the market, in danger from the threat of drugs, AIDS, and abuse, surrounded with pornography and consumerism at every turn—their silent cries echo through the nation: Is there anybody who loves me? Is there anybody who really cares? Is there anybody who wants to stay home with me? Is there anybody who wants to be with me when I am not in control, when I feel like crying? Is there anybody who can hold me and give me a sense of belonging? Is there anybody to tell me the stories of God, of Jesus, who left ninety-nine to come after the one?

Read these words, this poignant paragraph by college student Doug Coupland from his book, *Life After God*. He speaks for all youth:

> Now here is my secret: I tell it to you with an openness of heart that I doubt I shall ever achieve again, so I pray that you are in a quiet room as you read these words. My secret is that I need God—that I am sick and can no longer make it alone. I need God to help me give, because I no longer seem capable of giving; to help me be kind as I no longer seem capable of kindness; to help me love as I seem beyond being able to love.

"I need God." That is the unrecognized yearning of all youth. They—and we—need a God who claims and reclaims. We need to feel confident when we pray, "O God of the Second Chance, here I am again!" They, and we, need to know the stories of redemption. They, and we, need to know, as we all struggle with our temptations and imperfections, about a God so wide, so big, so strong, so caring, so loving that this God can embrace our imperfections as he embraced powerless little children, broke bread with sinners, and forgave latecomer thieves.

They, and we, need to know the stories of Paul who, while his hands were still red with Stephen's blood, could be knocked from his horse and gaze into the face of Christ; of Magdalen, who could be called from promiscuity and look into the eyes of pity; of the prodigal son, the good thief, the woman caught in adultery, and the out-of-wedlock father Augustine, who picked up the Scriptures, wended his way to Milan, fell at the feet of Ambrose, made his confession, and was restored in God.

All of us need to hear the story of Dorothy Day, who was called from her atheism and communism, and became an apostle of the poor. We need to know about Thomas Merton, who wondered while on his knees in a Catholic church in Greenwich Village, gazing at a statue of Christ, what he was doing in his wickedness; about Malcolm Muggeridge, a playboy, who became a convert because in Mother Teresa he saw something of the divine; about Charles Colson, a convicted felon from the Nixon administration, who now serves Jesus in prison ministry.

A story for children

This round-about gospel story can speak well of imperfections to children:

> Once upon a time some grandparents were in a little gift shop looking for something to give their granddaughter on her birthday. Suddenly, the grandmother saw a precious teacup. "Look at this lovely teacup, Harry. Just the thing!" Grandad picked it up, looked at it and said, "You're right. It's one of the nicest teacups I've ever seen. We must get it." At this point the teacup startled the grandparents by saying, "Well, thank you for the compliment, but, you know, I wasn't always so beautiful." The grandparents, still surprised, said, "What do you mean you weren't always so beautiful?"
>
> "It's true," said the teacup. "Once I was just an ugly, soggy lump of clay. But one day a man with dirty and wet hands threw me on a wheel and started turning me around and around till I got so dizzy that I cried, 'Stop! Stop!' but the man with the wet hands said, 'Not yet.' Then he started to poke me and punch me until I hurt all over. 'Stop! Stop!' I cried but he said, 'Not yet.' Finally he did stop but then he did something worse. He put me in a furnace and I got hotter and hotter until I couldn't stand it any longer and I cried, 'Stop! Stop!' but the man said, 'Not yet.'
>
> "And finally, when I thought I was going to get burned up, the man took me out of the furnace. Then, some short lady began to paint me and the fumes were so bad that they made me sick to my stomach and I cried, 'Stop! Stop!' but the lady

said, 'Not yet.' Finally she did stop and gave me back to the man again and he put me back in that awful furnace. I cried out, 'Stop! Stop!' but he only said, 'Not yet.' Finally he took me out and let me cool. And when I was cool a very pretty lady put me on a shelf, right next to the mirror. And when I looked into the mirror, I was amazed! I could not believe what I saw. I was no longer ugly, soggy, and dirty. I was beautiful and firm and clean. And I cried for joy!"

The little ones, the ugly ducklings, must know that God, the Divine Artisan, is at work in their lives.

A story for teens

Older kids and teenagers will relate to this true story, told by Mark Link, SJ:

When I was growing up, I lived near Collingswood in south Jersey. In that town, I knew of a young boy by the name of Eugene Orowitz—a skinny, one-hundred pound sophomore at Collingswood High School. He didn't have much going for him—and if your name was Eugene Orowitz, you'd better have something going for you.

One afternoon the gym coach held classes in the middle of the track infield. He wanted to show the kids how to throw a javelin. After the coach finished his instruction, he let the kids try their hand at it. One by one, they threw a six-foot-long spear. The longest throw was thirty yards. When everyone but Eugene had tried, the coach looked over at him and said, "You want to try to throw it too, Orowitz?" Eugene nodded. "Well, go ahead," he said impatiently. The other kids laughed at Eugene. "Hey, Ugly, can you lift it?" someone shouted. "Careful! You'll stab yourself," shouted another.

A strange feeling came over Eugene as he stood there holding the long spear. He pictured himself as a young warrior about to battle the enemy. He raised the javelin over his head, took six quick steps, and let it fly. It soared twenty, thirty, forty, fifty yards. Then it crashed into the empty bleachers. Eugene's throw went twice as far as the others. When Eugene retrieved the javelin, he saw the tip had broken as a result of its crash against the bleachers. The coach looked at it and said, "What the heck, Orowitz, you broke the thing. You might as well take it home with you. It's no good to the school any longer."

That summer Eugene began throwing the javelin in a vacant lot. Some days he spent six hours throwing it. By the end of his senior year, Eugene threw the javelin twenty-one feet farther than any other high school student in the nation. Eugene was given an athletic scholarship to the University of Southern California. He began dreaming of the Olympics. Then one day he didn't warm up properly, and he tore the ligaments in his shoulder. That put an end to javelin throwing, his scholarship, and his dreams.

All his hard work went down the drain. It was as if God had slapped him in the face after he had performed a minor miracle with his puny one-hundred-pound body. Eugene dropped out of college and took a job in a warehouse. He worked in the warehouse for a while. Then one day he met a struggling actor who asked him to help him with his lines. Eugene got interested in acting himself and enrolled in an acting school. His big break came when he was cast as Little Joe in "Bonanza." That show ran for fourteen years. Later he got the lead in another long-running TV show, "Little House on the Prairie."

You guessed it. Eugene Orowitz, the imperfect, skinny boy from New Jersey, became Michael Landon.

Gene knew that a well-known actor could make a difference. He also knew he had one shot at life. He was dismayed at so much of the trash on TV so he conceived and produced "Highway to Heaven," a series that showed people the value of kindness.

When he got cancer and his life was cut short, he knew that he had lost his life to decency and goodness—and in doing so had found it.

A story for adults

Finally, this story tells of a very imperfect boy—he was abandoned and had polio—and a Christ-figure, an old black lady of the South. The boy, now a man, tells it in his own words:

I was a timid six year old with braces on my legs, a frail, lost, lonely little boy when I first arrived at the farm in Georgia. Had it not been for an extraordinary woman, I might have remained that way. She lived in a two-room cabin on the farm where her parents had been slaves. To an outsider she looked like any of the black people on the farm, in her shapeless gray dress. But to those who knew her she was a spiritual force whose influence was felt everywhere. She was the first person called when there was sickness; she made medicines from roots and herbs that seemed to cure just about anything. She had a family of her own, but all the children in the area felt that they belonged to her.

Her name reflected this. In the soft speech of the Georgia lowlands, the word "maum" is a slurred version of "Mama." We called her "Maum Jean." Maum Jean talked to the Lord often and we all suspected that when she did he stopped whatever he was doing and listened and took appropriate action. Her heart reached out to small, helpless things, so she took particular interest in me from the start.

When I was stricken with polio at the age of three, I'm sure my parents didn't know what was the matter with me. All they knew was that times were hard and suddenly they had a crippled child on their hands. They took me to a New York City hospital, left me, and never came back. The people who took me into their foster home had relatives on the Georgia estate where I was sent in the hope that the warmer climate might help. Maum's Jean sensitive emotional antenna instantly picked up the loneliness and withdrawal inside me. Moreover, her marvelous diagnostic sense surveyed the polio damage and decided that, regardless of what the doctors might have said, something more ought to be done.

Maum Jean had never heard the word "atrophy," but she

knew that muscles could waste away unless used. And so every night when her tasks were done she would come to my room and kneel beside my bed to massage my legs. Sometimes, when I would cry out with pain, she would sing old songs or tell me stories. When her treatments were over, she would always talk earnestly to the Lord, explaining that she was doing what she could but that she would need help, and she asked him to give her a sign when He was ready.

A creek wound through the farm and Maum Jean, who had never heard of hydrotherapy, said there was strength in running water. She made her grandsons carry me down to a sandy bank where I could splash around pretty well. Slowly I grew taller, but there was little change in my legs. I still used crutches. I still buckled on the clumsy braces. Night after night, Maum Jean continued the massaging and praying.

Then one morning, when I was about twelve, she told me she had a surprise for me. She led me out into the yard and placed me with my back against an oak tree. She took away my crutches and braces. She moved back a dozen paces and told me that the Lord had spoken to her in a dream. He had said that the time had come for me to walk. "So now," said Maum Jean, "I want you to walk over here to me."

My instant reaction was fear. I knew I couldn't walk unaided. I had tried. I shrank back against the solid support of the tree. Maum Jean continued to urge me. I burst into tears. I begged. I pleaded. Her voice rose suddenly, no longer gentle and coaxing, but full of power and command. "You can walk, boy! The Lord has spoken! Now walk over here!" She knelt down and held out her arms. And somehow, impelled by something stronger than fear, I took a faltering step, and another, and another until I reached Maum Jean and fell into her arms, both of us weeping.

It was two more years before I could walk normally, but I never used the crutches again. For a while longer I lived in my twilight world. Then a circus came through town and when it left, I left with it.

This man's crippled state was no barrier to Maum Jean's love. Our crippled state is no barrier to God's love. There is a sequel to this story, so let's continue:

> For the next few years, I worked with one circus or another. Then the night came when one of Maum Jean's tall grandsons knocked on my door. Maum Jean was dying. She wanted to see me. The old cabin was unchanged. Maum Jean lay ill in bed surrounded by silent watchers, her frail body covered by a patchwork quilt. Her face was in shadow, but I heard her whisper my name. I sat down and touched her hand.
>
> For a long time I sat there. Now and then Maum Jean spoke softly; her mind was clear. She hoped I remembered the things she had taught me. Then the old voice spoke, stronger suddenly. "Oh," said Maum Jean with surprise and gladness, "It's so beautiful!" She gave a little contented sigh and died. And then something quite unbelievable happened. In the semidarkness, her face seemed to glow. No one had touched the lamp. There was no other source of light. But her features, which had been almost invisible, could be seen plainly and she was smiling. It lasted for perhaps ten seconds.
>
> It was most strange, but not at all frightening. I couldn't account for it then and I can't account for it now. But I saw it. We all saw it. Then it faded and was gone. That happened a long time ago. But I still think of Maum Jean often. And I will always remember the main thing she taught me: that nothing is a barrier when love is strong enough. Not age. Not race. Not death. Not crippled state. Not sin. Not imperfection. Not anything!

Maum Jean is a Christ figure. We are the imperfect, abandoned, crippled boy. But the truth is that our very need catches Maum Jesus' attention: "How often I have desired to gather your children together as a hen gathers her brood under her wings..." (Mt 23:37). Our flaws force us to cry out, our imperfections qualify us for Jesus' mercy and healing. So let us remember our three points:

First, imperfection does not disqualify us from God's love. If anything, it makes us more open to it.

Second, our sins, our imperfections, must not be used as a defense against God's yearning, mighty love and God's invitation to heroism and holiness.

Third, imperfection need not defeat us, for imperfection is the wound that catches God's eye. "Come to me, all you that are weary and carrying heavy burdens, and I will give you rest" (Mt 11:28). "Those who are well have no need of a physician, but those who are sick; I have come to call not the righteous but sinners to repentance" (Lk 5:31–32).

Tell that to your heart and to your children.

Questions for reflection

1. What lessons has life taught me?

2. What is my body image? My mind image? My soul image?

3. Do I use my imperfections as an excuse to hide from the grace of God?

4. "God doesn't need us to meet his needs." How do I feel about this statement?

5. "Imperfection is a wound through which God can enter." How does this relate to my life?

FIVE

THE TIN MAN

Wounded Hearts

Pilgrims, like Chaucer's motley crew, carry some heavy emotional and spiritual baggage on their journey. In this and the next chapters we're going to reflect on some of those people and their burdens: the wounded, the guilty, those with poor self-esteem, and the sinfully strayed. In this chapter, we begin with the Tin Man, who had no heart, and with the wounded hearts that make our journey so painful at times. It is a rather demanding reflection, I might add, but worth the effort—so stick with it.

We begin this topic with a truism: earlier experiences in our lives, especially in the beginning of our lives, do make us more vulnerable to hurts in the here and now. What happens during infancy and toddlerhood can predispose us toward a feeling of homelessness in our very being, of not feeling at home with ourselves. True, we must hasten to add, history is not destiny—too many people have overcome bad and sad beginnings—but we know from psychological studies that early experiences of hurt and deprivation in the first three years of life can, in fact, make us vulnerable to later difficulties with self-esteem, with relationships, and with our spiritual journey.

And so, following the words and outline of Rachel Callahan and Rea McDonnell in their audiotape, *Welcome Home: Healing Your Broken Heart*, we will begin by mentioning those particularly sensitive times in our journey: our beginnings, the first days and years of existence.

This is when we go through the developmental stages of identity and intimacy, when we have to negotiate the various losses (daddy's gone to work or to war or, worse, to the divorce court) and leave-taking (mommy's gone to the store) that are a normal part of the human journey. Some people do well with this period in their lives, but for others such normal transitional periods may have been hurtful.

How the heart gets hurt

For the purposes of our reflection, we will use six words, all starting with the letter "F," to describe the developmental injuries that may wound the heart at various stages. The first four conditions are the frigid heart, the frightened heart, the frenetic heart, and the faulted heart; these evoke a predominant feeling that usually begins in early life, but manifests itself in later life. Two other conditions can occur at any stage of life; those are the fractured heart and the freighted heart.

> *Frigid:* numb, not much circulation, paralyzed, rigid.
> *Frightened:* anxious, fearful, needy, wanting comfort.
> *Frenetic:* driven, performance conscious, perfectionism,
> demanding of self and of others.
> *Faulted:* incomplete, partial, carrying a spiritual vacuum.
> *Fractured:* broken, rejected.
> *Freighted:* burdened, just plain discouraged.

1. *The frigid heart.* We all come into being with a certain set of genes, which give us not only our physical characteristics but personality traits as well. But nurture and our environment—the people and places and events of our lives—also profoundly shape the person we eventually become. Certain early experiences form not only our childhood but also our inner child, in both a psychological and spiritual way.

The infant in the womb and the dependent newborn have four basic needs: safety, feeding, comfort, and touch—all of which have to be met in order for the infant to survive, much less thrive. The question arises: what happens if such basic needs are not met? The sad answer is that such an absence of physical or emotional bonding sends to the child the message that the world is a painful place to be. Herein are the origins of the frigid heart.

Early experiences of rejection (think of some of the children of celebrities you see on TV and how they often turn to drugs or suicide because their famous parents' careers allowed no time for them) and pain (child neglect or outright abuse), for example, get registered powerfully in the child's preverbal memory. Or, if his or her caretakers are not trustworthy and consistent—breaking promises all the time, not being there for them, mood swings—they soon learn not to trust and not to feel.

Mothers especially are critical here. Indeed, they cannot be God, but they really need to be good enough. Of course, they can be tired, preoccupied, or suffering from addiction and deprivation themselves. But if these burdens keep them from meeting the child's earliest needs at least well enough, or if these burdens cause them to reject the infant as too much of a burden or bad, then this early experience of rejection and deprivation can leave a person not even sure of his or her right to exist. It can leave one, in fact, with a profoundly internalized sense of inadequacy or just plain badness.

Such pain as this is intolerable for an infant, so what does the infant unconsciously do? He or she very soon learns to simply shut down on life to protect itself from its own pain—and alas, unknowingly, from its glory.

We call this wound the frigid heart because it makes victims unavailable to the zip and zest of life. Feelings get frozen, denied, because to experience them would be too painful. As adults, such deprived children may experience deep self-loathing, anxiety, fear, or some aversion to others; and, in extreme form, which occurs more and more in fatherless families, rage which leads to sociopathic behavior. Think of the many teen or child killers we read about who have backgrounds where abuse occurred.

2. *The frightened heart.* The next critical stage in the development of a self, in becoming a separate person, comes in those early excursions away from the lap; you know, crawling, standing, and the first steps—and here is where the frightened heart may be born. Take

some time to watch a baby in these early toddler months. Fascination with fingers and toes turns to fascination with everything. Everything is to be explored, touched, tasted. But watch the baby during this time. There is also a consistent need for mother to be available, ready for comfort, affirmation, and refueling.

Maybe this scenario exists: mommy can either be unavailable, tired, preoccupied, or depressed. On the other hand, mommy can be overly overprotective, resisting those excursions off the lap, even, as a matter of fact, resenting baby's passage from contented and cuddling to active and exploring. The result is that if there is no one there to encourage, affirm, and give comfort when the child falls down and goes boom, to introduce the child to a benign world, to offer a consistent guide to depend on as he or she explores the world, then the child will find the world a frightening and unreliable place.

Inconsistency or unavailability in having our dependency needs met at this time can create in children (and later, adults)—again in the preverbal memory, which is a feeling memory—a profound hunger for what they did not get. This deep-down memory leaves these people much more vulnerable to fears of abandonment and much more prone to fears of leaving a relationship even when it is clearly not a life-giving one. The frightened heart may try to deny dependency needs, or to react against them with compulsive care-taking behaviors of co-dependency. This frightened heart is also vulnerable to depression and addictive behaviors: compulsive eating or drinking, shopping, religiosity, working—anything to fill the hole in one's sense of emptiness.

3. *The frenetic heart.* Between fifteen and twenty-four months, the toddler's self enters a new world of exploration and attempt at mastery. Newly discovered mobility and language skills delight the hearts and hands and often, the feet of the caretaker. Her majesty, the baby, likely will never again simultaneously experience the grandiosity and the vulnerability of being alive and being a separate human being in quite the same way.

Listen to the loud and imperious "No!" of a two year old which sig-

4

4

extf

nals as much a declaration of separateness as of negativity. But our question here is: what if the "no" is never tolerated? You know the phrases: "Nice children don't do that!" "You should know better." "Big boys don't cry." What if the young child's trials and explorations are met with ridicule or putdowns, and only the nice, quiet behaviors are tolerated? What if, finally, all of the creative and spontaneous gestures that two and three year olds always do get squelched? Here is a benign example:

> The whole family went out to dinner one evening. Menus were passed to all including Molly, the eight-year-old daughter. The conversation was an "adult" one, so Molly sat ignored. When the waiter took orders, he came to Molly last.
> "And what do you want?" he asked.
> "A hot dog and a soda," she said.
> "No," said her grandmother, "she'll have the roast chicken, carrots, and mashed potatoes."
> "And milk to drink," chimed in her father.
> "Would you like ketchup or mustard on your hot dog?" asked the waiter as he walked away, taking the parents aback.
> "Ketchup," she called out.
> She then turned to her family and added, "You know what? He thinks I'm real!"

A delightful story, but it carries our point. If ridicule and humiliation meet what a child naturally experiences, that toddler will gradually learn the behavior and responses which do win parental approval and applause. Now you have the birth of a pleaser. Of course, the price of such conformity is to gradually become cut off from the spontaneity and range of feelings, and the creativity of the true self goes into hiding.

As a result, to win approval, such people learn to perform and achieve, and so become "human doings" rather than "human beings." They become truly frantic and frenetic. In an effort to compensate for childhood disapproval, they have learned to measure self-worth by achievement and perfection—or, in our market, media-dominated world, by what they own. Lacking inner strength and identity, their possessions are saying, "Look at me! I'm important!"

The burden of Joan Brumberg's book, *The Body Project*, is to show how girls of the past were taught the priority of internal qualities. These girls were therefore less susceptible to societal pressures of external beauty in order to win acceptance. But as families floundered and parents were less and less present and the media more and more intrusive, a girl's sense of self-worth shifted from the inside to the outside, with anorexia and bulimia the extreme symptoms of trying to measure up to the media's impossible external ideals. Absorbed by the frenetic pace to prove our worth, we lose the capacity to be nourished by the juice and joy of ordinary life.

4. *The faulted heart.* Next, there is the faulted heart—as in a geological fault, a split, a schizophrenia, or a lack of wholeness. This is the heart that early on, and maybe all through childhood, did not observe—and so did not learn—how fully authentic human beings live but, on the contrary, observed immoral, conniving, materialistic ways of life. Here are the influences from the unspoken but observed messages that speak louder than words, as this little bit of wisdom tells us:

> When you thought I wasn't looking, I saw you hang my first painting on the refrigerator, and I wanted to paint another one.
> When you thought I wasn't looking, I saw you feed a stray cat, and I thought it was good to be kind to animals.
> When you thought I wasn't looking, I saw you make my favorite cake just for me, and I knew that little things are special things.
> When you thought I wasn't looking, I heard you say a prayer, and I believed there is a God I could always talk to.
> When you thought I wasn't looking, I felt you kiss me good night, and I felt loved.
> When you thought I wasn't looking, I saw tears come from your eyes, and I learned that sometimes things hurt, but it's all right to cry.
> When you thought I wasn't looking, I saw that you cared and I wanted to be everything that I could be.
> When you thought I wasn't looking, I looked...and wanted to

say thanks for all the things I saw when you thought I wasn't looking.

But what if, when you thought I wasn't looking, I observed abuse and foul language, put-down sentences, cruelty, cheating, indifference, and vulgarity, a materialistic home devoid of any religion or spirituality, and they became part of my context and crept into my soul, making it hard—like the conscience-less kids who kill without a thought—or cold or unanchored? This, in a word, is the heart existing in a spiritual vacuum, the spiritual void of one's upbringing, which is abetted by a public media that has no room for religious realities and every room for consumption and banality, and a culture that produces empty marriages, rudderless children, and hollow lives governed by the clever motto "Shop till you drop."

5. *The fractured heart.* Then there is the fractured heart, the heart of rejection, the hard rejection such as divorce or the soft but deadly rejection such as neglect. You catch the soft rejection often in the songs and cries of the youth whose parents or significant adults are not there emotionally or physically, as in Harry Chapin's song, "The Cat's in the Cradle," where a father is always just about to be there for his son, but never quite makes it. At various stages of his childhood and teenage years, the son asks, "When're you coming home, Dad?" Each time the father replies, "I don't know when. But we'll get together then." But, as time goes by and the father is finally ready and eager to spend some time with his son, the son has learned how not to be there for his father. Thus, when the father asks his adult son, "When're you coming home, son?" his son replies, "I don't know when. But we'll get together then." The fracture goes on.

Or how about Stan Gerbhardt's poignant piece, "But You Didn't":

> I looked at you and smiled the other day;
> I thought you'd see me but you didn't.
> I said "I love you" and waited for what you would say;
> I thought you'd hear me but you didn't.
> I asked you to come outside and play ball with me;
> I thought you'd follow me but you didn't.

I drew a picture just for you to see;
I thought you'd save it but you didn't.
I made a fort for us back in the woods;
I thought you'd camp with me but you didn't.
I found some worms 'n such for fishing if we could;
I thought you'd want to go but you didn't.
I needed you just to talk to, my thoughts to share;
I thought you'd want to but you didn't.
I told you about the game hoping you'd be there;
I thought you'd surely come but you didn't.
I asked you to share my youth with me;
I thought you'd want to but you couldn't.
My country called me to war,
and you asked me to come home safely;
but I didn't.

The heart of rejection never quite heals completely.

6. *The freighted heart.* Finally, there is the freighted heart, the heart weighted down with discouragement. Discouragement is no laughing matter, but let us start on a light note.

You can tell it's going to be a bad day when:
You wake up face down on the pavement.
You call Suicide Prevention and they put you on hold.
You see a *60 Minutes* news team waiting in your office.
Your birthday cake collapses from the weight of the candles.
You turn on the news and they're showing emergency routes out of the city.
Your twin sister forgot your birthday.
Your car horn goes off accidentally and remains stuck as you follow a group of Hell's Angels on the freeway.
Your boss tells you not to bother to take off your coat.
The bird singing outside your window is a buzzard.
You wake up and your braces are locked together.
You call your answering service and they tell you it's none of your business.

Your income tax check bounces.

You put both contact lenses in the same eye.

Your wife says, "Good morning, Bill," and your name is George.

We all have days like that. But when the heart is freighted, laden down with discouragement, the sadness exists at deeper levels. We work at something for a long time and still do not get the result we want. Or we need a job: we send out countless resumes and follow up with phone calls, yet it all seems to just disappear into somebody's wastepaper basket. Sometimes it is not a job but a life partner we seek. We have gone through years of failed relationships, with fallow periods in between. Nothing has panned out; we might as well just give up.

We study hard for an exam or labor long over a paper, satisfied we have done well. Back comes a low grade, and we are crushed. Or we have gone through months of therapy and have begun to feel better about our life when something happens, and we find ourselves feeling and behaving exactly the way we did before. Our heart sinks. Or we have poured all our energies into raising our children well, sacrificed and spent and patiently toiled. They seem to be doing well, then suddenly they drop out of school, or get in trouble with the law, or tell us angrily how poorly we have parented them. We are devastated.

Sometimes several problems hit at once. A man was scraping along financially when his truck broke down. His truck was his livelihood, so he had no choice but to borrow the money to fix it. Then his dog, a companion of many years, fell sick and died. Not long afterward he threw out his back at work and was sidelined for several weeks. Then his relationship with his girlfriend ended painfully. He was on the verge of despair, and who could blame him? What an extraordinary flood of misfortune! No wonder people get depressed.

A recent article in a national magazine reported that depression and despair are at epidemic proportions. Nearly 30,000 Americans kill themselves each year in overt acts of suicide. Another 100,000 attempt to take their own lives. Countless more are killing themselves slowly by less obvious means such as overeating, alcohol and drug abuse, addiction to work, and the like. In addition to these overt forms of acting out depression, there are millions more who daily seek to diminish themselves through humiliation and other psychological forms of punishment.

It would certainly seem that discouragement is the worst enemy of the human spirit, and heavily weighs down the heart. Hurting hearts can lead to hurting or hurtful behaviors, yet they don't have to. In fact, many people who have been very badly hurt are the ones who work the hardest to make sure that the same thing doesn't happen to anybody else. But the unhealed child within us can recreate what was done to us or left undone to us. Abuse, we know, breeds abuse, violence begets violence, children of divorce are more likely to divorce than children from intact families. Not having been taught boundaries can leave one unsure of appropriate limits for work, play, food, or any behavior, unsure of when to say "No" to either legitimate or excessive demands.

These, then, are a few of the "heart hurts" which can lead to disease in adult life. You might want to pause now to think about the hurt within your own heart.

Healing the heart

So, we have set up the issue: if our hearts hurt and carry wounds from the past or from more recent times, what can we do? We cannot undo our past, that's for sure; but we can take the poison out of the past. We can make the present and the future better. We will always have the scars, but we can be healed. We can have a restoration, not in the sense of a sudden and miraculous cure that makes everything as it was before, but in the sense that we have the opportunity not to have it as it was before. That is, we have a chance in our hurts and heart-wounds and failures to move on. We have a chance for healing on a much deeper level, a healing that leaves us scarred but different from what we were before.

Still, we know that healing is something that cannot be forced. It requires a certain process for it to happen, and this process has seven steps—the "seven Cs," I call them. We will explore these now.

1. *Control.* The first step in healing the wounded heart is control.

We must come to a realization that even if we could not have controlled the past, we can control the present and the future. It is said that wisdom is making peace with the unchangeable. We are not responsible for our past heart wounds, whether they be from neglect, abuse (physical or sexual), divorced parents, cancer, joblessness, or the loss of a child, just as we are not responsible for the economic situation into which we are born or our DNA. But we *are* responsible for what we do with the effects, for what we build with the rubble fate has made of our lives. The only hand we have to play is the hand God (or fate) deals us.

So we needn't be victims of our biological fate. Stephen Hawking, crippled with Lou Gehrig's disease (ALS), is a good example of how a phoenix can rise from the ashes. Helen Keller was struck blind, deaf, and dumb, and yet, through the feisty persistence of her teacher, Annie Sullivan, she achieved a breathtaking depth of spirit. Milton went blind and Beethoven wrote great music after he'd gone deaf. Dostoyevsky was an epileptic. Only temporary greatness lies in the body; permanent greatness is lodged in the soul. We needn't be prisoners of our psychological fate. As psychiatrist Victor Frankl starkly and firmly asserts: "Faulty upbringing exonerates nobody."

Those brought up in heartless homes are surely victims of others' misuse of their humanity, but it is not an inescapable burden they were delivered, and they need be no more hamstrung by it than Abraham Lincoln was doomed by poverty. For those mired in self-pity or alcoholism or defeatism, there is a way out. We are all free to crawl ever so slowly toward the light—or to wallow in the darkness. Don't blame the system or others or God.

We needn't be prisoners of our situational fate, walled in by its "laws," living a provisional existence, seeking mere survival. People who went down on the Titanic went down singing. People have gotten off third-generation welfare. People survived Dachau, Auschwitz, the Gulag, Teheran, and Bosnia because they knew (if only in their guts) that others can savage our body and even take our life, but they cannot take our soul—not without our permission. Apropos are the words of psychiatrist David Ricchio:

It is important to remember a distinction: the people or situations of our past may be accountable for some of our present distress, but are not responsible for it. To be accountable means to have played a part in the formation of a fear or a deficiency. To be responsible means to have caused it, that is, to be the blame. The past is not causing nor has it caused our feelings.

As adults, our work is to recognize our pain and to work with it for change. To hold onto it is a choice against change and growth and for such a choice we are the ones responsible. The work of recovery can never truly proceed as long as anyone else is to blame, because we then become passive victims, unable to help ourselves. Only able (though wounded) adults can do this work for themselves on themselves.

2. *Care.* So often, when hearts are hurt, we neglect care, particularly self-care. Maybe we think we don't have a right to care for ourselves. Maybe we don't have the energy for it. Maybe we can't find the time because of all the claims life is making on us right now. Maybe we've been told it's not a good thing, it's selfish. But all of the holistic programs today tell us that healing begins with self-care.

For example, it is imperative to create a balance between food, exercise, rest, meditation, prayer, meaningful work, and personal relationships. We have to create the space for all those ways in which daily life can nourish us. We should learn those self-healing, self-comforting ways that help. Focusing on one's breathing, meditation, progressive relaxation, guided imagery, slowing down our pace—all are proven ways to reduce stress and anxiety.

And we have to learn to say "no" more often. The heart that takes on too many burdens because it can't say no is a heart that won't ever heal. In her book, *A Home for the Heart*, psychologist Charlotte Kasl writes:

> When you won't play the role of the one who gives all, or the nice guy, other people might feel hurt or be angry with you. Remember, whenever we carry others on our backs, both become cripples. By taking people off your back, you free them to learn to walk and you will feel lighter, happier, and more able

to feel the breath of spirit. Most of all, as you get more comfortable in saying no, you can relax, laugh, and start saying a true "Yes!"

Next, find a "Barnabas." Barnabas was introduced in the Acts of the Apostles as a companion who traveled with Paul on his journeys. His given name was Joseph but his nickname was Barnabas, which means "encourager." He was just that type of man, one who encouraged people and gave them a lift. The best health insurance of all is a relationship with a Barnabas. Who can you find to encourage you on your journey?

Also, we can begin to develop the capacity to notice the positive. When hearts have been hurt we can get into the habit of focusing on the negative, waiting for the other shoe to drop. But we should learn to focus on all the small ways that life can nourish, learn to slow down and smell the flowers, literally and figuratively. A good way to do this is to savor sensate delights like a child does.

Take the time to experience the wonder of nature: a tree, a flower, the sunset. Experience the joy of walking barefoot on different kinds of surfaces: grass, sand, rugs. In a 1988 study, University of Michigan psychologists Stephen Kaplan and his wife, Rachel, co-authors of *The Experience of Nature*, found that workers whose offices fronted a natural setting were more enthusiastic about their jobs, had fewer symptoms of ill health, and felt less pressured that those whose offices overlooked a parking lot. Take a brisk, ten-minute walk. Savor your favorite scent, from perfume to cooking: lavender, rosemary, or the spicy scent of warm apple pie (actually proven to be beneficial). Savor the taste of your favorite food.

Give yourself a treat. Practice self-care.

3. *Career.* When our wounded hearts reduce us to tears, we must say, as the mystics do, "what is the weeping asking of me?" That is, we must search for meaning in the pain and suffering and mistakes and failures of our lives. If we are preoccupied with our sins or past upbringing or bad fortune, and stay paralyzed in fear or self-recrimination or self-pity; if we are preoccupied with running away from our wounded hearts, from moral or physical pain, we are not likely to dis-

cover the meaning that might be found in running with that pain. For the truth is that when failure is present there is also a call to discover a new facet in ourselves.

In other words, it is not enough for us to recognize that we share a common brokenness with all who are sinful and hurting and wounded, and it's not enough simply to tell our tales of woe over and over again. It is only when somehow our wounds and mistakes are internalized in a meaningful way that they have the possibility of bringing us to some new place in life.

Failure may seem to break us, but unless our lives are not only broken but broken into as well, we shed tears "that turn no mill," as the poet says. Our mistakes and life-blows and heart-hurts must move us to a different place. We have to discover their meaning for us. To see no message behind the wounded heart is to wallow in paralysis. To see the message is to move on. Which is to say, wounded hearts can lead us to a second career.

When we speak of second careers, one story that comes to mind is the Old Testament account of the boy Samuel who was called three times in the temple. Old Eli, the high priest, finally caught on to what was happening and told Samuel to answer, "Speak, Lord, for your servant is listening." But recall the story's embarrassment: Eli himself was a failed parent. The Scripture says quite plainly that his sons were a disgrace who "did not walk with the Lord." People wondered among themselves: how could Eli run the religious nation when he couldn't control his own sons? His failure as a parent must have been a heavy burden for Eli, the high priest.

But Scripture also points out that in spite of failure, God will not be without a voice and without a witness. And God will use anyone— even a failed or disappointed parent—to achieve this. And so the boy Samuel, who became a great prophet of Israel, had his mind and spirit opened and sensitized by old Eli, the failed parent. This Eli, who could not open the minds and hearts of his own sons, who could have been caught in the paralysis of self-pity, shame, and failure, broke through and taught another to listen to the voice of God. And what a difference that lad made!

There is redeeming hope offered in the story of Eli and Samuel.

It says that any of us—children or parents, spouses or friends—who have experienced disappointed or failed relationships, who have had childhood traumas or deprivations, any of us can still do much good with our lives. Why? Because God offers us, always and at all times, a second career.

It is as simple and powerful as that: we are always offered a second chance. We can show the way to others and be there for them, even if we weren't successful with those closest to us. We can be teacher, guide, confidant, mentor, counselor, consoler, pray-er, and fellow pilgrim. And we will have even more impact and be more influential because our care and guidance and wisdom all come from the hurts we have felt, the wounds we have known, the depths we have plumbed.

In a word, all people with wounded hearts can discover inner depths, new spiritual dimensions, and become the wounded healers of others—take on a second career. The wounded heart, as Simeon predicted for Mary, can either break or be broken into by the Spirit.

4. *Consolidation.* Yes, consolidation is our fourth principle. All of us are partial even at our best. But when we hurt, when we suffer losses, physical or mental, when our hearts are broken, we can take our partial piece of life and try to match it up with someone else's partial piece and create a synergy of healing and wholeness. This idea is what's behind organizations such as Mothers Against Drunk Driving (MADD). In that case, parents who have suffered the terrible loss of their children through an automobile accident caused by a drunk driver can consolidate their grief into something useful. That is also the story of Alcoholics Anonymous: addicted people who use their wounds creatively for mutual help and healing. Or take the story of these two delightful ladies:

> In the spring of 1983, Margaret Patrick arrived at the Southeast Senior Center for Independent Living to begin her physical therapy. As Millie McHugh, a long-time staff member, introduced Margaret to people at the center, she noticed the look of pain in Margaret's eyes as she gazed at the piano. "Is anything wrong?" asked Millie. "No," Margaret said softly. "It's just that seeing a piano brings back memories. Before my stroke, music

was everything to me." Millie glanced at Margaret's useless right hand as the black woman quietly told some of the highlights of her music career. Suddenly Millie said, "Wait right here. I'll be back in a minute." She returned moments later, followed closely by a small, white-haired woman in thick glasses. The woman used a walker.

"Margaret Patrick," said Millie, "meet Ruth Eisenberg." Then she smiled. "She too played the piano, but like you she's not been able to play since her stroke. Mrs. Eisenberg has a good right hand, and you have a good left, and I have a feeling that together you two can do something wonderful."

"Do you know Chopin's 'Waltz in D flat'?" Ruth asked. Margaret nodded. Side by side, the two sat on the piano bench. Two healthy hands—one with long, graceful black fingers, the other with short, plump white ones—moved rhythmically across the ebony and ivory keys.

Since that day they have sat together over the keyboard hundreds of times—Margaret's helpless right hand around Ruth's back, Ruth's helpless left hand on Margaret's knee, while Ruth's good hand plays the melody and Margaret's good hand plays the accompaniment. Their music has pleased audiences on television, at churches and schools, and at rehabilitation and senior citizen centers. And on the piano bench, more than music has been shared by these two. For it was there, beginning with Chopin and Bach and Beethoven, that they learned they had more in common than they ever dreamed—both were great-grandmothers and widows (Margaret's husband died in 1985), both had lost sons, both had much to give, but neither could give without the other.

Sharing that piano bench, Ruth heard Margaret say, "My music was taken away, but God gave me Ruth." And evidently some of Margaret's faith has rubbed off on Ruth as they've sat side by side these past five years, because Ruth is now saying, "It was God's miracle that brought us together." And that is the story of Margaret and Ruth, who now call themselves "Ebony and Ivory."

Remember that wonderful film, *Driving Miss Daisy*? A proud Jewish woman and an illiterate black man learn to consolidate their individual weaknesses—her physical weakness and his educational weakness—into communal strengths and deep friendship.

There is another common sense principle under the category of consolidation; that is, to seek help and support for the ongoing journey. All of us need help in order to move out of our moral fears and spiritual paralysis. St. Paul is a good example. Remember when he was knocked off his horse on the road to Damascus? He heard a voice saying, "Get up and go into the city and there you will be told what you are to do." And in the city he meets a little nondescript man named Ananias, who in no way wanted to meet Paul because he heard that he was going around killing Christians. But Ananias overcame his fear, cured Paul of his blindness, and introduced him to the faith.

All of us need an Ananias, a spiritual guide, a friend or, as the Irish put it, a soul-friend. And in turn we have to be Ananias for others. All of us need help toward restoration, whether it be through a friend, a therapist, a spiritual counselor, or a support group. We all need help to overcome spiritual paralysis. Like religion itself, "moving on" is a communal, not a solitary, adventure.

5. *Ceremony.* When we hurt, when we are burdened with scars of the past, when the inner child cries with pain, ritual will help heal. I don't think we Americans really understand how powerful rituals are. We've done away with most of them or have had them replaced by commercialized ones designed to make us buy things. But rituals are very healing. Listen to Sr. Jose Hobday:

> My mother, who was a Native American, taught me all kinds of
> wonderful ways to pray when I was a child. A very special one was
> the Sacrifice Flower prayer, which she adapted from the heritage
> of her people, the Seneca Iroquois. She taught me to say this
> prayer when I was feeling low or had a burden I wanted lifted.
> Later, I learned to use it for happy occasions and when I had a
> special request I wanted to make of God. Like all mothers, she
> could always tell when something was bothering me. She'd say
> to me, "All right, Jo. I think it's time you went outside and found

yourself a Sacrifice Flower. It's time you get your burden lifted from your heart and give it to God."

So I would go looking for a flower. Sometimes Mother would go out with me to help me with my flower or talk about what was bothering me. Sometimes, too, she had something weighing on her heart and she would find a Sacrifice Flower of her own. That flower was supposed to be special, one that meant a lot to me. As a girl, I liked dandelions, hollyhocks, and daisies. So I usually picked one of them. In addition, Mother said I was to be very careful with the flower because it had been selected for a holy purpose. I lovingly cupped it in my hands so nothing would happen to it.

When I got home, I did as my mother instructed and told the flower what burden I wanted lifted and taken to God. How was the flower to do this? Remember, this was a Sacrifice Flower, one that was going to die. The idea was that as life went out of the flower, it would carry my prayer to God. That meant, of course, the flower was not to be placed in water. I had a shelf in my room that I liked to use for my Sacrifice Flower because it was sort of private and yet I could see it as I went in and out.

Every time I saw the flower, I could see it giving its life for me and I could imagine my prayer being carried to God. That was true even when I was elsewhere and was just thinking about the flower. Either way, I had a strong sense my prayer was being heard. My flower and I were in union. Sometimes it took a few days, sometimes a couple of weeks. When the flower finally died, I would take it outside, say good-bye to it, and thank it for giving its life for me and for delivering my prayer. Then I would bury it so it would have a chance at a new life, and I always hoped it would come back as an even nicer flower.

In this simple, graphic way my mother taught me how uplifting prayer can be. And, in the process, she taught me about life, too—how basic both dying and rising are to living and how important it is that we become Sacrifice Flowers for each other.

Here's another Jose Hobday story:

My mother taught me many prayers when I was young. Often they were prayers of comfort, in contrast to those of my father. His prayers taught me to meet life's challenges. I did not always think of my mother's prayers as prayers, even though that's what she called them. Sometimes I just went through them with her to satisfy her. Nevertheless, because they were based on experience, many of them stuck with me.

This is one of my favorites. I was about six years old at the time I learned this one. I was sitting outside on a block of concrete, and I was crying. I don't even know why. I was just crying and crying. My mother came along and said, "What's the matter?" I said, "Nothing. Leave me alone!" She did—and then I really started crying. About fifteen minutes later she came back and sat beside me. "You know," she said, "I have to tell you something. There are going to be a lot of times in your life when you are going to cry, and you won't know why. You won't understand and neither will anybody else. You can marry the nicest man in the world, but at times like this, he won't know what to do to help you stop crying."

Then she said she was going to teach me a prayer for the times when I was crying and didn't know why. She made me get off the cement block and stand up. She said, "Now put your arms around yourself." I did, but it wasn't good enough for her. "You're just folding your arms," she said. "Put them all the way around yourself. Cuddle your body. Hold yourself the way you would hold a baby in your arms. Now after you have a real good hold of yourself, close your eyes and begin to rock yourself. Rock yourself real good, the way you would a baby, and just keep doing it.

"When you grow up, no matter how old you are, and you find yourself crying and you don't know why, I want you to rock yourself just like this. And as you do it, remember that you are God's little girl, and that God understands why you are crying even if no one else does. And remember, too, that God holds you close just the way you are holding yourself, because God loves you very much. Then just keep rocking yourself and be comforted."

Isn't that a good prayer? I still say it today when I feel bad. I recommend it for you, too. Just stand wherever you are—in the kitchen, in the shop, or in the bathroom—and wrap your arms around yourself as tightly as you can. Rock yourself. Before long you will be able to feel God holding you in the same way you are holding yourself. You will be comforted the way you were comforted as a child when your mother held you in her arms and rocked you.

We Americans are so deprived of rituals today. But they move the body, the imagination, the fluids of life into something more creative than our hurts.

6. *Contemplation.* Contemplation basically means tapping into the stories of other people, people with wounded hearts who turned around, like sinner Augustine or deaf Beethoven or others.

One morning a small boy living on a North Dakota farm awoke in great pain. Recognizing that their son was deathly ill, his parents were greatly alarmed. Rushing him to the nearest hospital, seventy-five miles away, it was discovered his appendix was ruptured. Peritonitis had set in and poison was spreading rapidly through his body. A tube was quickly inserted into his side to siphon away the deadly toxin. Feverish days turned into frightening weeks. Miraculously, the boy survived.

Through the long months of isolation and recuperation in the family's farmhouse, a growing conviction grew within the youth that God had spared him. "It seemed to me that God had given me a second chance at life and I prayed for guidance to use my life in ways that would please him most," he would later write. To pass the time, the boy began to play sounds on his father's old accordion. The more he played, the more he enjoyed it.

Had it not been for the "terrible" experience of a ruptured appendix, the boy might have remained a North Dakota farmer. Instead, he emerged from that experience with a deep faith in God and in himself. Following his interest in the accordion, Lawrence Welk left his North Dakota farm, becoming a gifted musician and host to one of television's most popular programs.

Key to Welk's future success was the fact that as a youth he chose to face the light in his life rather than curse the darkness. Instead of placing the focus on the danger, disaster, and disappointment which clouded his young life, the boy chose to place his energies on healing, recovery, and opportunity.

Unfortunately, when misfortune strikes some people, they squander their time and energy lashing out at fate. Because they are unable to turn away from the darkness and face the light, they become bitter, angry, hostile. They need to contemplate stories of people like Lawrence Welk. They need to delve into biblical stories, like those that tell of a sterile Sarah who bore a son, or a rejected Joseph who became ruler of Egypt, or a David chosen over his brothers, or a virgin who conceived, or a Jesus betrayed, tortured, and risen from the dead, or a murderous Saul who became Paul. Then there are the contemporary stories, like those of a libertine named Merton who became a monk, or an unwed mother named Dorothy Day who became a beacon for the poor.

7. *Christ.* Finally, last and far from least, is Christ. Turn to God and to Jesus, God's sign of tender care and presence. For the fact is, we need to be reborn, re-parented—some of us would like that—and God says, all right. I will rebirth you in my womb. God has sent Jesus to heal what has been hurt in our past and present. Remember, it is the outcast to whom Jesus comes: the one who feels alone, abandoned, burdened, rejected, alienated, or unreconciled with God and with others. Jesus wants to welcome home our hearts. He wants us to show him where it hurts. Recall these words from the mystics: "God is greater than our accusing hearts." All God wants is for us to surrender to him, to become the stream in this ancient Sufi tale:

Once upon a time a stream was working its way across the country, experiencing little difficulty. It ran around the rocks and through the mountains. Then it arrived at the desert. Just as it had crossed every other barrier, the stream tried to cross this one, but it found that as fast as it ran into the sand, its waters disappeared. After many attempts it became very discouraged. It appeared that there was no way it could continue the journey. Then a voice came in the wind: "If you stay the way you are you cannot cross the sands; you cannot become more than a quagmire. To go further you will have to lose yourself."

"But if I lose myself," the stream cried, "I will never know what I'm supposed to be."

"Oh, on the contrary," said the voice. "If you lose yourself you will become more than you ever dreamed you could be."

So the stream surrendered to the sun. And the clouds into which it was transformed were carried by the raging wind for many miles. Once it crossed the desert, the stream poured down from the skies, fresh and clean, and full of the energy that comes from storms.

So, say the saints and mystics, we must let go and let God. Ponder the words of Henri Nouwen:

Yes, you are ill, but you are Beloved.
Yes, things are going wrong in your life, but you are Beloved.
Yes, you are fed up, disgusted, hurt, but you are Beloved.
Yes, you are hungry—hungry for love and acceptance—but you are Beloved.
Whatever is happening to you, there is one constant: you are Beloved.

So, here we are, the wounded hearts:

- frigid
- frightened
- frenetic
- faulted
- fractured
- freighted.

But, as we have seen, there are responses and processes:

- control

- care
- career
- consolidation
- ceremony
- contemplation
- Christ.

Running through this reflection are these fundamental questions: What do loss and failure reveal about me? What is my wounded heart asking of me? What does it tell me of my need for God? How can my mistakes move me from one place to another, to being a fuller, more whole person? To being the saint God created me to be?

What is the wounded heart's message, its meaning, and its promise of a better future? How can I become a wounded healer of others? For that is what we are all called to be. If we see our losses and failures as defining us forever, we succumb to spiritual paralysis and our journey slows down or stops. But if we look at our failures, claim them, and hand them over to Jesus to be used as building blocks, then we are on the way to recovery. We get back on the path. Freed from our paralysis, we shall dance once more and sing Mary's song of praise along with her:

My soul magnifies the Lord
And my spirit rejoices in God, my Savior.

For he has looked on the lowliness and nothingness of someone no more than a servant—a "Miss Nobody"—a mother whose heart was pierced with a sword, but still, still…

He who is mighty has done great things for me.

And holy is his name!

Questions for reflection

1. Is mine the frigid heart? Was I neglected or rejected as an infant? Do I have throat-constricting anxiety?

2. Am I the frightened heart? Was I someone who did not receive a lift when I fell or a towel for my tears?

3. Is mine the frenetic heart, always on the move, always trying to prove myself, always seeking the approval of others because I was not approved, was not allowed to explore the world or my feelings?

4. The faulted heart—is it mine? When they thought I wasn't looking, I saw nothing of kindness, forgiveness, or faith and I feel the emptiness.

5. Is mine the fractured heart? I've been rejected and neglected. My sibling was the favorite; someone else got the part in the play or the promotion at work; my "special someone" chose to marry another. People don't see me—they see past me.

6. Am I the freighted heart, weighed down with discouragement? Nothing seems to have gone right in my life, even my spiritual life.

Come to me, all you that are weary and are carrying heavy burdens, and I will give you rest. Take my yoke upon you, and learn from me; for I am gentle and humble in heart, and you will find rest for your souls (Mt 11:28–29).

7. *Control.* Others may be accountable for my wounded heart, but I am responsible for what I do with it. Pray over this.

8. *Care.* Do I take proper self-care? Or do I think that's an indulgence, a sinful selfishness? Do I take time for the healing benefits of sensate delights or do I have a touch of puritanism in me?

9. *Career.* What is the weeping asking of me? What is to be discovered in my brokenness? What other career beckons? Where are the possibilities for grace to occur?

10. *Consolation.* What partial part of me can I join to another's to create wholeness?

11. *Ceremony.* Do I use rituals that heal?

12. *Contemplation.* Do I savor and enter into the stories of redemption?

13. *Christ.* Do I, like the stream, let go and let God?

SIX

THE WIZARD

Four Questions

Landscapes can become disfigured: we have all seen that happen. Lovely parks are now filled with condos, open spaces loaded with fast-food places. Ocean views are obstructed by highrises for the wealthy, and tree-lined roads are dotted with billboards. Then there is the ugliness of city blight, pollution, and smog.

Our spiritual landscapes can become disfigured and suffer, as well. Cut off from aesthetics and beauty and nature, the soul shrivels and becomes one-dimensional. It becomes hard for us to detect the presence of angels. And when our spiritual landscape suffers, we can become sick: soul sick. We then need to be made well. But we don't need the type of curing which usually refers to the body: for a headache, the broken leg, cancer. We need healing, which has to do with repairing the soul, mending our bond with the self, at the deepest levels of who we are.

As the medical profession is discovering more and more these days, you really cannot cure the body unless you also heal the soul. In fact, the body may become sick because the soul is. It is estimated that eighty-five percent of our bodily illnesses come from distress in the soul. It is indeed an accepted fact that eighty-five percent of the reasons that people visit their doctor are mind-body related. And it is no wonder: today there is a terrible loss of soul. People are soul sick. Community is fractured. God is absent and enchantment has disappeared from the face of the earth. As Thomas Moore writes in his book, *The Re-Enchantment of Everyday Life*:

> We have been ingenious in this century in finding ways to hide from nature, and in the process we have let enchantment recede piece by piece. Then we wonder why we now have a religious and spiritual crisis. We blame each other for not having the moral fortitude to maintain traditional values and sustain church commitments, but we don't complain about the commercial obliteration of nature by the great screen of advertising that lines every American town or road, or by the ever present noise and light of an insensitive culture that keeps nature's presence blissfully blocked out.
>
> The only explanation for our acceptance of these commercial insensitivities is that we have forgotten that nature is the prime source of the spiritual life. Block it out, and we obliterate the source of the spirit that the soul thrives on. Erect another billboard, another neon sign, another rack of halogen lights, and we push spirituality farther into repression.

Such exploitation, driven by the always present and always dominant "bottom line" has, in Moore's words, left us with a low consciousness of the Presence, with a sense that nothing is sacramental and sacred, nothing lurks behind reality. There are no rumors of angels, only raw human power to manipulate the human machine. All this starves the soul. And that leaves us all at bay, especially the youth. Let me reach back to chapter four and repeat Doug Coupland's cry:

> Now here is my secret: I tell it to you with an openness of heart that I doubt that I shall ever achieve again, so I pray that you are in a quiet room as you hear these words. My secret is that I need God—that I am sick and can no longer make it alone. I need God to help me give, because I no longer seem capable of giving; to help me be kind, as I no longer seem capable of kindness; to help me love, as I seem beyond being able to love.

And that is the cry of so many people. Our lifestyles, broken relationships, child abuse, crass commercialism, the felt absence of

God—all are symptoms of a deep illness. People lose their bearings on life's journey because they are suffering from what we might call a loss of soul, or soul sickness. But let me share this: in other cultures, people who show the symptoms of soul sickness and who have a desire to be healed go to the "wizard," an indigenous healer or spiritual guru. All over the world the soul-sufferer is invariably asked four deep and universal questions, one by one. These four questions frame the reflections of this chapter.

Singing

The first deep question is: "When in your life did you stop singing?" When did you lose your voice? Who or what made you feel that it was no longer safe to give voice to your own truth, thus submerging your real self? As a result, your soul has contracted and your identity has been lost.

Jules Pfeiffer, the satirist and playwright, has a wonderful parody that appears in a series of cartoon panels. They show a boy named Danny who says:

> Ever since I was a little kid, I didn't want to be me. I wanted to be like Billy Whittleton, and Billy didn't even like me. I walked like he walked; I talked liked he talked. I signed up for the same high school he signed up for, which was when Billy Whittleton changed. He began to hang out around with Herbie Vanderman. He walked like Herbie Vanderman; he talked like Herbie Vanderman. And it dawned on me that Herbie Vanderman walked and talked like Joey Hamerlin. And Joey Hamerlin walked and talked like Corky Fabinson.
>
> So here I am, walking and talking like Billy Whittleton's imitation of Herbie Vanderman's version of Joey Hamelin trying to walk and talk like Corky Fabinson. And who do you think Corky Fabinson is always walking and talking like? Of all people, dopey Kenny Wellington—that little pest who walks and talks like me!

We all go through that: the gentle muting of our inner songs. Other times it is not so innocent. A few years ago I read a wonderfully poignant novel by the Irish writer, Molly Keane. It was called *Good Behaviour*, a sad story about what we would call today a dysfunctional family. The story centers around a daughter who, in her mother's eyes, is a non-entity, a zero; a daughter, therefore, who is desperate for love and acknowledgment and recognition by her parents—by anybody. Symptomatic of their relationship is this scene, which the daughter, who narrates the events in this novel, describes. The household is retiring for the night:

> The staircase at the mansion parted right and left under a high window. From there, two separate flights took one upwards on light, shallow steps. They embraced the hollow to the hall below them. A single flight went on to the next story of the house, and above that was the glazed bell of the dome. I took the left stair upwards, and Mummy took the right, so that when we got to the bedroom corridor there would be no need to speak or kiss. She wafted up her side, I trudged up my side. "Goodnight," we said, "Goodnight." And we turned gratefully away from one another.

The whole novel is like this: the story of this emotionally starved girl and her unwise projections of love because no one has touched her or affirmed her. A riveting scene takes place when, towards the end of the novel, her father has a stroke. The mother, who is a self-centered socialite type, is running around distraught, looking for the maid, who is named Rose. What happens is described by the daughter:

> Breaking into the void of (the) silence of the afternoon, a voice came calling, distantly, then nearer, "Rose!" it called. "Rose! Rose!" Mummy, of course, forgetting that the servants had gone out, that was quite like her. So she rang the library bell. So nobody answered the library bell. So she called distractedly, demanding. "Let her," I thought, as I opened my bedroom door. "Let her go on calling."
>
> Then as I reached the staircase I could hear panic, high and faint in her voice. What a fuss. What nonsense. I proceeded in a calm, sane way downstairs, my hand on the rail, my head still held high.

Then I saw her, pattering and running, stripped of her poise, awkward as an animal in clothing.... And this was Mummy, always so cool, so balanced, and here she was, her hair flying loose out of her hat, her mouth grimacing. "Rose!" she called. "Rose!"

Then she saw me. "Oh, it's you."

Her passionate disappointment infuriated me and kept me outside her terror. "Find somebody!" she said. "Find somebody! He's dying!" She tottered on and ran towards the swing door, away from me. She didn't have to say it. I knew it was Papa. "Where is he?" I went after her, but she didn't tell me where to find him, only ran before me, following her hands, her feet fumbling on the flagstones, calling "Rose!" into the dark pantry door, and the lamp room, and the boot room; and "Rose! Rose!" into the hot, empty kitchen.

I stood in the doorway before she could escape me. I caught her by the shoulders, something impossible I had never done. I shouted at her, "Where is he?" "He's terribly ill. He can't get up. Find Rose! Oh, you fool! Find Rose!"

What about me? There was no "me" here: the daughter was invisible to her mother. Alienation. Estrangement. The daughter's song had long ago been suppressed.

Was there any time in your life that someone was yelling for Rose when you were standing there all the while? That will make you lose your voice. I can think of another muting: the one who is forced into a job or calling he or she does not want. I recall a priest long ago who caused much scandal when he left the priesthood. He never wanted to be a priest. His Irish mother had the vocation, not him. His sister, a whiz in math, was made to teach English out of "holy obedience." Again we see the lack of affirmation, the put-downs.

In his autobiography, that incredible writer, Frederick Buechner, relates an incident that occurred when he was six years old awaiting his favorite grandmother's visit. He decided to surprise her with a feast of cold string beans, causing the grandmother to make a caustic remark which the boy overheard. Buechner writes:

I do not remember what she said then exactly, but it was an

aside spoken to my parents or whatever grownups happened to be around, to the effect that she did not usually eat much at three o'clock in the afternoon or whatever it was, let alone cold string beans of another age, but that she would see what she could do for propriety's sake. Whatever it was, she said it dryly, wittily, the way she said everything, never dreaming for a moment that I would either hear or understand.

But I did hear, and what I came to understand for the first time in my life, I suspect—why else should I remember it?—was that the people you love have two sides to them. One is the side they love you back with, and the other is the side with which, even when they do not mean to, they can sting you like a wasp, the first telltale crack in the foundation of the one home which perhaps any child has when you come right down to it, and that is the people he loves.

There is a well-known Irish play called *Translation.* It is a story about what happens to a people when not only the rule but the language of a foreign nation is imposed upon them. The play opens with a hedge-school teacher (the hedge-school teachers were the people in old Ireland who used to grab the children, hide them in the hedges, and teach them their heritage because the British forbade them to teach the Irish language and culture), who is coaxing and encouraging a young woman to overcome her speech impediment; and at least learn to say her own name. Her agonized struggle to form simple words that express her identity are finally successful. Her transformation is clearly reflected in her face, which shows a new dignity that at last she can publicly profess her identity and who she is.

But in the last act of the play, there is a bullying military officer of the occupying force who has gathered these people, this young girl included, to interrogate them because an officer has been killed and he suspects that some of them are harboring the killers. She is so frightened and intimidated by his bullying ways that once more she loses the power of speech. And it becomes clear, as you watch the play, that the girl is not only the girl, but she represents all the people who have been rendered dumb by the violation of their dignity and their culture. They lose their voice.

Or maybe for us the case is that we experienced a rather bloodless authoritarianism in our parents or teachers or other significant adults in our lives. Maybe our lot is a loveless marriage, a divorce, a shallow relationship that makes it hard to share the deepest secrets of the heart. Walker Percy captures this evasiveness in a chilling scene from his novel *The Second Coming*:

She spoke with the quietness of people after a storm which had drowned out their voices. What struck him was not sadness or remorse or pity but the wonder of it. How can it be? How can it happen that one day you are young, you marry, and then another day you come to yourself and your life has passed like a dream? They looked at each other curiously and wondered how they could have missed each other, lived in the same house all these years and passed in the hall like ghosts.

Then there are the cruelties of convention, imposed by the media and reinforced by our circle of friends, who tell us what we must wear and eat and hold dear in order to be accepted. Anthony DeMello is quite direct in this regard:

Look at your life and see how you have filled its emptiness with people. As a result they have a stranglehold on you. See how they control your behavior by their approval or disapproval. They hold the power to ease your loneliness with their company, to send your spirits soaring with their praise, to bring you down to the depths with their criticism and rejection.

Take a look at yourself spending almost every waking moment of your day placating and pleasing people, whether they are living or dead. You live by their norms, conform to their standards, seek their company, desire their love, dread their ridicule, long for their applause, meekly submit to the guilt they lay upon you; you dare not go against the fashion in the way you dress or speak or act or even think. And observe how even when you control them you depend on them and are enslaved by them. People have become so much a part of your being that you cannot even imagine living a life that is unaffected or uncontrolled by them.

All these conditions and more suppress the voice, make us feel quite unsafe to express our own truth. We are immobilized by the thought of what others will say. The fear of our peers silences our voices. And so, over time, the soul becomes ill and contracted. Before you know it, the singing has stopped and you just go along. No wonder the spiritual guru's first question is: when in your life did you stop singing? When did you feel it was no longer safe to voice your own truth? Do you even realize that you are no longer singing?

Dancing

The second question is this: "When did you stop dancing?" When did you begin to lose touch with your body? Children dance spontaneously all the time. How did it happen that we stopped dancing? We hide our bodies, are ashamed of them or punish them or rearrange them through cosmetic surgery. After all, they sag and age, give off unpleasant odors and, perhaps worst of all, have demanding sexual yearnings. So, no more spontaneous dance.

We soon learn: don't make a fool of yourself. Be respectable. And if you're elderly or near elderly—forget about dancing. People see us—and I count myself, grudgingly, as a senior citizen—as if we were beyond feeling and dreams, as if we didn't have a rich inner life or current passions and desires and a taste for romance and a craving for arms around us in bed. Beth Ashley speaks for many of us when she recounts:

> The little cruise ship was crowded with people, many of them retired, all of them off for three days of pleasure. Ahead of me in the carpeted passageway was a tiny woman in brown polyester slacks, her shoulders hunched, her white hair cut in a short, straight bob. From the ship's intercom came a familiar tune, "Begin the Beguine," by Artie Shaw.
>
> And suddenly, a wonderful thing happened. The woman, unaware that anyone was behind her, began to shimmy and

shake. She snapped her fingers. She swiveled her hips. She did a quick and graceful Lindy step back, shuffle, slide. Then, as she reached the door to the dining salon, she paused, assembled her dignity, and stepped soberly through. She became a hunched old lady again.

That visual fragment has returned to mind many times. I think of it now as I recall another birthday and an age where most people would not believe that I still shimmy, too. Younger people think folks of my years are beyond music, romance, dancing, or dreams. They see us as age has shaped us: camouflaged by wrinkles, with thick waists and graying hair. They don't see all the other people who live inside. We present a certain face to the world because custom indicates it. We are the wise old codgers, the dignified matrons. We have no leeway to act our other selves or use our other selves.

She's right, isn't she? There's more to us older folks—more dreams and desires and passions; more memories, wit, and intelligence than meets the eye—and we resent being categorized as formless "senior citizens" to be distracted like children and not engaged as persons. But in a market-driven society, where we are no longer "useful" for production or reproduction, we are patronized, not revered, for who we are.

When did you stop dancing? When did you lose touch with your body? When did you learn to hate it, even though God thought the human body worthwhile enough to embrace it with incarnation? A shamed, constricted body is a shamed, constricted soul. Body hatred is soul hatred; soul hatred is soul sickness; and sickness can make the spiritual journey joyless.

Stories

The third deep question is: "When did you stop being enchanted with stories?" Stories are the greatest healing and teaching art we have. Through stories we transmit values, traditions, memories, and identity. But in the course of history they have been undermined. On one hand, education set in. And propositions. And doctrine. And rules. And lesson plans. And outlines. And scientific thinking. And linear expression. And the bottom line. And thus we began to lose our stories, the stories that enchanted us, that spoke to us, that moved deep into the soul because somehow the story was us.

So we begin to lose our identity, curtail our ability to dream, and worst of all, shrink our pool of healing images. In the meantime, global corporations have become so powerful that they have supplanted our traditional stories with their commercially-honed market stories, all of which are designed to encourage consumerism. These stories supply the images and metaphors for popular consumption. Martin Copenhaver catches it well:

> In our time, the stories that most occupy us and may most influence us are the stories that come to us through the media, particularly television. These are the stories of our culture, the stories that tell us who we are and what we are to value. The news programs and soap operas, the sporting events and situation comedies—they are the default catechism of our children. There may be some good things and some bad things on television, but in the end they are all the same in this respect: they are brought to us by people trying to sell us things. The underlying story that unites them all is the message that we are supposed to learn how to be good consumers.

Therein lies the disaster. It is—or should be—the images that arise from the ancient stories and poetry that determine our outlook. Images, you must know, are where the therapy is. The images of the soul impact the body and vice versa. Images move in and out of the mind-body unity and soothe it. Therapists know this truth: change the image and you heal the soul. Change how you imagine reality and you make whole what is fragmented, you enable the soul, mind, and body to interact.

Here's a very simple example. I went to someone's home for dinner one night, and watched while the wife prepared dinner. She had made pork, which her husband hated because he said it made him sick. So she did what a good wife might do: she made the pork in a wonderful sauce and told him it was something else. All during the meal he enjoyed it immensely. About an hour later, after complimenting his wife on the wonderful dinner, she confessed that it was pork. He then promptly threw up. Talk about a mind-body relationship! Talk about the power of image!

Or, if you want a more sophisticated example, listen to psychologist Joan Boryshenko:

> [When I was in training at Harvard] there was very little in the way of treatment for people with stress-related illnesses, and most physicians had very little time for them. I found that out because I was one of those people. Part of my stress had to do with the gap between what my parents wanted for me and what I wanted for myself. I was raised as the archetypal Jewish American princess—groomed from birth to grow up and marry a doctor.
>
> When I rebelled at an early age, saying I would rather be a doctor than marry one, I became a big disappointment to both my parents, particularly my mother. The difference between what your parents envision for you and what you want for yourself is often linked to self-esteem; the farther apart those visions are, the lower your self-esteem is likely to be. Because I was constantly aware of how different my path was from the one my parents had chosen for me, my self-esteem was quite low.
>
> [As a result], within my first year of graduate school, my migraines became so severe that they often lasted for two or three days, and I would become dehydrated from the constant vomiting. I also had irritable bowel syndrome, which is like having a migraine in your belly. I developed high blood pressure, as well as a cardiac arrhythmia that was so severe I was afraid of fibrillating and dying. It also became clear that something was very wrong with my immune system—I had chronic bronchitis that kept turning into either pleurisy or pneumonia. For most of the time, I was on antibiotics; occasionally, my problems became so acute that I had to be hospitalized....
>
> A fellow student of mine, a long-time practitioner of transcendental meditation, took me aside and said, "You have all the

symptoms of hyper-arousal of your sympathetic nervous system. You are forming images in your mind of everything you fear in life and your physiology is carrying out your fearful images because your body cannot tell the difference between what you're imagining and what is happening." I said, "So what should I do?" He said, "Learn to meditate. Meditation will help you clear fearful images from your mind and teach you instead to be present to what is." He was right. I learned how to meditate, and within a period of about six months, all of my illnesses disappeared.

Simply put, Boryshenko had replaced her images. Meditation and stories can help to do that.

I want to point out what many of you might know by experience. A study of one hundred Roman Catholics showed that for each person, self-esteem was connected to how he or she thought of God. Those who believed in a loving and merciful God had much higher self-esteem than those who saw God as being judgmental and punitive. This, in turn, was related to the way they were raised. Those who were brought up in a very authoritarian and punitive environment developed low self-esteem, which they, in turn, projected onto the world; they created a punitive God in the image of their parents.

Now you know why psychologists ask you to draw pictures. They want to see what your images are, particularly your self-image. Poor images contort the soul. So this third question becomes critical: who told you your first stories? The images in your head and heart—where did they come from? At what point did you hold onto the negative images and not replace them?

Which leads us back to the question: when did you stop being enchanted with stories? Or, for Christians: when did you stop reading the Jesus stories—really reading them with your heart? The prodigal father who took the initiative; the foolish shepherd reversing the odds of ninety-nine to one; the healer who dried up flowing wounds; the man who talked to the woman as an equal at the well; the conversationalist with a crucified thief? When did you stop being enchanted with stories? Stories like this one:

One day a young sailor was in the library getting a book when he noticed that there were pencil notations in the margin. And they were so deep and loving that he decided then and there that he would have to meet the person who wrote such beautiful thoughts. He went to the librarian and got the name of the woman who had written those lovely words.

The day after his introductory letter to her as pen pal he was shipped overseas. But for the next year the two corresponded regularly back and forth, exchanging a great deal of pleasure in revealing their deepest thoughts. At different times the sailor asked for a picture of his correspondent but he never received one. But still, their feelings for each other grew.

It was finally time for him to return to the United States. He and his pen pal arranged a rendezvous for seven o'clock, in Grand Central Station. How would he know her? She wrote back that he would know her by the red rose she would wear in her lapel.

Well, shortly after entering the station, a tall, beautiful blonde, in a pale green suit sauntered by. Almost magnetically, the lonely young man was drawn toward this woman, and her alluring vitality and sensuality. She smiled at him and even murmured, "Going my way, sailor?" as she passed by. But her spell over him was broken when he suddenly saw behind her a woman wearing a red rose in her lapel. His heart sank because she was as plain as the blonde had been stunning. She was fortyish, roundish, grayish, but with two sparkling eyes in a gentle face.

As the blonde walked away, the young sailor hesitated for a moment, but then turned his back on her beauty and strode over to the simple woman who was wearing the red rose in her lapel. Looking at her, he faced the disappointed realization that their relationship could never really be a romantic one. And yet, on the other hand, he was buoyed by the memory of their letters and of the prospect of having at least a lifelong friend, one whose wit and spirituality and intelligence he already knew from their correspondence.

And so, the young sailor introduced himself and suggested

that they go out to dinner. But the woman just smiled at him with amusement and told him, "I don't know what this is all about, son, but the young lady in the green suit who just went by begged me to wear this rose on my coat. And she said that if you were to ask me out to dinner she is waiting for you in the restaurant across the street. She said it was some kind of a test."

Think about that one. Now, here's another story:

Once upon a time in a forest, three young trees were growing side by side. As they grew, they shared with each other their dreams of what they would become when they grew up to be big trees. The first tree said, "My dream is to become part of a luxurious home, where many famous people come and go, and admire the grain and the color of my wood." The second young tree said, "My dream is to become the tall mast of an elegant sailing vessel that journeys to the seven seas." And the third said, "Well, my dream is to become part of a great tower, so high that it will inspire people who look at it. People will come from all over the world to see it." And so the young trees dreamed.

Eventually, the young trees grew to maturity and were cut down. The first didn't become a part of a luxurious home as it had dreamed; instead, some of its wood was fashioned into a simple manger, a wooden trough to hold the hay that animals ate. The second tree didn't become the tall mast of an elegant ship as it had dreamed; instead, it became the sides of an ordinary fishing boat, like many another on the Sea of Galilee. The third didn't become part of a tall tower as it had dreamed; instead, it was fashioned into the beams of a cross and used for a crucifixion.

Rerouted dreams can find glory in unexpected places. Now, permit me one more story:

Just over one hundred years ago, Adolph Hitler was born. In his fifty-six years on the planet he did incredible harm, and was responsible for millions of terrible deaths. Yet in all of the horror that he unleashed, there are pinpoints of light and nobility.

A German soldier, Private Joseph Schultz, was one such pinpoint of light. He was sent to Yugoslavia shortly after the invasion. He was a loyal, young German soldier on patrol, and one day the sergeant called out eight names, his among them. They thought they were going on a routine patrol, and as they hitched up their rifles, they came over a hill, still not knowing what their mission was. There were eight Yugoslavians there, standing on the brow of the hill; five men and three women. It was only when they got about fifty feet away from them, when any marksman could shoot out an eye of a pheasant, that the soldiers realized what their mission was.

The eight soldiers were lined up. The sergeant barked out, "Ready!" and they lifted up their rifles. "Aim," and they got their sights. And suddenly in the silence that prevailed, there was a thud of a rifle butt against the ground. The sergeant, and the seven other soldiers, and those eight Yugoslavians, stopped and looked. And Private Joseph Schultz walked toward the Yugoslavians. His sergeant called after him and ordered him to come back, but he pretended not to hear him. Instead, he walked the fifty feet to the mound of the hill, and he joined hands with the eight Yugoslavians.

There was a moment of silence, then the sergeant yelled, "Fire!" And Private Joseph Schultz died, mingling his blood with those innocent men and women. Later found on his body was an excerpt from St. Paul : "Love does not delight in evil, but rejoices in the truth. It always protects, always trusts, always hopes, and always perseveres" (1 Cor 13:6–7).

These, then, are the images and stories that should fill our minds and hearts. But all too often they are, as we said, pushed out by the commercialized media stories of greed and violence, lust and consumerism, that shrivel the soul.

When did you stop being enchanted with stories?

Silence

The final question the spiritual guru would ask is, "When did you

stop being comfortable with the territory of silence?" Silence is recognized by all cultures as that place where we can connect to mystery.
Is it any wonder, then, that our culture is soul sick? So much noise;
so many commercials; so much incessant rock music, loud and deafening; so much striking violence; so persistent the ever-present TV
that many people don't even know it's on.

Yes, in our culture silence is often impossible to come by. This is a
tragedy, for silence allows us to replenish ourselves so that we can
then give back to the world around us. The lack of generosity that we
often experience in the world—even our physical tiredness—may be
due to the fact that so few of us have adequate solitude within which
to replenish ourselves. Savor this reflection on silence from Belden
Lane:

> Occasioning this whole line of thought for me is a phrase that
> has rumbled for several years in and out of my consciousness
> like a nagging koan. "We are saved in the end by the things that
> ignore us." I found it in a book by Andrew Harvey, an
> Englishman from Oxford writing about Buddhist meditation,
> the landscape of northern India along the borders of Tibet,
> and his own pilgrimage in search of a self he meant to lose.
> Near the Land of Snows, at the roof of the world, he traveled
> with eager anticipation from one monastery to another, passing
> rows of large stone stupas erected along the high passes, spin-
> ning the copper cylinders or "prayer wheels" that symbolically
> intone the ancient mantra, *om mani padme hum.*
>
> Moved by the magnificence of mountain landscape and the
> esoteric mystery of the lamas, he found himself searching for a
> Great Experience, wanting to be transformed by what he saw,
> desiring as a tourist some deep, spiritual memento of his trip.
> Yet this self-obsessed "wanting" was precisely what kept him
> from obtaining enlightenment. Only as the vast grandeur of the
> land drew him beyond himself did he begin to discover what he
> sought.
>
> Walking one day toward a remote monastery at Rde Zong, he
> was distracted from his self-conscious quest for spiritual attain-

ment by the play of the sun on stones along the path. "I have no choice," he protested, "but to be alive to this landscape and this light." Because of his delay, he never arrived at the monastery. The beauty of the rocks in the afternoon sun, the weathered apricot trees, the stream along which he walked, all refused to let him go. He concluded that "to walk by a stream, watching the pebbles darken in the running water, is enough; to sit under the apricots is enough; to sit in a circle of great red rocks, watching them slowly begin to throb and dance as the silence of my mind deepens, is enough."

Most compelling to his imagination was the fact that the awesome beauty of this fierce land was in no way conditioned by his own frail presence. It was not there for him. The stream would continue to lunge over the rocks on its way to the valleys below long after he'd gone. The apricot trees would scrape out a spare existence and eventually die entirely apart from any consideration of his having passed that way. Only in that moment of afternoon sunlight in Ladakh, as he abandoned any thought of hurrying on to the monastery, did he receive back something he'd already unconsciously offered.

Hence he declared, "The things that ignore us save us in the end. Their presence awakens silence in us; they refresh our courage with the purity of their detachment." Becoming present to a reality entirely separate from his own world of turmoil strangely set him free. By its very act of ignoring him, the landscape invited him out of his frantic quest for self-fulfillment.

To be saved by the things that ignore us requires silence. Now here is one more story from Sister Jose Hobday:

One summer Saturday morning when I was twelve, I was waiting for my friend Juanita to come over. We had planned a morning together, and she was quite late. I was fretting and complaining, and generally making a nuisance of myself. In fact, I was becoming rather obnoxious to everyone else in the house.

Finally, my father said to me, "Get a book, a blanket, and an apple, and get into the car!" I wanted to know why, but he only repeated the order. So I obeyed. My father drove me about eight miles from home to a canyon area, and said, "Now get out. We cannot stand you any longer at home! You aren't fit to live with. Just stay out here by yourself today until you understand better how to act. I'll come back for you this evening." I got out, angry, frustrated, and defiant. The nerve of him! I though immediately of walking home; eight miles was no distance at all for me. Then the thought of meeting my father when I got there took hold, and I changed my mind.

I cried and threw the book, apple, and blanket over the canyon ledge. I had been dumped and I was furious. But it is hard to keep up a good, rebellious cry with no audience, so finally there was nothing to do but face up to the day alone.

I sat on the rim, kicking the dirt and trying to get control of myself. After a couple of hours, as noon approached, I began to get hungry. I located the apple and climbed down to retrieve it— as well as the book and the blanket. I climbed back up, and as I came over the top I noticed the piñon tree. It was lovely and full.

I spread the blanket in the shade, put the book under my head, and began to eat the apple. I was aware of a change of attitude. As I looked through the branches into the sky, a great sense of peace and beauty came to me. The clouds sat in still puffs, the blue was endless, and I began to take in their spaciousness. I thought about the way I had acted and why Daddy had treated me so harshly. Understanding began to come, and I became more objective about my behavior. I found myself getting in touch with my feelings, with the world around me.

Nature was my mother, holding me for comfort and healing. I became aware of being part of it all, and I found myself thinking of God. I wanted harmony. I wanted to hold the feeling of mystery. I wanted to be a better person. It was a prayerful time, a time of deep silence. I felt in communion with much that I could not know, but to which I was drawn. I had a great sense of discovering myself as great, of seeing the world as great, of touching the holy. This sense lasted a long time, perhaps a couple of hours. I found I liked being alone, enjoyed the rich emptiness, held the stillness. It was as if I had met another person—me—who was not so bad after all.

By the time my father came to get me, I was restored. Daddy did not press me about the day. He asked no questions and I gave him no answers. But I was different and we both knew it. My father had dumped me into solitude and had challenged me to grow. Before I got out of the car, I thanked him.

And from that day on, especially during the summers, I would take a day to go out alone. I loved those times of solitude, of contemplation, of prayer. I loved the person, the world, the God I had met that day. Without silence we dry up. Many of us know that experience, and that experience is a symptom of soul fatigue, of soul sickness.

In her book, *Amazing Grace: A Vocabulary of Faith*, Kathleen Norris offers this reflection on silence:

Over the years when I worked as an artist in elementary schools, I devised an exercise for the children regarding noise and silence. I'll make a deal with you, I said—first you get to make noise, and then you'll make silence.

The rules for noise were simple: when I raise my hand, I told them, you make all the noise you can while sitting at your desk, using your mouth, hands, and feet. The kids' eyes would grow wide—and the teacher's as well—so I'd add, the important thing is that when I lower my hand, you have to stop. I found that we'd usually have to make two or three attempts to attain an acceptable din—shouting, pounding, stomping. The wonder is, we never got caught. Maybe because the roar lasted for just a few seconds and school principals assumed that they'd imagined the whole thing.

The rules for silence were equally simple. Don't hold your breath and make funny faces, I learned to say, as this is how third graders typically imagine silence. Just breathe normally but quietly: the only hard thing is to sit so still that you make no noise at all. We always had to try this more than once. A pencil would roll down someone's desk, or someone would shift in a seat. But in every case but one over many years, I found that children were able to become so still that silence became a presence in the classroom.

Some kids loved it. I believe it was a revelation to them, and certainly to their teachers, that they could be so quiet. "Let's do it again," they'd say. Others weren't so sure. "It's scary," a fifth grader complained. "Why?" I asked, and I believe that he got to the heart of it when he replied, "It's like we're waiting for something—it's scary!"

There was only one time when I encountered a class that was unable to reach a point of stillness, and I learned the reason why when I happened to arrive early for class one day. Their teacher was shrieking commands at them: write, don't print your name in the upper right-hand corner of the paper; set a left-hand margin and keep it; use a pencil, not a pen; line the paper up with the edge of your desk for collection. These children had so many little rules barked at them all day long by a burned-out teacher that they had stopped listening, which surely is a prerequisite for silence.

What interests me most about my experiment is the way in which making silence liberated the imagination of so many children. Very few wrote with any originality about making noise. Most of their images were cliches such as "we sound like a herd of elephants." But silence was another matter: here, their images often had a depth and maturity that was unlike anything else they wrote. One boy came up with an image of strength as being "as slow and silent as a tree"; another wrote that "silence is me sleeping, waiting to wake up. Silence is a tree spreading its branches to the sun." In a parochial school, one third grader's poem turned into a prayer: "Silence is spiders spinning their webs, it's like a silkworm making its silk. Lord, help me to know when to be silent." And in a tiny town in western North Dakota a little girl offered a gem of spiritual wisdom that I find myself returning to when my life becomes too noisy and distractions overwhelm me: "Silence reminds me to take my soul with me wherever I go."

As Brennan Manning writes in his book, *Abba's Child*: "Silence is not simply the absence of noise or the shutdown of communication with the outside world, but rather a process of coming to stillness. Silent solitude forgets true speech. I'm not speaking of physical isolation; solitude here means being alone with the Alone, experiencing the transcendent Other and growing in awareness of one's identity as the beloved."

The well

If you want an image that is useful for describing the necessity for replenishing ourselves, it is that of a well with buckets around it. Our soul—our deep source—is the well. We fill our buckets from that well and then pour out to others what is needed from our buckets. In order to protect that source, we have to be sure that we give from the buckets and not from the well itself; and that when those buckets are empty, there is a time for replenishing, a time to refill before we give again.

Unfortunately, the frantic pace of our lives often requires that we begin to give not just from the buckets around the well but from the well itself. Some of us, I'm afraid, are squeezing the last few drops of liquid from the moss at the bottom. Soul work requires that we give ourselves adequate time for replenishment: time to deepen and integrate, time to come back to the center of our lives. That is why meditation is a powerful way to provide our souls with adequate solitude and silence. In meditation, you can most easily access your authority and power. Merton was right when he wrote: "It is in deep solitude and silence that I find the gentleness with which I can love my brothers and sisters."

I hope this refection has provoked you to find some time for soul-searching. If your soul is out of kilter, if your body is tired, if your spirit is depressed, ask yourself the Wizard's questions:

1. At what point in my life did I stop singing?
2. When did I stop dancing?
3. When did I stop being enchanted with stories?
4. When did I stop being comfortable with silence?

These are the four universal questions for spiritual seekers everywhere, and at all times.

Soul searching can happen during seasons such as Advent and Lent, as well as during retreats and days of recollection. It can be aided by reading Scripture daily so that the Jesus story might rest in the soul. The stories of Scripture offer us the possibility of freeing the voice—remember stuttering Moses and dumb Zechariah? They offer us the possibility of dancing—remember the woman at the well? They offer us stories—remember the prodigal son? They offer us silence—remember the desert and the nights Jesus spent in prayer? They offer us examples of just how far God's love for us will go—remember Calvary? Scripture offers us images of forgiveness, wholeness, and redemption, especially in the life and death of Jesus. He himself is, as St. Paul says, the very image of God.

So like the world's spiritual gurus, I leave you with these four questions. But they are not to be pondered alone. They are best pondered while you imagine Jesus sitting in a room with you, helping you to find the answers to your soul's sickness and offering himself for your soul's healing, for he is the only way to wholeness.

Questions for reflection

1. When in my life did I stop singing? When did I begin to feel that it was no longer safe to give voice to my own truth? Can I sing again, feel free to express my opinions, my feelings, without fear of ridicule or reprimand? Jesus, free my voice as you did that of the deaf mute.

2. When in my life did I stop dancing? When did I learn to hate or fear my body? measure it against the impossible images of the media? distrust my sexual feelings? When did I learn shame? Jesus, make me what St. Paul reminded us we were: temples of the Holy Spirit.

3. When in my life did I stop being enchanted with stories? When did I learn to be head-orientated only, weaned away from tales that touch the soul? What do I read? What images enter?

What is my image of myself? Jesus, I come to you like a child; tell me your stories again.

4. When in my life did I stop being comfortable with silence? Am I a "successful" American, always on the go? Do I feel guilty about the times—or are there any—when I am not doing anything? Do I feel I must always "produce"? (That is the market talking to you.) Do I feel it is enough simply to "be"? (That is Jesus talking to you.)

SEVEN

THE WITCH'S BROOM

The Elusive God

This is not my chapter. I shall explain shortly. Meanwhile, recall the first encounter between the motley quartet and the Wizard. The wizard they meet is not the Wizard. Through bursts of fire and smoke, they are seeing an image on a screen. They do not encounter him directly.

Yet frightened as they may be, they are nevertheless there with their imperious demands for a home, a brain, a heart, and a dose of courage. They do not know that, loaded down with their own expectations, their own preoccupations, they will never see the Wizard they desire to see. (They also do not know that he is seeing them, peeking out from behind his protective curtain.) So he makes a seemingly silly demand: bring back the broom of the Wicked Witch.

The Wizard has no use for the broom. Unlike Dorothy's ruby slippers, it has no magic. But the task of acquiring the broom will require an emptying out of each one's desires; it will require risk, a chastening, an adventure. If the four succeed—and we know they do—they return humbled, with broom in hand, the Witch destroyed, her minions liberated. Only then will they encounter the real Wizard.

Within this innocuous scenario lies a deeper truth, which we will explore in this chapter. The quartet are seekers, as we all are. Behind the home and the brain and the heart and the courage which they are immediately seeking, however, is something deeper: they seek the

Wizard. And in this the four are symbolic of those who seek God. What they, and we, don't know is that the Wizard—God—is seeking them. What they, and we, don't know yet is that they have to let go in order to be grasped by the divine reality, which remains elusive and mysterious and cannot be won by their efforts or desires. Going after the broom is basically a call to apprenticeship, to learning the patience, humility, and process of emptying necessary for an encounter with the divine.

The way we come to encounter the divine on our spiritual journey constitutes such a profound truth that I must turn to someone who, with greater depth and elegance and insight than I am capable of, exquisitely unfolds it for us. That is why, as I wrote before, this chapter belongs to another. Part of one chapter of an evocative book, *Now I See...*, by Fr. Robert Barron, has a piece that is relevant to our thoughts here. In this section he explores William Faulkner's story from 1942, "The Bear," taken from Faulkner's collection titled *Go Down, Moses.* "The Bear" is the coming-of-age story of a young man. More importantly for our concerns, it is the story of a mystical encounter with the reality of God. So read on and savor the words of Fr. Barron.

The bear

The story begins with an evocation of a boy and a bear. The boy, Ike McCaslin, is ten, and he has been invited for the first time to join the men as they go on a late fall hunting foray into the deep woods. They will shoot for quail and deer, but the ultimate goal of their quest is Old Ben, the legendary bear who roams an area one hundred miles square and who has, for years, terrorized the villages around the woods, ruining corn cribs, slaughtering pigs, and even carrying calves bodily into the forest. The bear has lived in the boy's dreams and imaginings for many years: this great beast "too big for the dogs which tried to bay it, for the horses which tried to ride it down, for the men and the bullets they fired into it." Long captivated by the image of the bear, the boy is, at one and the same time, frightened and fascinated at the prospect of facing it.

When he arrives at camp, deep in the forest, Ike enters into an experience not unlike that of a novice in a religious community. He is met by Sam Fathers, part Indian, part black, who will be his mystagogue in the ways of the hunt. He becomes accustomed to the rude lifestyle of the hunter, to the simple and poorly prepared meals, to the damp and cold of the stands where he waits, through long hours, for the rush of deer through the woods. He learns that "patience and humility" are essential for survival in the forest, that the overeager or cocky hunter never lands a kill. Ike feels that he is "witnessing his own birth" as he follows Sam into a new realm of experience.

Then one morning, during the second week of his novitiate, while he waits on his lonely hunting stand, Ike hears the unusually high-pitched yipping and barking of the dogs, and, with some trepidation, he readies his gun. Sam Fathers tells him, "It's Old Ben," and the boy stiffens in anticipation and excitement. The two listen and watch until finally Sam knows that the bear has slipped back into the woods. "He do it every year," Sam explains. "He come to see who's here, who's new in camp this year, whether he can shoot or not, can stay or not." The boy has been dreaming of the bear for years, reaching out to him in imagination and will, and now the bear has established contact with the boy, sizing him up and monitoring his readiness for a richer encounter, gazing mysteriously from the shadows of the woods, seeing without being seen. The hunted, Ike realizes, is himself a hunter.

Sam teaches the boy how to track the bear, and he manages to find a vestige of the beast, Old Ben's footprint in the mud, bigger and more fascinating than he had imagined. Then, sometime later, having moved deeper into the dark of the forest, stationed at another lonely stand, Ike listens carefully, and he hears no baying of the dogs, only the solitary drumming of a woodpecker. When even that sound stops, he knows that the bear is, once again, looking at him. He has no idea whether the animal is before or behind him, whether he is far or near, and he stands still, the useless gun at his side, the taste of fear like brass in his mouth. And then, just as abruptly, it is over, the bear is gone. When Sam emerges from the woods a few minutes later, the boy excitedly tells him of the encounter, but he adds, somewhat puzzled, "I didn't see him; I didn't, Sam." And the old man replies, "I know it; he done the looking." Wisely and mysteriously, the bear has, once more, sought out the young man and watched him, but this being seen awakens in Ike the even more intense desire to see: "So I will have to see him; I will have to look at him."

The encounter

And so the next June he returned to camp, this time with his own rifle. While the men hunted, Ike ranged out into the woods, using his compass as Sam had taught him, identifying landmarks, tracking animals, even finding, once more, Old Ben's crooked footprint, but the bear himself he did not encounter. He spent hours and hours every day exploring the woods with increasing confidence, returning later and later to camp, amazing the men who had roamed the forest for years and had never attained the boy's level of competence. When he tells Sam Fathers of his exploits and of his frustration at not having seen the bear, the old man knowingly responds, "You ain't looked right yet." When the boy protests that he has been following all the recommendations of his mentor, Sam cuts him off: "I reckon that was all right. Likely he's been watching you." But the reason, he explains, that the bear has not come out into the open is the gun that the young man carries: "You will have to choose," Sam explains, between the safety the gun provides and the experience of seeing the bear close up.

The next morning, before light, the boy set out into the woods, consumed by the desire to commune with Old Ben. Purposely he left behind his weapon and entered the woods armed only with a stick to ward off snakes and a compass to find his way back. He remembered that Sam had told him to "be scared but not afraid" since nothing in the woods would hurt him unless it was cornered or smelled fear. By noon, he had wandered further into alien country than he had ever gone, and he knew that he would make it back to camp only after dark had fallen. Still there was no sign of the bear. He stopped to wipe his brow and to glance at the compass. Perhaps, he thought, the surrendering of the gun was not enough; perhaps the bear demanded that he leave behind everything, all weapons of defense and all instruments of direction. And so he hung the compass on a nearby bush and he leaned the simple snake stick against it, and, stripped of any of the accouterments of civilization, he entered deeper into the forest.

Before he knew it, he was lost, enveloped by the woods. But he did not panic, for Sam Fathers had taught him ancient Indian techniques for tracking in the woods. While he was without the aid of his compass, executing one of Sam's maneuvers, he saw the familiar crooked and enormous footprint, but this time it was not old; as he looked at it, it was still filling with water, proving that Old Ben had just been there. Frightened but fascinated, Ike followed the prints, though he knew the reckless decision to follow Old Ben into the trackless woods, hours from his home camp, would leave him either dead or hopelessly lost. Still he pressed on, "tireless, eager, without doubt or dread," following the prints to a lovely open space, a glade deep, deep in the woodland. And then he saw the bear. "It did not emerge, appear; it was just there, immobile, fixed in the green and windless noon's hot dappling, not as big as he had dreamed it but big as he had expected, bigger, dimensionless against the dappled obscurity, looking at him." Next the animal moved across the glade, pausing ever so briefly in the direct light of the sun and then, as it passed into the obscurity of the woods, it glanced once over its shoulder and spied the boy. Finally, it sank into the deep darkness of the forest just as a great bass sinks, almost motionlessly, into the depths of a pool.

The interpretation

The sketchy summary that we have provided here can only begin to hint at the richness and mysterious beauty of Faulkner's account. Like Ike himself, the reader is lured by Faulkner's snaky prose, gradually and achingly, into the arcana, the technique, and the mystique of the hunt. He too is being disciplined, readied for the encounter. And the very elegance and solemnity of the story show that we are being drawn into a sacred space, a confrontation with the deep things of God. Therefore let us now view this lovely tale through the interpretive lens of a religious consciousness.

We begin with a hunt, a quest to find and to kill. The great old bear is a menace to life and property, and something must be done to stop it. But beneath this practical concern, there is, among the hunters, something of an aesthetic fascination, a desire simply to commune with the bear, to revel in its size and strength, to return and tell stories of it. This ambiguity in the intentionality of the hunters corresponds to the ambiguity in the feelings of sinful human beings vis-à-vis the mystery of God, the split in consciousness that we have already referred to. To the sinner who has made herself the unconditioned center of the universe, God is necessarily experienced as a threat, as the one who plunders and carries off the goods of her realm. Like the bear, God, the authentically unconditioned, breaks into her sinful soul with awesome and disquieting power, unsettling her complacency, stirring her to fear and violent response. This rivalrous God must, accordingly, be either hidden from or ruthlessly hunted down and eliminated. The hunting down of God is, of course, in a Christian context, of enormous importance, since, when the divine appeared in human flesh, he was pursued and eventually killed by the power of sin. The crucified and hunted Christ reveals, as it were, how the sinful ego responds in the presence of the sacred.

But, as Faulkner suggests, this is only half the story. Even the boy knows that the hunters really never intend to kill Old Ben, that, at least with regard to the bear, the hunt is more of a pil-grimage, an attempt to commune. Though they are frightened of the beast, they are, even more, compelled by it, captivated. Rudolf Otto, of course, taught us long ago that trembling and fascination were the twin poles of the natural human response to the divine, a fearful awe in the presence of that which judges and a dazzled awe in the presence of that which overwhelms and lures. The fascination before the divine—the pull toward the wonder of God despite all fearful pushing away—is a func-tion of what we have been calling the *imago Dei*. We are afraid of God, but we are also irresistibly drawn to God, our sense of beauty stirred. And so, like the hunter/pilgrims of Faulkner's tale, we all go out, with split souls, to meet the sacred.

Now Faulkner purposely orients his reader to the perspec-tive of the boy, Ike McCaslin, as he is introduced into the ways of the hunger, and he uses the evocative language of monastic novitiate or shamanic initiation to describe the process. As the boy endeavors to join the party of hunter/worshippers, there is a disciplining of consciousness required, an entry onto the path of "humility and patience." Like most children, Ike probably wants to leap into the fray, to encounter the bear quickly and effortlessly, and this childlike enthusiasm, left unchecked, would have been his undoing. In some ways, he is like Dante at the beginning of the Divine Comedy, desirous of a quick ascent of the mountain and in fact in need of a chastening discipline. And so his Virgil arrives, the half-black, half-native American Sam Fathers, the wisdom figure who will be his spiritual guide, fathering him into the mystery of God.

The discipline

Just as there are disciplines and techniques that enable a per-son to survive in the trackless wood, so there are disciplines and techniques in the spiritual life, that is to say, ways of orienting oneself in the dark wood of the divine reality. Accordingly, Bonaventure gives us his *Itinerarium mentis in Deum* ("The Mind's Journey into God"), and Ignatius offers us the Spiritual

Exercises, and Juan de la Cruz guides our ascent of Mount Carmel. All of these ascetic disciplines, practices of prayer, focusings of consciousness, moral endeavors, etc., are attempts by some of the shamans of Christianity to tame the often erratic spirit of the sinner and to give direction to its quest. And at the heart of so many of these shamanic disciplines of the Christian tradition are the twin virtues that young Ike McCaslin learns: patience and humility.

Though we are ravenously hungry for God, the divine is not something that responds to our demands and on our timetable. God appears when he appears, and for his own reasons. Thus we must be humble and docile in his presence, ready to wait, if necessary, through long hours, days, and years, prepared to hear the rush of God through the woods when it comes. As all spiritual searchers attest, there is a healthy tediousness to the religious life, a settling into routine that is necessary if one is to be ready when the divine chooses to show itself. We think here of the novice in a Benedictine monastery being put to the tasks of setting tables or cleaning toilets and being compelled to stand, with his brothers, through long hours of chanting and silence every day. Perhaps, our tradition wagers, God will not appear until the fallen ego is ready to see.

After considerable waiting, Ike finally hears the overexcited barking of the dogs, and he knows that the bear is close, but the great animal itself he does not see. When the ego has been chastened and readied, the divine deigns to come closer, perhaps knowing that its presence will be properly appreciated. But it is still known only through signs, hints, indications. If God appeared unambiguously to a consciousness at this still primitive level of development, God would devastate it: no one sees the face of God and lives. It is only analogously and elusively through his creatures that God first speaks. Thomas Aquinas compares the initial experience of the divine to a man who approaches a house and concludes that it is burning though he never sees the fire. What he feels is the ever increasing heat as he moves from porch to foyer to drawing room. So the patient and humble spiritual seeker begins to receive signs of God in his created effects.

The one who seeks the seeker

But most interestingly, Sam Fathers tells Ike that it is the bear who has been doing the seeing. This is the great reversal that is usually shocking to the sinful ego: the divine one whom I have been seeking (or hunting) is in fact seeking and hunting me. The psalmist knew the experience to be both uplifting and deeply troubling: "Lord, you search me and you know me; you know my resting and my rising, you discern my purpose from afar" (Ps 139). The sinner is convinced that the spiritual life is his game and that God is a prey to be stalked, a prize to be won. The unsettling fact is that we are mastered, we are stalked, and the very condition for the possibility of our finding is that we have already been found. While we desperately seek after God, God is already even more desperately seeking after us, and what most spiritual writers eventually urge on us is a surrender to the divine hunt. The Curé of Ars once described his liturgical spirituality in these words: "I look at Him and He looks at me." So while Ike peers through the woods to see Old Ben, the bear is already and much more successfully peering through those same woods to see the boy.

Excited by his first contacts with the world of the hunt and by his mystic encounter with the power of the bear, Ike returns the next summer, supplied with compass, woodsman's skill, and a shiny gun. He stands now for the spiritual apprentice sure of his game, the seeker who has been touched by the sacred and is ready for fullness of contact. His grace and skill in the forest evoke the growing adeptness in the ways of the spirit. Ranging deep into the woods, he is the mystic confidently moving in the black forest of the divine presence, finding hints of the sacred (the footprint of Old Ben) through prayer and fasting and study. Chastened, humbled, disciplined, he is relatively successful in the ways of the spirit, far more so than his older contemporaries. But the decisive moment is reached only when his mystagogue tells him of the choice, the decision he must make between the safety of the gun and the ecstasy of the vision of the bear. The bear will not show itself as long as the boy carries with him the instruments of guidance and violence, in other words, those things that contribute to his mastery of the situation. With his compass and rifle, he is in control, he is doing the seeing, and he can determine the quality of his encounter with Old Ben.

These tools are evocative of the frightened and grasping conscious consciousness of Adam and Eve, the fearful and God-hunting state of mind. Both Sam Fathers and Ike realize that letting go of these accouterments of egotism is dangerous—the boy could easily be lost or killed—but absolutely necessary if the bear is to be encountered close up. The ego must drop the aggressiveness and defensiveness that flows from its self-elevation; it must abandon all those descendants of the loincloths of Eden, those instruments of protection. It must realize that any semblance of the hunting of God must be eradicated. Alone, naked, unafraid (as Sam pointedly reminds Ike), the soul must present itself to the Mystery.

Letting go

And so the boy lets go of the compass, the stick, and the gun, and, with fear just beginning to rise in him, he enters the deepest part of the woods. And it is there, in that place and in that state of soul, that he sees: in a glade, a small clearing in the forest, the bear is simply there. Intriguingly, the animal first appears in the "dappling," the playful mixture of dark and light so characteristic of forest scenery. God is always seen and not seen, visible but ever more invisible, available but ever elusive, epistemologically and metaphysically in the dappling; the power of Being itself cannot be unambiguously understood by the rationality of the ego, forced into the glaring light of science and analysis. The implicit goal of Enlightenment science—the mastery of nature through knowledge—is, quite simply, irreconcilable with the goal of spiritual knowing, namely, the experience of being grasped by the very ground of reason.

The bear moves across the glade and only for an instant is in the direct light of the sun before fading once more into the half-light. This momentary illumination signifies the passing, fleeting quality of the vision of God available in this life: occasionally we see, with frightening clarity, but before we can even begin to reflect on such a vision of the divine, it fades, receding into the dark. How often in Moby Dick (a story to which Faulkner's "The Bear" has a more than passing resemblance) the white whale tantalizes the sailors, rising just for a moment above the roiled surface of the ocean, only to sound once more into the murky depths. So with the God who passionately seeks us, but refuses to be mastered by us.

Just before disappearing into the woods, Old Ben pauses, ever so briefly, and looks at the boy once more "across one shoulder." When, in the book of Exodus, Moses asked to see Yahweh, God placed his servant in the cleft of a rock and then told him to close his eyes as the divine presence passed (Ex 33:18–23). Only when God had gone by was Moses permitted to look and see the hindquarters of the sacred. When we are ready, when we have divested ourselves of the tools of hunting and manipulating, when our egos have been sufficiently humbled and disciplined, God sometimes appears, looking at us across one shoulder, allowing us to see something of his being, tantalizing and seducing us to deeper vision and more thoroughgoing surrender. Hence, control and evasion—the twin strategies of sinful Eden—are foiled by the odd mode of God's self-offering. The Bear is neither trapped nor avoided.

Back to the Yellow Brick Road

Fr. Barron's interpretation of the Faulkner story is worth pondering. The events of "The Bear" echo the initial encounter with the Wizard in the Oz story. Dorothy and her friends "saw" the Wizard—but didn't really see him. They needed "emptying" just as Ike had to leave his compass and rifle behind in order to get a truer vision and, more to the point, to realize that he was the one being seen. And so it is with us. We are both pursuers and the pursued: "How often have I desired to gather your children together as a hen gathers her brood under her wings…!" (Mt 23:37); the shepherd who leaves ninety-nine to seek out the lost one.

We all get glimpses at one time or another of the divine, of the Mystery that envelops us. In our search, we sometimes sense that we are being sought after by the Hound of Heaven. The trouble is that sometimes we are too laden with our own agendas to make progress in our search, and too laden with our own agendas to be discovered. As Fr. Barron says, when we are divested of our tools of manipulation, when we have been humbled enough, we may get a glimpse of the One who aches for us.

The mission on which the Wizard sent the four friends—to bring back the Witch's broom—was one of purification. After the "emptying"—that is, the trial—the quartet (with the help of Toto!) get to see the Wizard. We won't press this image too far, for the Wizard in the movie is a gentle manipulator with good in his heart. But, then again, come to think of it, so is God.

Questions for reflection

1. Am I like Ike, so intent on seeking the divine that I do not even know I am being sought? "In this is love, not that we loved God but that he loved us" (1 Jn 4:10).

2. Ike could not see Old Ben because he was carrying too many items, his gun and compass. What encumbers my life and prevents me from discovering God? What helps me to overcome hindrances to seeing the divine?

3. "Let go and let God" is a Christian truism. Do I follow this saying in the way I approach life?

4. Lost in the woods, Ike nevertheless presses on. Do I persevere through dry times in my pursuit of God?

5. God is the One Who seeks the seeker. Do I believe this?

EIGHT

ELMIRA GULCH

Self-esteem

In the opening scenes of *The Wizard of Oz*, Elmira Gulch is pedaling furiously towards Dorothy's house with a complaint and a court order. Toto the dog has nipped Elmira and she is there to take him to the pound. Uncle Henry trades mild insults with her and Auntie Em finally tells her off. But Dorothy is devastated and runs away in tears as Miss Gulch—"you wicked old witch," cries Dorothy prophetically—rides off triumphantly with Toto. Talk about feeling bad. Talk about being buffeted by life's unfairness. Talk about low self-esteem. Well, all these characteristics are the topic of this reflection, which we will treat under the general category of self-esteem.

Of course, none of us has perfect self-esteem; it usually ebbs and flows with moods and circumstances. Self-esteem is always under pressure during transition times, like moving from the secure to the insecure, for example, going to college or getting a job promotion. Aging and illness also subvert self-esteem, as people begin to lose health, movement, and abilities. The general rule holds that the more our self-esteem is in the hands of external circumstances, other people, or situations outside ourselves, the more fragile it is. This fact affirms the importance of the spiritual life, of our relationship with Jesus, and of holding fast to the one major criteria of self-worth, which we shall explore shortly.

There is always a hesitancy to use the word self-esteem, even in

---

118

speaking about the spiritual life. The term conjures up what is all too often true: a narcissistic, self-centered stroking that ducks the harder issues of responsibility, hard work, discipline, and pain so that one won't feel bad about his or her self. Soft-hearted counselors and soft-headed policymakers or teachers or parents often promote self-esteem at the price of challenge, maturity, and growth. A recent article which appeared in the *New York Times* Sunday magazine—"an idea whose time has come...and gone" was the subtitle—took a critical look at self-esteem as an underlying principle for education today, especially in the public school system, where it reigns supreme. Often, the article points out, feelings are extolled at the price of learning.

The self-esteem movement also shows up notably in the avalanche of self-help and how-to books. The *New York Times* article quotes Albert Bandura, a psychology professor at Stamford, who concludes from his research: "self-esteem affects neither personal goals nor performance." Indeed, it has been shown that some students who feel bad about themselves nevertheless become academic and social successes. Others who brim with self-confidence do poor work. Testing done in the United States, China, Japan, and Taiwan shows that students in the Asian countries consistently outperform the students in the U.S., although the U.S. students felt better about themselves and their world. Research has further shown that even in the black community, blacks have no lower self-esteem than whites; in fact, most blacks have a remarkably good sense of self-esteem. Furthermore, self-esteem has been shown to have no connection with violence, crime, or other antisocial acts. As the *Times* article mentions, studies of gang members and criminals show that their self-esteem is as high as that of overachievers.

For this reflection, when I use the term "self-esteem" I basically mean "God-esteem." I mean that fundamental self-esteem rests not on any external criteria but on grasping the reality that we are beloved by God, are in a relationship of love with God: "You are my Beloved, with whom I am well pleased" (Mt 3:17; cf. Mk 1:11, Lk 3:22). We are the children of God. Frederick Buechner writes in his book, *The Magnificent Defeat*:

We are children, perhaps, at the very moment when we know that it is as children that God loves us—not because we have deserved his love and not in spite of our undeserving; not because we try and not because we recognize the futility of our trying; but simply because he has chosen to love us. We are children because he is our father; and all our efforts, fruitful and fruitless, to do good, to speak truth, to understand, are the efforts of children who, for all their precocity, are children still in that before we loved him, he loved us, as children, through Jesus Christ our Lord.

As Jesus said, "On that day you will know that I am in my Father, and you in me, and I in you" (Jn 14:20), and "I do not call you servants any longer, because the servant does not know what the master is doing; but I have called you friends" (Jn 15:15). Or, as the psalmist put it, "What are human beings that you are mindful of them, mortals that you care for them? Yet you have made them a little lower than God, and crowned them with glory and honor" (Ps 8:4–5).

The basis of our self-esteem therefore rests on the fact that indeed, in us dwells Father, Son, and Holy Spirit; that, in the words of St. Paul, "your body is a temple of the Holy Spirit within you" (1 Cor 6:19). For the Christian, self-esteem *is* God-esteem: God esteems us, takes up his dwelling in us, calls us beloved. That is what gives us our worth, the unchanging, infallible source of our dignity. When we forget this, when we forget that we are the beloved children of God, then we do negative things.

So when you read the phrase "self-esteem" in these pages, know that while the world puts the emphasis on the first word, Christians put the emphasis on the second word, esteem. We are esteemed by God. As St. Iraeneus said in the third century, "Know, O man, your dignity." The writer Miguel de Unamuno adds, "Cure yourself of the affliction of caring how you appear before others. Concern yourself only with how you appear before God, concern yourself only with the idea God may have of you." And thus, let us begin our reflection on self-esteem.

Competition and hostility

Do you know why some priests have such low self-esteem? It's because:

If a priest preaches over ten minutes, he's longwinded.
If his sermon is short, he didn't prepare it.
If the parish funds are high, he's a businessman.
If he mentions money, he's money mad.
If he visits his parishioners, he's nosy.
If he doesn't, he's snobbish.
If he has fairs and bazaars, he's bleeding the people.
If he doesn't, there's no life in the parish.
If he takes time in confession to help and advise sinners, he takes too long.
If he doesn't, he doesn't care.
If he celebrates the liturgy in a quiet voice, he's a bore.
If he puts feeling into it, he's an actor.
If he starts Mass on time, his watch is fast.
If he starts late, he's holding up the people.
If he tries to lead the people in music, he's showing off.
If he doesn't, he doesn't care what Mass is like.
If he decorates the church, he's wasting money.
If he doesn't, he's letting it run down.
If he's young, he's not experienced.
If he's old, he ought to retire.
If he dies, there was nobody like him and there will never be his equal again!

Talk about poor self-esteem! Rodney Dangerfield says that as a teenager he had so many pimples on his face that when he laid down his head and fell asleep on a table in the public library, a blind man began to read his face. When he got married and the judge asked if there was anyone who objected to this marriage, he looked around and her family had formed a double line.

Rodney Dangerfield notwithstanding, anyone who wants to grow to the fullness of their vocation has to work hard at self-esteem. And what is that vocation? All Christians are called to the triple commitment of holiness, community, and ministry. Let's look a bit more closely at these three calls to see how self-esteem functions.

When we look at holiness we see that the love of God begins and ends with the love of self. So proclaims St. Bernard—and Jesus. "You shall love your neighbor as yourself" (Mt 22:39; cf. Mk 12:33, Lk 10:27). When we belittle ourselves we insult the One who made us. Yet it's a severe temptation, isn't it? An unkind word, a devastating insult, failure—all conspire to tell us we are no good, and no good deep within. The advertising which appears in the media constantly presents us with impossible measurements of success and acceptance. And, of course, it simultaneously offers redemption and salvation from social sins and inferiority. How? Through consumption, of course.

The advertising industry preys especially on children and teenagers who, in striving to develop their self-esteem, are often driven into unhealthy behavior patterns: extreme dieting, smoking, alcohol, promiscuity. Parents certainly influence their child's sense of self-esteem, as well. As Gil and Tanya Gockley write in their book, *Loving is Natural, Parenting is Not,* many parents "wait for the A, they wait for the goal in sports, they look to have the clothing that makes them a worthwhile person…we focus on these things instead of on the goodness of the person." The goodness of the person: that is holiness, and the first place we should look for self-esteem.

According to Brother Loughlan Sofield, the two factors that can destroy a community, competition and hostility, are related to self-esteem (*Self-Esteem and Christian Growth,* Ave Maria Press). Like a see-saw, when self-esteem is low, competition and hostility are high; when self-esteem is high, competition and hostility are low. When we look at a community—be it a neighborhood, parish, organization, or family—self-esteem never grows and develops if competition and hostility are high. If we have a low sense of self-esteem, if we treat other people as if they were the enemy, we will consciously or unconsciously do things that will destroy the community. We will be hostile; we will have excessive competition. In order for people to build a successful and healthy community, the self-esteem of its members must be strong.

Pause and ask yourself: when have you best experienced community? In one form or another, the answer will always be, when people had a healthy sense of self-esteem. That is to say, they didn't have to be in competition with you; they didn't have to be jealous or undermining or hostile. If we are to work together, live together, and minister together we need a good sense of self-esteem.

Whenever I give a workshop and ask people what the obstacles are to working together, to shared and collaborative ministry, every answer that they give is directly related to low self-esteem. When people's sense of self-esteem is highest, they are better able to reach out to others in ministry. In human interactions, people with poor self-esteem often tend to be aggressive toward people in authority. Why? Because they are basically codependent on such people. They need to please them yet at the same time, in unconscious resentment, need to put them down.

A man went to his local barber. (The barber was one of those people with low self-esteem who is always cutting others down to size.) The man mentioned that he was taking a trip to Rome. "I hear that Rome is overrated," said the barber. "The hotels are substandard and overpriced. The streets are a nightmare. Italians are rude to Americans. You really won't like it." The man protested, "But I've been saving for years to make this trip. Besides, there is a good chance that I will be able to get an audience with the Pope." The barber gave him a skeptical look. "I wouldn't count on that if I were you," he said. "The Pope only gives audiences to really important people."

A couple of weeks later the man returned to the barber shop. "How was your trip?" the barber asked diffidently. "Oh, it was great!" the man answered. "The city was beautiful, the hotel was fantastic, Italian people were so friendly, and I got to see the Pope." The barber couldn't believe it. "You got to see the Pope?" he asked. "That's right," said the man. "I bent down and kissed his ring." "Wow!" said the barber. "Did he say anything?" "Yes, he did," replied the man. "He looked down at my head while I was kneeling and said, 'What a lousy haircut!'"

People with low self-esteem flit from -ism to -ism, from one new form of spirituality to another. They are always trying to impress you with their accomplishments. They are rigid and dogmatic in their thinking. They can tell you what is right and what is wrong. They have trouble with the gray areas. They cannot tolerate ambiguity, for their sense of identity comes from having the right answers.

Measuring self-esteem

Let's probe further. Right now, take some time to answer this question: if you were to rate your sense of self-esteem on a scale of one to ten, where would you put yourself? Secondly—and this is the more critical question—what criteria did you use to value yourself? (We'll come back to the question of criteria later).

Try this one: can you think a time of your life when your self-esteem was highest? Ask yourself, what made your self-esteem high? And how did you act when your self-esteem was high? When was your self-esteem lowest? Can you picture the time when it was lowest? What was going on in your life? Why was it so low? How did you behave? How did you treat the people around you? What have you done in your own life to help build a sense of self-esteem?

Our sense of self-esteem, like the wounded hearts we saw in chapter three, for the most part goes back to childhood. Perhaps others, knowingly or unwittingly, contributed to our sense of low self-esteem. To show how this works let's do a little exercise. It was designed originally by a psychologist to reveal the degree of child abuse, both mental and physical, that people have experienced in their lives, and may even have inadvertently passed on to their own children. Ideally find a friend—not a spouse—to do this exercise with you (that's the way it works best). Have this person ask you the following nine questions, but note: the heart of the exercise is that you have to answer "yes" to each question, even if you don't want to. You have to answer "yes" even though you want to scream out "no!" The point of answering "yes" is to get in touch with what you might be feeling when you say that "yes." Here are the nine questions:

> Will you give me all of your money?
> Will you let me punch you in the nose?
> Will you learn what I tell you to learn?

Will you believe what I tell you to believe?
Will you always do what I ask you to do?
Will you always tell me what I want to hear?
Will you let use you sexually?
Will you like me no matter how I treat you?
And finally, will you live your life for me?

Now, how did you feel each time you said "yes"? How might you feel if, in fact, you were someone who did at one time say "yes" to all these questions? As adults, most people feel badly that they let other people walk all over them. They realize how much abuse they have experienced because in some form or another, they have said "yes" to most of those questions. But here is a large caution: people who say "yes" to those questions should not beat themselves up over this and feel guilty—although they do.

Reflect a moment. Think of what would have happened if you, as a very dependent child, had answered "no" to these questions when you were growing up. Would you have risked rejection and aban-donment, or even physical harm by your parents or other people who were important to you, by saying "no"? I don't think so! Therefore, naturally and sensibly, from your point of view—a child's or adolescent's point of view—you chose to sacrifice yourself to their conditional love: "I will love you on condition that you say 'yes' to these questions" was the unspoken contract. Can you really say "no" to someone whom you need to survive? Can you really say "no" to your own parents or aunts or uncles or caretakers? No, it is simply not in the cards. For children especially, there's really not much of a choice: they must say "yes" or lose the love they so desperately crave.

Nevertheless, when we answered "yes" to abuse or put-down of any kind, we sensed that somehow we dishonored ourselves and lost a part of ourselves. Think of how a person like that must feel about his or her self-worth and how that person must feel about his or her own dignity and position with God. Each time he or she answered "yes," he or she was distanced from God a little bit more.

And so here are these people, perhaps deeply hurting inside, per-haps not ever having shared that they have been abused—physically, sexually, emotionally, or verbally—people who said "yes" to the questions without realizing that "no" was really not an option. And they feel unworthy and sinful; they suffer a great deal. Sometimes these people exhibit various addictions or acted-out behavior, from anorexia to promiscuity to obnoxiousness to withdrawal—all signs of low self-esteem.

But there is more. These people not only become victims of low self-esteem and turn inward but worse, they tend to measure everything by their emptiness, their undisclosed yearnings. Their mind locks into negativism and victimhood and they fall into the ten cognitive traps that Dr. David Burns describes in his book, *The Good Feeling Handbook.* Let's look at these now.

1. *All-or-nothing thinking.* People with low self-esteem see things in black or white categories. If a situation is anything less than perfect, they see it as a total failure.

Nick, our oldest child, was always a happy, energetic kid who would usually come running or skipping out of school. But one fall day, when Nick was six years old, I was parked at the curb when I saw Nick walking slowly toward me, his curly head hung low, his mouth turned down, a bunch of papers in his hand. Nick seemed to drag himself along the sidewalk. He slowly pulled open the car door and slumped into the seat.

"Hi, Nick. How are you doing?" I asked.

No response.

"What's goin' on? Did something bad happen today?"

Nick slowly nodded yes before turning his face away.

"Oh, come on, Nick. Tell your old dad what's wrong," I prodded.

"I'm bad," Nick said at last. "Bad? Why do you say that?" Nick handed over a crumpled paper.

Smoothing it out revealed rows of math problems. A big red "–3" dominated the top. "Look," Nick said, tears running down his cheeks, his lips quivering in an attempt at self-control. He pointed at the glaring red mark. "Look, Dad, I got a bad grade."

After considering for a long moment, I said, "That minus

three doesn't mean you're bad or that you got a bad grade, Nick. It means you missed just three problems on this whole paper. Your teacher wants you to learn from your mistakes. But that's not all that counts. How many did you get right?"

Nick had no idea. So I started counting up the correct ones that weren't marked, pointing at each one as I went. By the tenth correct one Nick had joined in the counting and by the time we'd gotten to twenty-seven, Nick's tear-stained cheeks were showing signs of happiness. I had him write a huge black "+27" next to the red "–3."

"There. Twenty-seven right." Nick absorbed the truth for a moment before his usual bright smile reinstated itself on his little boy face. The subject was changed and the day went on.

Nick was able to find a good lesson in the red "–3." But most of us never learn this lesson. Most of us grow up with a barrage of criticism.... Since we learn and adapt to what's familiar, our inner voice criticizes us automatically, and we learn to apply this criticalness to ourselves and the world. Frequently, we develop a radar system that takes for granted the things we do right, while it scans for what's missing or wrong in ourselves and in life. We come to feel that we (and maybe also our life, as well as others' lives) are "bad"—inadequate, incompetent, shameful, unworthy, or unlovable.

2. *Overgeneralization.* People with low self-esteem see a single event as a never-ending pattern of defeat by using the words "always" or "never" when they speak: "This always happens to me." "I always hit this light." "Things never turn out as they should."

3. *Mental filtering.* These same people will pick out a single negative detail and dwell on it exclusively. One word of criticism erases all the praise you've received: "What sets you up brings you down," as they say. If looks are important to you, "You look marvelous!" sets you up. "What's wrong? You look pale and sickly!" brings you down. I like to preach. "What a wonderful homily that was!" sets me up. "What kind of homily was that? It's your kind that's destroying the church!" brings me down.

A while back I gave a talk on New Age religions to a group of adults, and the organizers of the event sent me the participants' evaluations of my talk. Here are some comments:

> Fr. Bausch is consistently an excellent communicator.
> I love Fr. Bausch's ability to help us see the New Age longings and methods as something very related to our own traditions.
> What a great challenge! Most informative.
> He is my hero, always the very best.
> Bausch at his usual best, wonderful speaker with much to give; he gets right to the point.
> I needed this workshop desperately to help me understand my children's search for spirituality.
> Is there any area that he can not illumine with his intelligence, energy, and humor? He exercised all of these to the benefit of his audience.
> Good suggestions for bringing the attractions of the New Age to our own faith experience.
> Very informative and provocative presentation about what we could learn from New Age groups.
> Bill shared much of his research and knowledge of New Age. I feel that many aspects of New Age spirituality are helping us become more authentic Christians.
> Very negative; he missed an opportunity here.
> There was a lot of "scapegoating"; negative and flat.

A whole chorus of praise, except for the comments of these last two arrogant, dense, slow-witted, feebleminded, ignorant, mindless Neanderthal crackpots who pollute the earth by their very presence! Otherwise, I never even noticed. See what I mean? We all do mental filtering, but the one with low self-esteem brings it to an art.

4. *Discounting the positive.* People in this situation reject positive experiences by insisting that they "don't count." If they do a good job, they tell themselves that anyone could have done as well. Here's a variation on that:

> A son regularly called his widowed mother, who lived alone and

at a distance, to see how she was doing and to stay in touch. On one such occasion the conversation went like this:

"How are you, Mom?"

"Oh, I'm fine, but the kitchen pipes broke."

"Did you get them fixed?"

"No, the plumber said it would cost $105.00."

"Mom, for cryin' out loud, I'll send a hundred dollars right away."

"Thanks, son."

"Okay, bye."

"And, son?"

"Yes."

"Don't worry about the other five dollars. I'll find a way to pay for it myself."

5. *Jumping to conclusions.* This group interprets things negatively when there are no facts to support their conclusions. Two common variations are mind-reading (they arbitrarily conclude that someone is reacting negatively to them) and fortune telling (they assume and predict that things will turn out badly). Here is a funny story that depends for its humor on people jumping to the wrong conclusion—in this case, the reader:

A butler named James worked for a wealthy couple. The wife was very beautiful and much younger than her husband. One evening they told James that they'd be out late, but the wife came home alone earlier than expected.

"James," she said, "come to my room."

He followed her. She closed the door and said, "Take off my dress." He did so. "Now my stockings," she continued. He rolled them down. "And off with my lingerie." He removed all that too.

"Now, James," she said, looking him in the eye, "don't ever let me find you wearing my clothes again!"

6. *Magnification.* These people exaggerate the importance of their problems and shortcomings, or they minimize their desirable quali-

ties. This is also called the "binocular trick." You see this in the one-liner: "He's so big it takes two men and a boy to look at him."

7. *Emotional reasoning.* These people assume that their negative emotions reflect the way things really are: "I feel guilty. I must be a rotten person." As Father John Powell says,

> Each of us acts out of his or her self-image. For example, if I perceive myself as a loser, I act as a loser. I approach each new person or situation with a loser mentality. All my expectations are colored by this "loser" perception of myself. And, as we all know, the expectation is often the mother of the result. Our expectation of failure gives birth to our actual failures. And when in fact we do lose or fail, we are then confirmed in our original self-defeating attitude. "You see. I told you I was no good. I failed again!" It is indeed a vicious circle.

8. *"Should" statements.* Here people tell themselves that things should be the way they hoped or expected them to be. Many people try to motivate themselves with shoulds and shouldn'ts, as if they had to be punished before they could be expected to do anything. For some, that's a religious attitude.

9. *Labeling.* This is an extreme form of all-or-nothing thinking. Instead of saying "I made a mistake," they attach a negative label to themselves declaring, "I'm a loser."

10. *Personalization and blame.* These people hold themselves personally responsible for events that aren't entirely under their control. "If I hadn't sneezed that night, the Titanic would not have sunk." "If I hadn't gone out that night, Dad wouldn't have died."

In his book, *When Bad Things Happen to Good People,* Rabbi Harold Kushner tells of paying condolence calls on the families of two women who died of natural causes after living long, productive lives. At the first home, the son of the deceased woman told the rabbi, "If only I had sent my mother to Florida and gotten her out of this cold and snow, she would be alive today. It's my fault that she died." At the second home, the son told the rabbi, "If only I hadn't insisted on my mother's going to Florida, she would be alive today. That long airplane ride was more than she could take. It's my fault that she died."

So there you have it: ten common traps of low self-esteem that we all fall into at one time or another. I must add that, for some reason, religiously oriented people seem to suffer more from low self-esteem—especially Catholics. The answer seems to lie in the desire for perfection which says that we are only good when we are perfect. If we are less than perfect, we are nothing. This type of guilt-producing input reinforces our negative opinions of ourselves and makes us quite forget, in the words of Thomas Merton, to "surrender your poverty and acknowledge your nothingness to the Lord. Whether you understand it or not, God loves you, is present in you, lives in you, dwells in you, calls you, saves you, and offers you an understanding and compassion which are like nothing you have ever found in a book or heard in a sermon."

Building self-esteem

How do we build self-esteem? The formula is:

self-knowledge + self-acceptance = self-esteem.

Self-knowledge is critical, for how can we esteem what we do not know? But here we discover a certain ambivalence about self-knowledge. We may be afraid that if we really do get to know ourselves, we won't like what we see and so won't love ourselves. The fear is that if we get to the core of who we are, we won't find someone who is valuable, who is lovable. So we figure, ignorance is bliss. But there is a penalty for such "bliss." Simply put, a lack of self-knowledge causes us to forfeit self-identity, and therefore a sense of our strong and weak points. All of us must ask as objectively as we can: what are my areas of strengths? What are my weak points?

After self-knowledge comes self-acceptance. There are four enemies to self-acceptance. The first is its opposite, self-rejection. Ponder these words from Henri Nouwen, who writes in *Life of the Beloved*:

Over the years, I have come to realize that the greatest trap in our life is not success, popularity, or power, but self-rejection. Success, popularity, and power can indeed present a great temptation, but their seductive quality often comes from the way they are part of a much larger temptation to self-rejection. When we come to believe in the voices that call us worthless and unlovable, then success, popularity, and power are easily perceived as attractive solutions. As soon as someone accuses me or criticizes me, as soon as I am rejected, left alone, or abandoned, I find myself thinking, "Well, that proves once again that I am nobody…[My dark side] says I am no good…I deserve to be pushed aside, forgotten, rejected, and abandoned." Self-rejection is the greatest enemy of the spiritual life because it contradicts the sacred voice that calls us "Beloved." Being the Beloved constitutes the core truth of our existence.

The second enemy to self-acceptance is scorekeeping. You know how it goes: we tally up our sins and virtues, and inevitably find the sin column much longer. We see ourselves as did Mae West: "I used to be Snow White—but I drifted." We make silly bargains with God: I will do this if you do that. We multiply our devotions and prayers in the hope that they will outweigh the sins. Thomas Merton's advice is appropriate here: "Quit keeping score altogether and surrender yourself with all your sinfulness to God, who sees neither the score nor the scorekeeper but only his child redeemed by Christ."

The third enemy to self-acceptance is the failure to take responsibility for ourselves. If we do not assume responsibility for our happiness, then we will spend our lives as victims and our conversations will be filled with blaming. Listen to the conversations of people who are dysfunctional or codependent or have been victimized, who walk around with poor self-esteem and lots of anger: years later—ten, twenty, thirty years later—they haven't moved away from blame, from an attitude of "poor us, lousy them." Because they are locked into their anger, they are never free.

Well, we all have a choice: we can spend our lives resenting some priest or sister or parent or relative who died thirty years ago; but if we do, who is paying for the resentment? We are. Or we can realize that the negative experiences of our past do not have to be an obstacle between us and God and our return to a more wholistic life.

Remember these wise words we quoted previously from David Ricchio:

> It is important to remember a distinction: the people or situations of our past may be accountable for some our present distress, but are not responsible for it. To be accountable means to have played a part in the formation of a fear or a deficiency. To be responsible means to have caused it, that is, to be the blame. The past is not causing nor has it caused our feelings.
>
> As adults, our work is to recognize our pain and to work with it for change. To hold onto it is a choice against change and growth and for such a choice we are the ones responsible. The work of recovery can never truly proceed as long as anyone else is to blame, because we then become passive victims, unable to help ourselves. Only able (though wounded) adults can do this work for themselves on themselves.

We can be freed from the past by becoming aware of our responsibility for our own lives. To do this we may find guidance from others, whether spiritual or psychological, to be of help in our recovery.

In the Genesis account in the Bible, you will recall that when God calls Adam to account for eating of the tree of knowledge, Adam blames Eve and Eve blames the serpent. All descendants of Adam and Eve have inherited this propensity for shifting responsibility to others. But the fact remains that self-esteem is inseparable from responsibility. By not accepting responsibility for our destiny, for our actions and all their consequences, we are prevented from feeling ownership of our lives. And without this sense of ownership, we remain chronically insecure. The more we expect others to do what we are able to do for ourselves, the more we diminish our sense of pride in what we can accomplish for ourselves.

Nothing is more important for effective living—whether spiritual or otherwise—than taking full responsibility for ourselves. We receive the strength to do this from knowing that God forgives our past, accepts our present, and welcomes our future. Our self-esteem increases substantially the moment we begin holding ourselves accountable for whatever goes on in our lives, the moment we let go of victimhood. God calls each of us to our own destiny, expecting us to own our lives and live up to our potential to the best of our ability.

As Christians we believe that in final judgment God will hold us, and only us, accountable for what we did with our lives. So accept responsibility for who you are, for what you have become, and for what you will be in the future. Make it a habit to repeat this affirmation: "I take responsibility for whatever goes on in my life. I accept my life and pledge that I will be accountable for how it unfolds." The Spirit is waiting to come upon us with grace for a better and happier life, but the Spirit cannot give birth to that life unless we are willing to take responsibility for it.

The fourth and final enemy of self-esteem is perfectionism, which says that you are only OK when you are perfect. Kathleen Norris rightly observes:

> Perfectionism is one of the scariest words I know. It is a marked characteristic of contemporary American culture, a serious psychological affliction that makes people too timid to take necessary risks and causes them to suffer when, although they've done the best they can, their efforts fall short of some imaginary, and usually unattainable, standard. Internally, it functions as a form of myopia, a preoccupation with self-image that can stunt emotional growth. Martha Stewart might be seen as the high priestess of Perfection: one dare not let the mask slip, even in one's home, where all is perfect, right down to the last hand-stenciled napkin ring.... To "be perfect" in the sense that Jesus means it ("You are to be perfect as your Heavenly Father is perfect"), is to make room for growth, for the changes that bring us to maturity, to ripeness.

Perfectionism denies the truth that we are just as good when we fail as when we succeed; that goodness lies, not in success, but in trying. God is as present in failure as in success. Ultimately, what it comes down to is that we are perfect if we continue to try, if we work at being better. We are never allowed to say, "but that's just the way I am," as a feeble excuse for not trying.

It is interesting to note the psychological mechanism that undoes us here. It's called the "ego-ideal," and it is the summary of all that we think we should be—the "shouldness" which comes from our parents and teachers and upbringing. The ego-ideal is every belief we have of what we think we should do in order to be a good person, a good Christian. You know, all those messages from long ago: "A good boy or girl does—or does not—do this or that." We have taken all of these expectations and dumped them into our ego-ideal.

Our self-esteem is closely related to how we live up to our ego-ideal. If this is what we think we should be then we are good persons if we do all these things. If we do something contrary to the ego-ideal, we feel anxious, guilty. The trouble is that many of these "shoulds" that have gone into making up the ego-ideal are unconscious thoughts: most likely, we have never taken them out and examined them. Do we still believe all the messages we heard in our childhood? Are they a valid part of our lives? Are they true?

Somewhere along the line, usually at midlife, we come face to face not with who we should be, but with who we are, our real selves. Then the challenge is to accept ourselves as who we are in light of our ego-ideal: if this is my ego-ideal, on one hand, but this is who I really am, can I accept the person I find—an incomplete, imperfect, sinful person? (Besides, if we were perfect, what challenge would be left for us—except driving everyone else crazy with our perfection?) Can we believe in the one reality, that we are good if we try? If we believe this, then we can replace the issue of perfection with the issue of "I try." And this is the way to grow.

So, for self-esteem to flourish you must first have self-knowledge, which comes from people who will give you honest feedback. Then you must accept yourself, believing that you are a good, loving person worthy of your own esteem. Psychiatrist Gerard May has it right when he says, "We have this idea that everyone should be totally independent, totally whole, totally together spiritually, totally fulfilled. That is a myth. In reality, our lack of fulfillment is the most precious gift we have. It is the source of our passion, our creativity, our search for God. All the best of life comes out of our human yearning, our not being satisfied."

The world's criteria

I asked you earlier in this chapter to rate your sense of self-esteem on a scale of one to ten. Then I asked, what criteria did you use? Let me share with you the five major categories which, according to social scientists, most people use to measure self-esteem. They are: significance to others; competence in terms of performance; virtue in conforming to what is right; power, that is, influence over people; and body image. Most people have developed their self-esteem around one or more of these criteria.

Significance. As we grow from childhood into adolescence, our self-esteem is more "other-esteem"; what others think about us ultimately leads us to think the same thing about ourselves. As we move into adulthood, the question becomes this: who has control over my own sense of self-esteem? If our self-esteem is low, a critic can cause us to be hostile. If our self-esteem is based on what one or two other people think about us, what happens if these people turn against us or are no longer in our lives? And so we act solely out of an effort to please these one or two people, in a mode of codependency. If we turn over our self-esteem to too many people and if all don't unanimously agree, then a few people can undermine us. Everyone praises the picture we painted—except three critics. Guess whose words you'll remember?

Competency. If my negative self-esteem is based on what I do, then my self-esteem will always be fragile. When work falters, self-esteem does as well, especially in our capitalistic culture which values people for what they can do, not for who they are. Priests, CEOs, managers, and the like are often praised for their competency but seldom praised simply for who they are; and there comes a time when being praised for competency is just not enough. Early on we begin to suspect that when we lose our competency, we will lose respect, lose value, and lose the esteem of others—including our own. We may even lose our identity.

A retired man, the founding genius of the company, went back after several years to visit the plant. The young receptionist did not have a clue who he was. When he mentioned that he had worked there for many years, she asked, "Oh? And who did you used to be?"

Virtue. Some people only value themselves when they live a perfectly virtuous life. But as we saw earlier, when one lives by these criteria and virtue fails, so does self-esteem. Or we do not measure up to what others consider virtuous, and our self-esteem lags when we fall short. Consider this old Cherokee fable of an imperfection that trampled self-esteem and almost deprived the world of a song:

> In the days when people and animals spoke the same language, there was a bird called Meadowlark, whose feet grew so big that he was ashamed of them. While the other birds flew through the air and sang in the treetops, Meadowlark hid himself in the tall grass where no one could see him. He spent all his time staring down at his big feet and worrying about them.
>
> "Provider must have made a terrible mistake," thought Meadowlark, turning his feet this way and that. No matter how he looked at them, all Meadowlark could see was how big his feet were. "Perhaps Creator thought this would be a funny joke to play," said Meadowlark. "I'm sure anyone who saw my big feet would laugh at them, but I do not think this is funny at all." And so Meadowlark continued to hide himself away in the tall grass.
>
> One day Grasshopper was going about his business, making his way through the tall grass, when he bumped smack into Meadowlark, sitting on the ground and staring sadly at his feet.
>
> "What are you doing here?" asked Grasshopper. "You are not one of those birds who live on the ground! You should be in the treetops with the other birds. Why do you not fly and sing as they do?" "I am ashamed," answered Meadowlark. "These feet that Provider gave me are so big and ugly that I am afraid that everyone will laugh at me!" Grasshopper looked down at Meadowlark's feet, and his eyes grew big with amazement. It was true; Meadowlark's feet were huge! Grasshopper did his best not to smile; he did not want to hurt Meadowlark's feelings.
>
> Finally he said, "Well, it is true that your feet are perhaps a bit larger than those of other birds your size. But Creator does

not make mistakes. If your feet are big, you may be sure that they will be useful to you someday. Big feet will not keep you from flying. Big feet will not stop you from singing. You are a bird and you should act like one!" And Grasshopper went on about his business.

After Grasshopper had gone on his way, Meadowlark sat and thought about his words. "Perhaps he is right," said Meadowlark. "The size of my feet cannot change the sound of my voice or the power of my wings. I should use the gifts Creator gave me." And so Meadowlark took Grasshopper's advice and flew out to sing. He landed in the top of a tree, threw back his head, and let his song pour from his throat. Meadowlark could really sing! Piercingly sweet and beautiful, the liquid notes of Meadowlark's song spread through the forest. One by one, the animal people stopped what they were doing and gathered to listen to Meadowlark's voice. Raccoon, Possum, and Skunk; Deer, Bear, and Wolf; even Rabbit paused in his scurrying about to listen in wonder to this marvelous singer. The other birds flocked around Meadowlark, listening. Even Mockingbird fell silent, entranced by the melody that Meadowlark sang.

When Meadowlark began to sing, he forgot everything else, even his big feet. He closed his eyes and lost himself in the joyful song Creator had given him. When at last he finished his song and looked around, there were all the other birds and animals, staring at him. With a rush of shame, Meadowlark remembered his feet. Thinking that the others were staring at him because he was so ugly, Meadowlark flew back down to the tall grass and hid. And this time he would not come out.

Not very far from the tall grass where Meadowlark hid, there was a wheat field planted by the Human Beings. Now there was a Quail who had made her nest and laid her eggs in the middle of this wheat field. Every day she sat on her nest and waited for her eggs to hatch. As the wheat grew ripe and her eggs had still not hatched, Quail began to worry. Sure enough, one afternoon she heard the people talking about how they were going to come out and cut the wheat the very next day. Quail knew that her nest would be trampled and her eggs crushed, and she began to cry.

Now Grasshopper heard Quail crying, and he came to see what was wrong. "The men are coming to cut the wheat," Quail cried, "and my family will die!" Suddenly, Grasshopper had an idea. "Wait here," he told Quail. "I think I know someone who can help." Grasshopper hurried to find Meadowlark. "Quail needs help to move her family," said Grasshopper, "and I think your big feet are the answer."

When Meadowlark heard of Quail's trouble, he agreed at once to try to help. He flew to Quail's nest. There he found that his big feet were just the right size to pick up Quail's eggs. Very carefully, Meadowlark lifted Quail's eggs and flew with them to the safety of the tall grass. There Quail built a new nest, and it was not long before the eggs hatched. As Meadowlark watched Quail tending her beautiful babies, he thought to himself, "My feet may be big and ugly, but they did a good thing. I should not be ashamed of them!"

And so Meadowlark flew out of the tall grass, back to the treetops where he began to sing. He is singing to this day, and his song is still so beautiful that everyone stops to listen.

Is lack of virtue preventing you from singing your song?

Power over others. This works for a while as a source of self-esteem. But as people begin to grow, they move to get out from under someone's power. And then what happens when you lose power? Who are you without it? In this context, Shakespeare's Othello was right: "Thou hast not half the power to do me harm/ As I have to be hurt."

Body image. In our age of slick commercialism where imagery is everything and a whole industry of spin doctors create illusions, one's body image is crucial for self-esteem. Obsessions with weight, skin, looks, and hair are a national pastime and have spawned a multibillion dollar market for the products that will "cure" whatever is "wrong" with our appearance. Bulimia and anorexia thrive as the dark side of this body-image culture. To have the right look, the current image, many people will suppress what is more noble in their lives. People will cripple the spirit to be "in."

A man goes to a tailor to buy a suit in a style that is all the rage. He tries the suit on in front of the mirror and notices that the jacket is a little uneven at the bottom. "It needs a hand adjustment," the tailor suggests. "Just pull it down with your hand." The man does this, looks in the mirror, and notices that the lapel has popped up. He is told it needs a chin adjustment. So he puts his chin on the popped-up lapel to keep it down. Finally, the pants are too tight in the crotch and have to be pulled down by a hand adjustment. Although he is bent over and crippled by the many "alterations," he buys the suit, for after all, it is the "in" style.

The next day he is walking through the park with his new suit. He passes two old men sitting on a bench. The first comments on how crippled the poor man is. The second one agrees and adds, "Yes...but I wonder where he got such a nice suit."

We all too easily recognize ourselves in this story. That's every one of us, at some time or another: shadow over reality, imagery over substance, body image over soul image.

Your criteria

We now circle back to the critical question for determining self-esteem: what do *you* use as your criteria? If you are caught in using any or all of the above as your standard, you now know that you must discover deeper criteria. For this, we look to what was suggested at the beginning of this chapter: your status as made in the image and likeness of God; your position as beloved of the Father, friend of Christ, and temple of the Holy Spirit; and the fact that you are brother and sister to Christ. Being your own person in Christ "who was no respecter of men" is what makes you who you are. "Who am I?" asks Thomas Merton. "I am one loved by Christ." How do we acquire this intimate knowledge, that we are loved by God? We come to this truth through prayer and through reading Scripture. These are the two time-tested means to help us bypass the world's criteria. Our value, our worth, reside in being children of God.

To excessively flirt with the perennially fickle standards of culture is to lose our identity and learn to play it small. True, none of us have perfect self-esteem; it will ebb and flow and become quite vulnerable to the shifting circumstances of life. But the general rule holds: the more our self-esteem is in the hands of external circumstances, other people, and situations outside ourselves, the more fragile is our self-esteem. The more it is in our own spirit, in the hands of God, the more firm it is. Henri Nouwen writes to a friend:

> All I want to say to you is "You are the Beloved," and all I hope is that you can hear these words as spoken to you with all the force and tenderness that love can hold. My only desire is to make these words reverberate in every corner of your being—"You are the Beloved."

We must always and at every moment define ourselves as radically loved by God. Let us end this reflection with the profound words of one of our modern prophets, Nelson Mandela, who said this at his inaugural address:

> Our worst fear is not that we are inadequate, our deepest fear is that we are powerful beyond measure. It is our light, not our darkness, that most frightens us. We ask ourselves, "Who am I to be brilliant, gorgeous, talented and fabulous?" Actually, who are you not to be? You are a child of God; your playing small doesn't serve the world. There is nothing enlightened about shrinking so that other people won't feel insecure around you. We were born to make manifest the glory of God within us. It is not just in some of us; it is in everyone. And as we let our own light shine we unconsciously give other people permission to do the same. As we are liberated from our own fear our presence automatically liberates others.

This is where self-esteem is to be found.

Questions for reflection

1. All Christians are called to holiness, community, and ministry. How do I see my self-esteem working in each of these three areas?

2. Where self-esteem is low, competition and hostility are high. Where do I most experience this in my life? in my faith?

3. Self-rejection is the first enemy of self-acceptance. Do I see myself as God sees me, as the Beloved? Or am I wont to dwell on my faults and failings rather than on my inherent Godliness?

4. Do I take responsibility for my life, my actions? Or do I continually blame others, both past and present, for my circumstances?

5. Am I guilty of perfectionism?

6. What is my criteria for success? Does it rest more with the world or with God?

NINE

SCARECROW

Failure & Guilt

Poor Scarecrow! He failed at the very thing he was supposed to do, scare crows, for the birds came and simply rested on him. But things got worse along the Yellow Brick Road. Scarecrow was terrified of fire, and so the witch taunted him with a flaming broom. He literally had the stuffing knocked out of him by the wicked witch's flying monkeys. Indeed, something was missing in his life. If he only had a brain.

The twin topics of this brief chapter are failure and guilt. To illustrate these two feelings, I have come up with five true but simple stories for your reflection. These stories, I tell you beforehand, all have one thing in common: they are "scarecrow" stories, that is, stories of failure and guilt. It is imperative that you read them with your heart as well as with your head, for my desire is that these stories will, in turn, provoke your story. Again, the best way to read them is to pause after each one in an examination of conscience. And so we begin.

I was a young lawyer then and, like everyone else, I called him "Old Governor Campbell." He was the undisputed chief of the village bums in the little southwestern town where I grew up. He hung around the courthouse, and knew many of the merchants and lawyers. He sponged quarters from me, from them. With the money he'd get something to eat but more to drink, for the fact was he was the town drunk and we all made fun of him.

In those days, the revival people used to sweep through these little towns with great regularity. And each time, Old Governor Campbell would go to the revival meeting and get converted. Then the news would spread from the courthouse to the barbershop and local bars that Old Governor Campbell got religion again. They would tell it as a great joke and the people would laugh knowingly. And sure enough, there would be Old Governor Campbell with his clothes pressed, hair combed, face shaved, standing erect on the street, full of pride for a few days. But never beyond a few days. Because as he strutted before us, some would call out, "How long this time, Governor? You'll never make it. How about a drink?" And all would laugh.

This one time, after one of those revival meetings and the Governor was sober, a group of us were standing around outside at lunch break, and for some reason he stopped before me. I knew that he liked me, and I also could sense that he was hoping that I, in front of all the men, would say something—well, positive. I could see longing and pleading in his eyes as if he were searching for some words of encouragement, some acknowledgment of dignity, some affirmation. I hesitated. I wanted to shake his hand and congratulate him and tell him he was on the right track. But the others were still heaping their sarcasm on him and I couldn't. Instead I found myself saying, "You'll never make the day out sober, Governor." Everyone laughed again and patted me on the back, and we went back to work. But inside, in my office, I felt shame, a deep shame, that I had left unspoken what I knew he wanted to hear, needed to hear.

Soon after you would see the stubble growing back on his face, the hair would be uncombed, the clothes would be disheveled, and he would be back in his role as the town drunk. People would pass him by and say, "How many days did you make it this time, Governor? How does it feel to be your old self again, Governor?" People would slip another quarter in his hand with a wink in their eye, and at the courthouse and at the barbershop they would say things like, "That's the trouble with religion. Those preachers keep trying to convert people like

Old Governor Campbell, and there he is again, stiff as a billy goat. He'll never change."

I moved away to practice law in Los Angeles. I don't know what happened to Old Governor Campbell. I heard later that he had died from cirrhosis of the liver. But I can still see him standing there before me practically pleading for a word of encouragement that would have made a difference, that told him I believed in him—and I never gave that word. I destroyed a life because of human pressure. I can't make it up to him. He still stays in the back of my mind. Call it guilt, if you will, but all I know is that I go once a week to the local AA meeting to give advice and counsel to the members of the group. I listen. I encourage. I direct. I owe that to Old Governor Campbell.

The late Lewis Grizzard was a newspaper columnist and essayist known for his offbeat, often outrageous Southern humor. Beneath the laughter, however, there was sadness—a life of personal suffering and loss. Some of Grizzard's pain came from his troubled relationship with his father, an alcoholic who left the family when Grizzard was a boy. He writes:

> Before he died, I asked Daddy a thousand times, "What is wrong? Why can't you stay sober? Why can't you stay in one place? What can be so bad you can't talk about it?" My father would never give a direct answer.
>
> One day, I pleaded desperately with my father to tell me what was wrong in his life. I told him that it didn't matter what it was, no matter how terrible, that I loved him whatever was the awful truth. But my father could not respond. He could only weep, sobbing out the words that he had made a mistake, "a bad mistake."
>
> That's all I ever got. The man died, as far as I know, with his secret. What terrible secret did he have? Did he kill somebody? Did he rob or cheat somebody? Was he a child molester? I can

think of no more unthinkables. No matter. Whatever his sin, his secret, I loved him—and I love him—anyway.

Whatever his sin, I loved him—and I love him—anyway.

"I am going home to Denmark, son, and I just wanted to tell you I love you." In my dad's last telephone call to me, he repeated that line seven times in a half hour. I wasn't listening at the right level. I heard the words, but not the message, and certainly not their profound intent. I believed my dad would live to be over 100 years old, as my great uncle lived to be 107 years old. I had not felt his remorse over Mom's death, understood his intense loneliness as an "empty nester," or realized most of his pals had long since light-beamed off the planet. He relentlessly requested that my brothers and I create grandchildren so that he could be a devoted grandfather. I was too busy "entrepreneuring" to really listen.

"Dad's dead," sighed my brother Brian on July 4, 1973. My little brother is a witty lawyer and has a humorous, quick mind. I thought he was setting me up for a joke, and I awaited the punchline—there wasn't one. "Dad died in the bed he was born in—in Rozkeldj," continued Brian. "The funeral directors are putting him in a coffin, and shipping Dad and his belongings to us by tomorrow. We need to prepare for the funeral."

I was speechless. This isn't the way it's supposed to happen. If I knew these were to be Dad's final days, I would have asked to go with him to Denmark. I believe in the hospice movement, which says: "No one should die alone." A loved one should hold your hand and comfort you as you transition from one plane of reality to another. I would have offered consolation during his final hour if I'd been really listening, thinking, and in tune with the Infinite.

Dad announced his departure as best he could, and I had missed it. I felt grief, pain, and remorse. Why had I not been there for him? He'd always been there for me. When I was nine years old, he would come home from working eighteen hours at his bakery and wake me up at 5:00 AM by scratching my back with his strong, powerful hands and whispering, "Time to get up, son." By the time I was dressed and ready to roll, he had my newspapers folded, banded, and stuffed in my bicycle basket. Recalling his generosity of spirit brings tears to my eyes.

When I was racing bicycles, he drove me fifty miles each way to Kenosha, Wisconsin, every Tuesday night so I could race and he could watch me. He was there to hold me if I lost and shared the euphoria when I won. Later, he accompanied me to all my local talks in Chicago when I spoke to Century 21, Mary Kay, Equitable, and various churches. He always smiled, listened, and proudly told whomever he was sitting with, "That's my boy!"

After the fact, my heart was in pain because Dad was there for me and I wasn't there for him. Again, no big scarlet sin. We're all busy. But it bothers us because we sense that we're less somehow for our neglect and the excuses for our neglect, which like so many small particles settle like dust on our soul.

My humble advice is to always, always share your love with your loved ones, and ask to be invited to that sacred transitional period where physical life transforms into spiritual life. Experiencing the process of death with one you love will take you into a bigger, more expansive dimension of beingness.

• ➤

I remember the day I learned to hate racism. I was five years old. The walk home from school was only about five blocks. I usually walked with some friends, but on this day I walked alone. Happy, but in a hurry, I decided to take the shortcut through the alley. Without a care in the world, I careened around the corner—too late to change course. I had walked into a back alley beating. There were three big white kids. In retrospect they were probably no more than sixth graders, but they looked like giants from my kindergarten perspective.

There was one black kid. He was standing against a garage,

his hands behind his back. The three white kids were taking turns punching him. They laughed. He stood silently except for the involuntary groans that that followed each blow. And now I was caught. One of the three grabbed me and stood me in front of their victim, "You take a turn," he said. "Hit the nigger!" I stood paralyzed. "Hit him or you're next."

So I did. I feigned a punch. I can still feel the soft fuzz of that boy's turquoise sweater as my knuckles gently touched his stomach. I don't know how many punches there were. I don't know how long he had to stand backed up against that garage. After my minute participation in the conspiracy, they let me go and I ran. I ran home crying and sick to my stomach. I have never forgotten. Thirty-five years later that event still preaches a sermon to me every time I remember it. One can despise, decry, denounce, and deplore something without ever being willing to suffer, or even be inconvenienced, to bring about change.

If there is one thing that Jesus taught us, it was how to suffer with and for others. Jesus walked the way of the cross. He taught us the meaning of suffering as a servant. Perhaps my first chance to follow that example came in the alley by a garage thirty-five years ago. I don't know if that black boy from the alley grew up, or where he lives, or what he does today. I never knew his name. I wish I did. I wish I could find him. I need to ask his forgiveness—not for the blow I delivered, for it was nothing, but for the blows I refused to stand by his side and receive. I think, that's what it takes.

• ⟶

Andy was a sweet, amusing little guy whom every one liked but harassed, just because that was the way one treated Andy Drake. He took the kidding well. He always smiled back with those great big eyes that seemed to say, "Thank you, thank you, thank you," with each sweeping blink. For us fifth-graders, Andy was our outlet; he was our whipping boy. He even seemed grateful to pay this special price for membership in our group.

Andy Drake don't eat no cake,
And his sister don't eat no pie.
If it wasn't for the welfare dole,
All the Drakes would die.

Andy even appeared to like this sing-song parody of Jack
Sprat. The rest of us really enjoyed it, bad grammar and all. I
don't know why Andy had to endure this special treatment to
deserve our friendship and membership in the group. It just
evolved naturally—no vote or discussion. I don't recall that it was
ever mentioned that Andy's father was in prison or that his mother took in washing and men. Or that Andy's ankles, elbows and
fingernails were always dirty and his old coat was way too big. We
soon wore all the fun out of that. Andy never fought back.

Snobbery blossoms in the very young, I guess. It's clear now
the group attitude was that it was all right to belong to the
group but that Andy was a member by our sufferance. Despite
that, we all liked Andy until that day—until that very moment.
"He's different!" "We don't want him, do we?" Which one of us
said it? I've wanted to blame Randolph all these years, but I
can't honestly say who spoke those trigger words that brought
out the savagery lying dormant but so near the surface in all of
us. It doesn't matter who, for the fervor with which we took up
the cry revealed us all.

"I didn't want to do what we did." For years I tried to console
myself with that. Then one day, I stumbled on those unwelcome
but irrefutable words that convicted me forever: the hottest corners of hell are reserved for those who, during a moment of crisis, maintain their neutrality.

The weekend was to be like others the group had enjoyed
together. After school on a Friday we would meet at the home
of one of the members—mine this time—for a camp-out in the
nearby woods. Our mothers, who did most of the preparation
for these "safaris," fixed an extra pack for Andy who was to join
us after chores.

We quickly made camp, mothers' apron strings forgotten.

With individual courage amplified by the group, we were now "men" against the jungle. The others told me that since it was my party, I should be the one to give Andy the news! Me? I who had long believed that Andy secretly thought a little more of me than he did the others because of the puppy-like way he looked at me? I who often felt him revealing his love and appreciation with those huge, wide-open eyes?

I can still plainly see Andy as he came toward me down the long, dark tunnel of trees that leaked only enough of the late afternoon light to kaleidoscope changing patterns on his soiled old sweatshirt. Andy was on his rusty, one-of-a-kind bike—a girl's model with sections of garden hose wired to the rims for tires. He appeared excited and happier than I had ever seen him, this frail little guy who had been an adult all his life. I knew he was savoring the acceptance by the group, this first chance to belong, to have "boy fun," to do "boy things." Andy waved to me as I stood in the camp clearing awaiting him. I ignored his happy greeting.

He vaulted off the funny old bike and trotted over toward me, full of joy and conversation. The others, concealed within the tent, were quiet but I felt their support. Why won't he get serious? Can't he see that I am not returning his gaiety? Can't he see by now that his babblings aren't reaching me? Then suddenly he did see! His innocent countenance opened even more, leaving him totally vulnerable. His whole demeanor said, "It's going to be very bad, isn't it, Ben? Let's have it." Undoubtedly well practiced in facing disappointment, he didn't even brace for the blow. Andy never fought back. Incredulously, I heard myself say, "Andy, we don't want you."

Hauntingly vivid still is the stunning quickness with which two huge tears sprang into Andy's eyes and just stayed there. Vivid because of a million maddening reruns of that scene in my mind. The way Andy looked at me—frozen for an eternal moment—what was it? It wasn't hate. Was it shock? Was it disbelief? Or, was it pity—for me? Or forgiveness? Finally, a fleet little tremor broke across Andy's lips and he turned without appeal, or even a question, to make the long, lonely trip home in the dark.

As I entered the tent, someone—the last one of us to feel the full weight of the moment—started the old doggerel:

Andy Drake don't eat no cake,
And his sister don't....

Then it was unanimous! No vote taken, no word spoken, but we all knew. We knew that we had done something horribly, cruelly wrong. We were swept over by the delayed impact of dozens of lessons and sermons. We heard for the first time, "Inasmuch as ye do it unto the least of these...." In that hushed, heavy moment, we gained an understanding new to us but indelibly fixed in our minds: we had destroyed an individual made in the image of God with the only weapon for which he had no defense and we had no excuse—rejection.

Andy's poor attendance in school made it difficult to tell when he actually withdrew, but one day it dawned on me that he was gone forever. I had spent too many days struggling within myself to find and polish a proper way of telling Andy how totally, consummately ashamed and sorry I was, and am. I now know that to have hugged Andy and to have cried with him and even to have joined with him in a long silence would have been enough. It may have healed us both.

I never saw Andy Drake again. I have no idea where he went or where he is, if he is. But to say I haven't seen Andy is not entirely accurate. In the decades since that autumn day in the Arkansas woods, I have encountered thousands of Andy Drakes. My conscience places Andy's mask over the face of every disadvantaged person with whom I come in contact. Each one stares back at me with that same haunting, expectant look that became fixed in my mind that day long ago.

Dear Andy Drake:
The chance you will ever see these words is quite remote, but I must try. It's much too late for this confession to purge my conscience of guilt. I neither expect it to nor

want it to. What I do pray for, my little friend of long ago, is that you might somehow learn of and be lifted by the continuing force of your sacrifice. What you suffered at my hand that day and the loving courage you showed, God has twisted, turned and molded into a blessing. This knowledge might erase the memory of that terrible day for you.

I've been no saint, Andy, nor have I done all the things I could and should have done with my life. But what I want you to know is that I have never again knowingly betrayed an Andy Drake. Nor, I pray, shall I ever.

Well, weighty stories, aren't they? A man who denied an old drunk a chance at redemption; a father who couldn't reveal his secret to a son who adored him; a son who ignored his father's reaching out to die in his arms, to be there for him as he was for his son; a kid who under pressure punched a kid whose only crime was that his skin was different; a boy who cut the heart out of his trusting friend.

What are these stories but jabs at our own consciences? They confront us. We think of the people we have hurt. Some of those people, perhaps deceased, haunt us to this day. They are never far from us and at certain times when we're alone, accuse us. What are we to do? What can we learn from these stories? We can apply four principles here.

First, we are all in need of redemption. All have sinned. "If we say that we have no sin, we deceive ourselves" (1 Jn 1:8).

A thief was sentenced to death by hanging for stealing a small package of meat. Before he was taken to the gallows, he was allowed to address the king. "Your majesty," the thief said humbly, "I am the only man who knows how to plant an apple seed that will grow and bear fruit overnight. To atone for my crime I would like to teach you and your court the secret. I will need a shovel, a handful of apple seeds, and a maiden who has not tasted love's first kiss."

Eagerly, the king, his thirteen-year-old daughter, and all his advisors gathered in an open field to learn this most wonderful secret. In the most elaborate manner possible, bowing and making dramatic gestures, the thief dug a small hole. "Now," said the thief, "the water must be poured into the hole by this tender maiden." The king's daughter stepped forward and carefully poured a small container of water in the freshly dug hole.

"We are ready for the actual planting," the thief said, addressing the assembled group. "The seed can only be placed in the earth by someone who has never taken a single item that did not belong to them, no matter how small or how long ago."

"I would like to have my most trusted advisor, the prime minister, be the one who plants this magic seed in the ground," the king announced.

Hesitating, the prime minister said meekly, "I am afraid that I am not eligible, your majesty. When I was young I took a jacket that was not mine."

"Perhaps it is best that our loyal treasurer be the one to plant the seed," the king said quickly.

"Majesty," the treasurer said with some embarrassment, "you forgot that in a previous position I foolishly kept a small amount of money that did not rightfully belong to me."

One by one the king's advisors coughed, sputtered, and explained meekly that they were not able to plant the seed. Finally, even the king admitted that he once took a small item which belonged to his father.

When each had spoken the thief addressed the king. "The members of your court are men and women of the highest ethical standards. They are recognized as devoted public servants, yet not one of them can say they have never taken something that did not belong to them. How is it that I am to be hanged for taking a bit of food?"

"You are a wise and crafty man," the king said to the thief. "I now give you a full and complete pardon."

All have sinned.

Second, go back to Scripture and read the stories of Peter and Judas. Both committed the same crime: they betrayed a friend. The result of this betrayal was every bit as hurtful as being punched in the stomach or being told, "Jesus, we don't want you," and seeing, like Andy, tears well up in Jesus' eyes. But the lesson in Scripture lies in what each guilty man did. One turned in on his guilt and took his life. The other turned to Jesus in his guilt, finding life. All of us have some measure of guilt, and this is not all that bad unless the guilt becomes self-absorbing and destructive. If, on the other hand, it leads us to a different life, then the guilt becomes life-giving.

So this is the second principle these stories reveal: play the role of Peter, that is, turn to Jesus. One way of doing this is to confess your sins. Go to the sacrament of reconciliation and say how you have hurt someone you shouldn't have, someone who had a claim on your love and your presence and you withheld these things from them. Confess. Get it off your chest, off your heart.

Third, remember that, even when your sin is absolved, you will always have scars, the scar of what you did, the uneasy memory. There is a tradition which says that Peter cried so much over his betrayal two grooves were worn in his cheeks forever. It is OK to feel some residual guilt. After all, we only feel guilty about what we value, and our guilt shows that a cherished value has been violated.

Fourth, remember that such guilt is productive if it leads to you to embrace sensitivity; that is, a sensitivity which leads to action, to a more caring, noble life as a wounded healer. Remember St. Paul's words: charity covers a multitude of sins.

Imitate the lawyer who counsels alcoholics, the man who works for racial justice, the man who never again will hurt an Andy Drake. Be like Eli of the Old Testament who, though a failed parent, ministered to another "adopted" son, little Samuel, who became the big prophet. Be like Peter who gave his life over to winning disciples for Christ. Be like the converted slave runner, John Newton, who gave us the wonderful hymn "Amazing Grace." Remember: imperfect people have the power to make all things new again.

Be ready now to add your story to the many stories of redemption already told and celebrated.

Questions for reflection

1. What are my stories of guilt?

2. The first step in healing is to admit both our guilt and our need of redemption. Have I done that?

3. The Bible is full of repentant sinners. Have I claimed their stories as my own, their example as encouragement?

4. Do my sins lead me to despair and paralysis, or are they a catalyst for renewal and charity, as were the sins of so many of the saints in our Catholic tradition?

5. John Newton wrote: "Amazing grace...that saved a wretch like me." Is this my song, too?

TEN

PROFESSOR MARVEL

Loss

That genial fraud, Professor Marvel, invites the fleeing Dorothy to his wagon to consult his crystal ball. Dorothy sits down and closes her eyes, awaiting the Professor's predictions. Meanwhile, he is looking through her basket, and in doing so, finds a photograph. When Dorothy opens her eyes, he pretends to read the crystal ball and exclaims, "What's this I see? A house and a picket fence and a weather vane…and a woman, her face is careworn. She's crying. Someone has hurt her."

"Me?" Dorothy asks. "What's she doing now?"

"What's this? She's putting her hand on her heart…."

"I've got to get to her right away," exclaims Dorothy, as she heads back home and into the approaching tornado.

This little scene invites us to consider in this reflection one of life's inevitable realities: as we travel life's journey we will suffer loss. Auntie Em lost a niece and is swooning from grief. Dorothy lost a dear aunt whom she has hurt by running away. Loss. There is no way around it.

A few years ago, Judith Viorst, columnist and writer, put together a collection of her columns and titled the book *Necessary Losses*. In one of her chapters she writes this:

The road to human development is paved with renunciation.

Throughout our life we grow by giving up. We give up some of our deepest attachments to others. We give up certain cherished parts of ourselves. We must confront, in the dreams we dream, as well as in our intimate relationships, all that we never will have and never will be. Passionate investment leaves us vulnerable to loss. And sometimes, no matter how clever we are, we must lose.... In fact, I would like to propose that central to understanding our lives is understanding how we deal with loss. I would like to propose that the people we are and the lives that we lead are determined, for better and worse, by our loss experiences.

This experience of loss is like a hemorrhage, a bleeding away of what we value and hold dear in life. It is the challenge of working through our losses and fashioning them into sustenance for our journey that frames our reflection.

The loss of separation

We don't often think of it, but one of the first and most pivotal losses that we experience is the loss of our mothers. Our mothers usually don't abandon us or die, but for every child as they grow up there is a separation from the mother on whom we depend. Fear of her loss is the earliest terror we know. Her presence stands for safety and we need her, cling to her even when, as sometimes happens, she abuses us.

During the atrocities that accompanied the Bolshevik revolution in Russia, thousands of bewildered suspects were randomly arrested, rounded up, stripped naked, and shot one by one in the back of the head. One eyewitness account captures the depth as well as the poignancy of our need to feel linked, joined together. "Most of the victims usually requested a chance to say good-bye and because there was no one else, they embraced and kissed their executioners."

So needy are we of our mothers that we will even seek the arms of one who hurts us. Still, we must lose our mother. She leaves before we can know that she will return. She "abandons" us to go to work or to the market or on vacation or to have another baby, or she is simply not there when we have need of her. She "abandons" us by having a life of her own, and we will have to learn to have one, too. Loss of our mother is as inevitable as it is necessary; it is a condition for our growth.

The loss of affirmation

Besides the loss of our mother, there is, for some, a second loss: the loss of the affirmation and acceptance so critical to our emotional and spiritual well-being and development. Contemplate this:

> I painted a picture—green sky—and showed it to my mother.
> She said that's nice, I guess.
> So I painted another holding the paintbrush in my teeth,
> Look, Ma, no hands. And she said
> I guess someone would admire that if they knew
> How you did it and they were interested in painting, which
>   I am not.

> I played the clarinet solo in Gounod's Clarinet Concerto
> With the Buffalo Philharmonic. Mother came to listen and said
> That's nice, I guess.
> So I played it with the Boston Symphony,
> Lying on my back and using my toes,
> Look, Ma, no hands. And she said
> I guess someone would admire that if they knew
> How you did it and they were interested in music which
>   I am not.

> I made an almond souffle and served it to my mother.
> She said, that's nice, I guess.
> So I made another, beating it with my breath,
> Serving it with my elbows,
> Look, Ma, no hands. And she said
> I guess someone would admire that if they knew
> How you did it and they were interested in eating which
>   I am not.

> So I sterilized my wrists, performed the amputation, threw away
> My hands and went to my mother, but before I could say
> Look, Ma, no hands, she said

I have a present for you and insisted I try on
The blue kid gloves to make sure they were the right size.

Some still feel the sting of the loss embedded in rejection or indifference.

The loss of innocence

Another loss is what we call the loss of innocence. This can mean many things. It means discovering clay feet in the ones we love and look up to, their humanness and weakness. Father was unfaithful, Aunt Bea a closet drinker. Trusted people were caught in a lie. People didn't keep their word. Promises were broken. The fairyland of childhood sprung some weeds. Flaws were discovered and high ideals were compromised—including your own. There was jealousy over the best friend who did better, the one who went on to achievement, the one who got the highest marks, not you. The perceived diminishing from sibling rivalry and its moment of truth:

> A little girl discovers, when she wakens on Christmas morning, the present she had longed for—a glorious doll's house, its tiny rooms neatly carpeted, wallpapered, hung with chandeliers and filled with furniture. She is gazing at it, enthralled, when her mother gives her a gentle nudge and asks a very simple, terrible question: Could she be grown up and generous enough to share her gift with her younger sister Bridget?
>
> I thought. That question, Mother's simple question…was to me the most complex question anyone had ever asked. I thought for a whole minute while my heart stopped and my eyes blinked and my face flushed with fury. It was a trick question, two-sided, flipping back and forth, now-you-see-it-now-you don't, the trick of the supreme magician who could—with cunning legerdemain under a silk handkerchief—transform a few seconds of tranquility into an eternity of chaos. The truth: no, I did not, under any circumstance whatsoever, wish to share the doll's house with Bridget….Or the truth: yes, of course I wanted to share the doll's house with Bridget, because not only would that please Mother and demonstrate how generous and

grown up I really was but because I knew that I loved Bridget very deeply and identified with her yearning as she tentatively touched the miniature grandfather's clock in the miniature hallway. (Get your fingers out of there, I wanted to scream, until I give you permission.) Bridget was blissfully oblivious of my pain, my conflict. I had not, before that question, ever been conscious of hating her or of loving her so absolutely. I never felt, or had the ability to be unaware of feeling, the same way about my sister again. And I could never bring myself to play with the doll's house. Eventually it had to be given away.

For some, the loss of innocence comes with abuse: verbal, physical, sexual. In her memoir book, *The Liar's Club*, Mary Karr writes:

Sometimes, when my parents were raging at each other in the kitchen, Lecia and I would talk about finding a shack on the beach to live in. We'd sit cross-legged under the blue cotton quilt with a flashlight, doing parodies of their fights. "Reel six, tape fifty-one. Let her roll," Lecia would say. She would clap her arms together like a 'gator jaw as if what we were listening to was only one more take in a long movie we were shooting. She had a way of shining the flashlight under her chin and sucking in her cheeks, so her eyes became hooded and her cheekbones got as sharp as Mother's. She also had a knack for Mother's sometime-Yankee accent, which only came out under stress or chemical influence....

Sometimes she'd just cry, and Lecia's imitation of that was cruelest: there's no hope, there's no hope, she'd say with a Gloria Swanson melodrama, her wrist flung back to her forehead like it had been stapled there. I always did Daddy's part, which didn't require much in the way of thought, since he was either silent or his voice was too quiet to hear. The only thing he ever shouted clearly was, "You kiss my ass...."

Sometimes we'd hear a crash or the sound of a body hitting the linoleum, and then we'd go streaking in there in our pajamas to see who had thrown what or who had passed out. If they were still halfway conscious, they'd scare us back to bed. "Git

back to bed. This ain't nothing to do with you," Daddy would
say, or Mother would point at us and say, "Don't talk to me like
that in front of these kids!"

When I stepped out the front door into sunlight after a night
of their fighting, the activities of the neighbors who looked up
from their trash cans or lawn mowers always seemed impossibly
innocent.... I never quite got over thinking that folks looked at
us funny on mornings after Mother and Daddy had fought.

What an upbringing to have in your memory bank! If this weren't
enough, at seven Karr was raped:

> And it was one of these times...that all the other kids poured
> out and scattered to their separate homes for supper, so this big
> boy and I were left alone. It was going dark when he got hold
> of me under God knows what pretext. He took me into some-
> body's garage. He unbuttoned my white shirt and told me I was
> getting breasts. Here's what he said: "You're getting pretty little
> titties now, aren't you." I don't recall any other thing being said.
>
> His grandparents had chipped in on braces for his snaggly
> teeth. They glinted in the half dark like a robot's grillwork. He
> pulled off my shorts and underwear and threw them in the cor-
> ner in a ball, over where I knew there could be spiders. He
> pushed down his pants and put my hand on his thing.... At
> some point, he tired of that. He got an empty concrete sack and
> laid it down on the floor, and me down on top of that.... It
> couldn't have taken very long.
>
> The rest of the houses were dark. You could see the spotlights
> from the Little League park and hear the loudspeaker announc-
> ing somebody at bat. I wondered if this boy had planned to get
> ahold of me way in advance, if he'd picked the time when every-
> body would be at the game. Which was worse—if he'd only
> grabbed me at the opportune moment, or if he'd plotted and
> stalked me? I couldn't decide. I didn't want to be taken too eas-
> ily, but I had been, of course. Even at seven I knew that. On the
> other hand, the idea that he'd consciously chosen to do this,
> then tracked me down like a rabbit, made me feel sick.

He walked me home not saying anything, like he was doing a babysitting chore. Then I was standing on my porch by myself. I could hear his tennis shoes slapping away down the street. I watched the square of his white T-shirt get smaller till it disappeared around the corner.

The loss of dreams

Then there is the loss of dreams. The job was a good job, but after a while it got boring or lacked challenge. There was the friendship that was a good friendship, but the years have gone by and I haven't seen my best friend, oh God, in I can't tell you how long. Or worse for some, there was a marriage to which I was dedicated, a person in my life to whom I literally gave myself, body and soul. And now, after these years, the marriage is no more and we're apart. And here I am, broken and lost.

Or there are maybe my children, so full of promise, so cunning; and maybe one or two or more of them have grown up to disappoint me. Now he's out of the church, or living with somebody. She's given up the Catholic faith, belongs to another religion or no religion at all. All the things I value, all the things I've hoped for, all the things I've prayed over, are not a part of their life. My children and I love each other, we meet each other cautiously; but it pains me that I cannot approach the altar with my flesh and blood. That I have a grandchild who's not even baptized, who doesn't even know how to bless herself. And this is a hemorrhage and a loss because my religion means much to me.

The loss of confidence

Anna, in *The King and I*, sang it for us all:

>Whenever I feel afraid, I hold my head erect,
>And whistle a happy tune so no one will suspect
>I'm afraid.
>While shivering in my shoes, I strike a careless pose,
>And whistle a happy tune so no one ever knows
>I'm afraid.

The result of this deception
is very strange to tell,
For when I fool the people I fear,
I fool myself as well.

We are fearful and anxious and lack confidence.

The loss of time

And then, of course, there is the slow and relentless hemorrhaging of
health and vigor by time. Little by little, the limbs give way along with
a bit of the memory. Where once we counted up the years, we now
count up the decades. The hearing, the sight, the walk, the gait. We
look into the mirror and say, "Is this the boy or girl who went to the
prom? It wasn't that long ago, was it?" Or we look into the refrigerator and ask the great theological question, "What am I here for?"

Consider again the words of Judith Viorst:

What am I doing with a mid-life crisis?
This morning I was seventeen.
I have barely begun the beguine and it's
Good-night, ladies
Already.

While I've been wondering who to be
When I grow up someday,
My acne has vanished away, and it's
Sagging kneecaps
Already.

Why do I seem to remember Pearl Harbor?
Surely I must be too young.
When did the boys I once clung to
Start losing their hair?
Why can't I take barefoot walks in the park
Without giving my kidneys a chill?
There's poetry left in me still and it
Doesn't seem fair.

> While I was thinking I was just a girl
> and my future turned into my past.
> The time for wild kisses goes fast and it's
> Time for Sanka.
> Already?

And there are the illnesses, both our own and those of our loved ones. Belden Lane describes his mother's sickness:

> In the beginning you weep. The starting point for many things is grief, at the place where endings seem so absolute. One would think it should be otherwise, but the pain of closing is antecedent to every new opening in our lives.
>
> When my mother was diagnosed with bone cancer, she was given six months to live. It seemed such a sudden and abrupt ending, so unarguable. But she was eighty years old and signs of Alzheimer's disease had begun already to appear. The doctor's words were given with what he meant to be a comforting assuredness, and I wanted to receive them as such. There was comfort in thinking limits were being assigned to her pain, as well as to my grief. I'd feared for some time that her body might go on for years longer than her mind could last.
>
> In the coming weeks I would travel with her through surgery, radiation treatments, the painful experience of being uprooted from her house and placed in a nursing home. Roles were reversed, as I (an only child, the last of my family) became mother to my mother, wondering at mid-life who would be left to mother me. It was an experience of discovering an unlikely grace in a grotesque landscape of feeding tubes and bed restraints, wheelchairs and diapers, nausea and incontinence.
>
> During those first few months I watched my mother work as hard at dying as I'd ever seen her work at anything in her life. I sat beside her bed, wondering at this middle passage through which she journeyed, looking for hints from the other side, listening for the wisdom she was weaving from the gathered threads of a long and troubled life. I was studying an athlete in training, a desert monk wholly absorbed in ascesis, the intimate

exercise of holy living (and holy dying). It was not easy for either of us. She longed to have the work done, seeking release from the burden of death. I, too, wished to put it behind me, hating the pitch of uncertainty at which my life was now lived.

The loss of life

And, finally, there is the loss of life that comes with death. "It is as natural to die as to be born; and to the little infant, perhaps, the one is as painful as the other." So wrote Francis Bacon and so we all know. Each of us who is born waits for the inevitability of death, the final surrender. What does it mean to die? What does it mean for me to die? Father Walter Burghardt puts it elegantly:

> What does it mean for a human being to die? A respected medical doctor once called death an "insult." My instinctive Christian reaction was to deny it, to say "no, no, a thousand times, no." Till I reflected more profoundly.
>
> In death a unique "I," an irreplaceable "thou," is destroyed, a wondrous wedding of spirit and senses. I who lift my eyes to mountains and the moon; I who catch with my ears the tenderness and the thunder of Handel's *Messiah* and throb to the music of a loved one's voice; I who breathe life-giving air in the smog of Washington and whose nostrils twitch to the odor of spaghetti bolognese; I who cradle Christ on my tongue and gently caress the face of a friend; I whose mind travels over centuries and continents to share Plato's world of ideas, Augustine's vision of God's city, and Gandhi's passion for peace; I who laugh and love, worry and weep, dance and dream, sing and sin, preach and pray—this "I" will be lost to the world, this "thou" lost to those who survive me.
>
> I say it without arrogance: This "I" God will not replace, cannot replace. I am not just someone: I am this one. Through three and eighty years, for good or ill, I have touched, been touched by, a whole little world. I still love this world. Oh, not its sin and suffering, not its pain and pornography. Rather, its love and self-giving, its yearning to build the single family of

God: the human person in love with God, with God's human images, with the creation that bears so diverse a trace of its Creator. But when I die, this warm, pulsating flame of human living and loving will die with me. Is it any wonder that I don't care to die, that I don't want to die?

Obstacles

When it comes to our losses, necessary and unnecessary, the question is: how do we handle them? What is our approach, our strategy, our reaction? Why do some grow stronger at broken places while others grow weaker?

Not surprisingly, one place to look for answers is where we have looked before in other reflections: to the family and the community we grew up in. They have shown us early on how to deal with loss. Both, in the course of time, have consciously or unconsciously provided us with physical ("brush your teeth"), emotional ("big boys don't cry"), and spiritual ("God is always with you") rules that shape our response to life in general and loss in particular. These teachings or rules were spoken or unspoken but, either way, they affected us.

Most of these rules were, of course, very good because they helped us to make sense out of experience and they set standards for us. Then came the day when you and I left our family circle, our town: we naturally and subconsciously took our home-bred, community-reinforced rules with us deep down in our souls. And often these rules meshed well with our adult life. They were sound and good. The rules that said: "Be thoughtful of others, Susie"; "Accept responsibility, Johnny"; "Remember, God will have the last word." Rules such as these translate well into mature adulthood and help us to deal with our losses.

But, on the other hand, there may have been some family rules that at a particular stage of our lives cause us tension, especially punitive and harsh rules. The fear of breaking these long-ago rules unconsciously operates in many people, causing them anxiety and sometimes depression. We have, as psychologists say, internalized these rules. There's a tape playing inside us that was recorded when we were one month, one year, two years, and five years old. And even though we're now fifty-five, the tape is still playing. As we indicated, some rules are helpful and healthy throughout life, and they can help us cope with loss. But others are not and paralyze us in time of loss. We can identify a few of those unhealthy rules as follows:

Unhealthy family rule one: *Do not express your feelings, especially sadness or weakness.* Good little girls don't show sadness. Good little boys don't show weakness. And you never, never show anger—above all, never with God. And so when losses come along, when we lose health or wealth or loved ones, we tend to swallow the feelings and keep them all inside, "bravely" and stoically, until they cause physical or emotional problems.

Unhealthy family rule two: *Do not become close to outsiders.* If you do, you'll be betraying the family. So every time we start to get close to someone else, we find an excuse to step back or to cause an argument because the old family rule is playing: "Let's stick to ourselves; don't get too close to outsiders." So why should I join a support group after my divorce or bereavement? My loss is my business.

Unhealthy family rule three: *Enjoying yourself is always wrong.* Always be productive; don't spend time "playing" or surely, not doing anything. Maybe half of us are afflicted by this rule. Say, for example, we have a couple of unexpected and unplanned free hours, where we could just go out and sit on the lawn and watch the clouds or read a good novel. But after about fifteen minutes we begin to feel an uneasiness, a sense of free-floating anxiety. If someone comes and rings our doorbell while we're doing nothing, we will jump up and grab a washcloth or a hammer and answer the door as if we were busy. We don't want our caller to find us just enjoying ourselves and doing nothing. God forbid we should answer the door holding our novel, wearing an old sweatsuit!

And what have we been doing? Nothing. And enjoying it. That is, until the old tape starts playing: "You mean you're not productive?" When it comes to loss, we are supposed to take it on the chin, wear black forever, stay at home, keep busy—but never take time out to heal the spirit through the joys of life.

Unhealthy family rule four: *Reaching out to others for help means you* *are weak.* Solve your own problems. You don't hang out your dirty laundry for all to see. So we don't confide, we don't share. The old family rule tape is playing: "Stand on your own two feet. It's a sign of weakness to seek help."

Along with this, if we seek to improve our own psychological and spiritual needs it means that we are demanding and selfish. This idea of improving ourselves elicits comments such as, "For crying out loud, accept your lot in life." "Who do you think you are, anyway, trying to improve yourself? Changing the color of your hair, or going back to college at fifty-six to take a course in gardening or nuclear physics or whatever?" And so people put us down. The underlying message is that taking care of ourselves, trying to grow, to "become more," means we are flying in the face of "God's will." Thus, a great many people who have tremendous potential never, never realize it because of the fear of reaching out to other people, of trying new things.

Unhealthy family rule five: *Anything that goes wrong in your life is your own fault and you probably deserve it.* "So don't blame anybody else. You put your own foot in it. You deserve what you get." "You suffered a loss: live with it!" Isn't this a great family rule? So on top of your loss, you get guilt for causing it.

Now, take family rules such as these and join them to the institution we call Holy Mother Church—who, at certain times in history, has also been known to propagate some fairly unhealthy rules—and you've multiplied the assault on our capacity to deal with loss.

Other obstacles

Besides the hidden family rules that sometimes make it hard to deal constructively with loss, there are other obstacles within ourselves. There is, for example, a tendency towards self-pity. We think: after all these years, I've spent all my savings on doctors, psychiatrists, and psychologists, on new ways and old ways, on this book and that book, on this retreat and that retreat. Yet I'm still not "perfect," still not happy. People have hurt me: can I trust again? Does God even care about me, for that matter? Does God find me lovable? No one else seems to find me lovable; at times I don't even find myself lovable. I'm afraid to pray. Will God spurn me, as well?

Another obstacle is our own inertia. We've learned not to expect too much from life, from love, from God. We've suffered so long our suffering has become a habit. And maybe we've come to think of it as our lot in life. We just can't seem to get going: better to stay put and let our life hemorrhage.

Then there is the subtle but incendiary fear of being healed. Why would we fear that? Don't all of us want to overcome our losses? Yes and no. Overcoming our losses, working through them, means that we will have to change our lives. And sometimes, our "poor me" attitude and the sympathy of others become, well, somewhat comfortable: they give us an identity. Working through our losses, on the other hand, can be challenging. We can no longer be a victim; we must now be an actor, an agent of change.

Are we ready for that? It will mean giving up the old dependencies, the old self-pities, the role of victim. It will mean new territory; it will mean hurt; it will mean restarting unused muscles; it will entail a certain fear of what lies ahead, of claiming new parts of oneself. It will mean holiness and wholeness. Are we ready for that?

A final obstacle to our healing and growth can be someone with a vested interest (often unconscious) in keeping us caught in our losses. There are some people—often family members—who "benefit" from our hurt, from our being bent down and staying that way. Any change in our lives, any constructive move forward, might be seen as an affront to them. What will they do if they lose the role of caretaker? How else can they be secretly superior?

I know of one woman, grossly overweight, who was often the object of her husband's jibes. One day she went away to a university which specializes in helping obese people. She spent a month there, came home with a significant weight loss, continued her regimen, and after a while came down to a more normal weight. She became an attractive person. Her new figure showed up her husband's somewhat overweight body, and he couldn't handle that. She had found both herself and a new life; he, meanwhile, had lost the target of his sarcasm and the source of his superiority. They soon divorced.

The late James Michener made his mark on the literary world with books such as *Hawaii*, *The Source*, and *Texas*. He drew on characters who were fleshed out with extensive genealogy and deep cultural roots, which lend great interest and strength to his books—as those of you who have read his books know. But James Michener was a man without a birth certificate who was abandoned as an infant. He never knew, never met, his biological parents. He was raised as a foster son in the Michener family, which was headed by a widowed woman. While he claimed to have come to some peace with the vacuum in his life, it is easy to understand why he found pleasure in creating characters with deep cultural roots and an extended genealogy.

Despite his generous spirit and kind nature, Michener's accomplishments raised the ire of one of his adopted clan. Over a period of time in Michener's life, some anonymous relative who never signed his or her name but only signed "a real Michener," felt impelled to send him notes whenever James Michener gained a little bit of fame. Even after he won the Pulitzer Prize, this poisoned-pen Michener wrote to him and said, "You have no right to use the name of Michener," and denounced him as a fraud. The closing line of these letters was always, "Who do you think you are, trying to be better than you are?"

Well, the final letter from this anonymous, unknown relative came in 1976 after President Ford had presented Michener with the Presidential Medal of Freedom. A note came as expected, saying, "Still using a name that isn't yours. Still a fraud. Still trying to be better than you are." James Michener later wrote that "these words are a cry that has been burned into my soul," but he turned their negativity into a positive power. Michener acknowledged his wound-licking kin, whoever he or she was, and said: "He was right in all of his accusations. I have spent my life trying to be better than I was, and I am brother to all who have the same aspiration."

Dealing with loss

Let's start with the most severe loss: death. Grief will not be easily stilled, or anger with God. Or doubt about God. In Ingmar Bergman's classic movie, *The Seventh Seal*, Death appears, in the form of a man, to a knight. A conversation follows in which the knight talks to Death about God. The conversation goes like this:

Knight: Why does God hide himself?
Why doesn't he reveal himself?
Why doesn't God stretch out his hand and touch us?
Why doesn't he at least say something to us?

Death: But God doesn't do this, does he?
He doesn't reach out. He doesn't speak.
He just remains silent.

Knight: That's right! He doesn't do a thing.
He doesn't touch us; he doesn't speak to us.
Sometimes I wonder if he's really out there.

Death: Well, maybe he's not there.
Maybe no one's out there.
Maybe we're here all alone.
Did you ever think about that?

The truth is that at one time or another, we have all thought about that.

A woman named Ann Weems thought about God's absence when she lost her son, Todd, killed less than an hour after his twenty-first birthday. Encouraged by a friend, she began to write some psalms of lament. Weems says that writing these brought her into contact with other people, whose "stories, like mine, were painful, too painful for any of us to try fitting our souls into ten correct steps of grieving. They knew what I knew: there is no salvation in self-help books; the help we need is far beyond self. Our only hope is to march ourselves to the throne of God and in loud lament cry out the pain that lives in our souls."

Here is one of her "loud laments":

O God, find me!
I am lost
in the valley of grief,
and I cannot see my way out.

My friends leave baskets of balm
at my feet,

but I cannot bend to touch
the healing
to my heart.
They call me to leave
this valley,
but I cannot follow
the faint sound of their voices.

They sing their songs
of love,
but the words fade
and vanish in the wind.
They knock,
but I cannot find the door.
They shout to me,
but I cannot find the voice
to answer.

O God, find me!
Come into this valley and find me!
Bring me out of this land
of weeping.

O you to whom I belong, find me!
I will wait here,
for you have never failed
to come to me.
I will wait here,
for you have always been faithful.
I will wait here,
for you are my God,
and you have promised
that you counted the hairs on my head.

In devastating loss, Weems teaches us that we must turn in abandonment to God even when we hate him. Like Jesus abandoned on
the cross, we must ultimately cry out, "Into your hands I commend
my spirit."

A man came around from his doubt to belief. He tells of his uncle's death when he was a little boy, then of the death of a playmate who died of cancer and, finally, of the death of his father when the man was thirteen years old. He writes:

> Eventually, in my eighteenth year, these experiences plunged me into a profound despair. What was the point of life that it should end in death? How could a blind cosmic evolutionary process, grinding along without purpose through untold billions of years, "hiccup" into such a wonderful thing as human consciousness—filled as it could be with such a poignant sense of treasured beauty in nature and human life—and then, by grinding on, snuff out such a consciousness as though it had never been? What kind of pointless bad joke was this? Rather we had never been born.
>
> In my despair I resorted to what, I would later discover, William James calls "the will to believe." Convinced that if death were ultimate, all pretense of sanity in the nature of things was insane self-delusion. I resolved that the only sane alternative was God. If God existed—as I had heard from friends and in a one-year fling with Sunday School in early childhood—then, somehow, death might not have the last word. Within the year I found myself in a church. Six months later I celebrated Easter, in a small choir singing my heart out; and six months after that I entered a seminary.

This man went on to lose his sister, who died at fifty-seven from cancer, and his twenty-two-year-old nephew, who died in a car accident. When friends asked him, "Where are you in your grief: denial? anger? bargaining?" he says,

> I hear myself saying with a vehemence that surprised me, "What makes you think death is on anybody's map, or can be plotted by such coordinates? Don't you know what death is? Death isn't on any of our maps; death is what punches holes in all our maps. I just trust that if I have the courage to look through the hole punched in my heart by Tony's dying, I may see the face of God."

Although we may be diminished by loss, we are given a chance for a radical turn in life, a realignment of priorities. Listen to this prayer of an elderly man:

> When I was poor I prayed to be rich. I learned that my true riches were in family and friends, in my faith and in my values. When I was sick I prayed to be well. It did not happen soon, not without suffering. But I learned that in sickness I needed others, and that health was a gift I should use well when it was given back to me. When I was older, I prayed for understanding. Not for youth, because it was gone. No, I prayed for wisdom to understand that all life, in every moment, is a gift. It is much too short to hold grievances. And it is is much too abundant not to look around and to enjoy.

Memories

One of the balms in loss is memories. Not that we become stuck in the past like Baby Jane, always reliving past glories and never growing into the present ones. No, we cherish memories as a salve for loss because they speak of the affirmations, joys, and little gifts of love that make us who we are. In his book, *The Mood of Christmas*, Howard Thurman writes:

> Whether your childhood was sad or happy as you look back upon it, there is one thing about it that is true. There were moments of intense and complete joy, which for the instant left nothing to be desired. It may have been your first new dress, or new suit; the thing about which you had dreamed for, oh, so many days was actually yours! Perhaps it was the first time you received a letter through the mail; your name was actually written on the envelope and it had come through the mail; yes, the postman actually brought it.
>
> It may have been your first time to visit a circus to see live tigers, lions, elephants, and big, big snakes; and there was the merry-go-round and the fluffy candy and the cold pink lemonade. Perhaps it was the time when your mother let you mix the dough for the bread or sent you on your first errand in the next

block alone. You may have been eavesdropping when the teacher came to call and you heard her say how smart you were and what a joy you were to teach. (And you wondered whether your mother would remember to tell your daddy what the teacher had said. At supper you managed to bring it up, so that your mother would be reminded.)

Your greatest moment of fullness may have come when, for the first time, you were conscious that your mother loved you— that swirling sense of sheer ecstasy when you were completely aware of another's love. Do you remember? It was a foretaste of something for which you would be in quest all the rest of your days: the matured relationships of friends and loved ones, of husband and wife; and that gradual or climactic moment of religious fulfillment when the heart and mind echo the words of Augustine: "Thou hast made us for Thyself and our souls are restless till they find their rest in Thee!"

The question to ask in loss—when you get around to it, and it may take a long time—is, "how can my loss bless others?" Physician Rachel Remen tells of a young man who suffered a terrible loss. He had bone cancer, and finally his leg was removed at the hip to save his life. She writes:

> He was twenty-four years old when I started working with him and he was a very angry young man with a lot of bitterness. He felt a deep sense of injustice and a very deep hatred for all well people because it seemed so unfair to him that he had suffered this terrible loss so early in life.
>
> I worked with this young man through his grief and rage and pain using painting, imagery, and deep psychotherapy. After working with him for more than two years there came a profound shift. He began coming out of himself. Later, he started to visit other people who had suffered severe physical losses and he would tell me the most wonderful stories about these visits.
>
> Once he visited a young woman who was almost his own age. It was a hot day in Palo Alto and he was in running shorts so his artificial leg showed when he came into her hospital room. The

woman was so depressed about the loss of both her breasts that she wouldn't even look at him, wouldn't pay attention to him. The nurses had left her radio playing, probably in order to cheer her up. So, desperate to get her attention, he unstrapped his leg and began dancing around the room on one leg snapping his fingers to the music. She looked at him in amazement and then burst out laughing and said, "Man, if you can dance, I can sing."

It was a year following this that we sat down to review our work together. He talked about what was significant to him and then I shared what was significant in our process. As we were reviewing our two years of work together, I opened his file and there discovered several drawings he had made early on. I handed them to him. He looked at them and said, "Oh, look at this." He showed me one of his earliest drawings. I had suggested to him then that he draw a picture of his body. He had drawn a picture of a vase and running through the vase was a deep black crack. This was the image of his body, and he had taken a black crayon and had drawn the crack over and over again. He was grinding his teeth with rage at the time. It was very, very painful because it seemed to him that this vase could never function as a vase again. It could never hold water.

Now, several years later, he came to this picture and looked at it and said, "Oh, this one isn't finished." And I said, extending the box of crayons, "Why don't you finish it?" He picked up a yellow crayon, and putting his finger on the crack he said, "You see, here—where it is broken—this is where the light comes through." And with the yellow crayon he drew light streaming through the crack in his body.

Our pain, our hurt, our brokenness, can be an instrument of change in us—for better or for worse. Madeleine L'Engle writes: "I look back at my mother's life and I see suffering deepening and strengthening it. In some people I have also seen it destroy. Pain is not always creative; received wrongly, it can lead to alcoholism and madness and suicide. Nevertheless, without it we do not grow."

We must pray, therefore, that light can come through the cracks of our losses. We must ask God to help us do so. One thinks of St. Ignatius of Loyola, limping from a gunshot wound badly managed by the doctors, or bereaved St. Elizabeth Ann Seton left with small children and indifferent in-laws, or orphaned St. Kevin of Ireland, or tubercular St. Thérèse of Lisieux. They all let light in through their losses. Nor should we neglect in our prayer the image of Jesus weeping. As Ann Weems expresses it:

Jesus wept,
and in his weeping,
he joined himself forever
to those who mourn.
He stands now throughout all time,
this Jesus weeping,
with his arms around weeping ones:
"Blessed are those who mourn,
for they shall be comforted."
He stands with the mourners,
for his name is God-with-us.

We must seek the answer to these questions: in our losses, how, ultimately, are we blessed? How do we bless others? Are we being called through loss to a different vocation? Is the loss making room for the God with whom we are, perhaps, angry, and who we may not be sure exists? Can the unbearable pain and humiliation make room for the Spirit? Do we see ourselves bearing the cross, like Christ, for the world? Can we see anew the meaning of Easter and how Jesus broke through the closed doors of doubt and fear and cried out the only word we ever really need to hear: "Peace!"?

Perhaps the one to turn to in times of loss is Mary. Early on, she lost her security when she had to flee from wicked people who sought to kill her infant son. Years later, the wicked finally succeeded, and she sobbed her heart out as she cradled his dead body in her lap. First her husband died, then her son.

Mary's first terror of loss may have been when her son was twelve years old, missing after a journey to the temple in Jerusalem. Where was he? Was he lost? Had he been kidnapped and sold into slavery—which was not uncommon in those days? Had he met with an accident and was moaning, lying in some ditch somewhere? Was he being physically or sexually abused? We can well imagine Mary's sense of panic as Joseph tried to calm her. She felt that gnawing sickness in the pit of her stomach. She was frantic.

These are the images of Mary that can guide us through our own losses: Mary fleeing, Mary seeking, Mary weeping, Mary mourning, Mary returning to an empty house. This might be our starting point for prayer, intercessory prayer offered to someone who has every sympathy with our loss.

Finally, the last question: can we ever say the "Loser's Prayer" with acceptance?

I asked God to take away my pride, and God said no.
He said it was not for Him to take away, but for me to give up.
I asked God to make my handicapped child whole, and God said no.
He said her spirit is whole; her body is only temporary.
I asked God to grant me patience, and God said no.
He said that patience is a byproduct of tribulation. It isn't granted; it's earned.
I asked God to give me happiness, and God said no.
He said He gives blessings. Happiness is up to me.
I asked God to spare me pain, and God said no.
He said suffering draws me apart from worldly care and brings me closer to him.
I asked God to give me self-esteem, and he said, "No.
You already have it because I dwell in you. Don't you realize you are my Beloved?"
I asked God to help me love others as much as He loves me.
God said, "Ah, at last. You finally have the idea."

Questions for reflection

1. What are the losses in my life—divorce, death, health, opportunity, virtue, friendships, a loveless marriage, disappointing children?

2. Where am I in the process of healing from my losses? Have I grown stronger at broken places? Am I still stuck in self-pity and grief?

3. Are there people in my life who unconsciously may need to have me remain in my losses, stay with the pain?

4. How can I let the light shine through the cracks in my life?

5. How do I bless others through my losses? How can I help others to heal?

ELEVEN

THE COWARDLY LION

Spiritual Fear

With a ruff and a roar the Lion attacks Dorothy and the Scarecrow. They cower until the Lion makes a mistake: he scares Dorothy's dog, Toto. Dorothy smacks the Lion on the nose and he bursts out crying. The moment of truth has arrived. The Lion is a coward. Not only that, but his lack of courage will lead him to reverse the journey several times, to run the other way as he does when the quartet arrives at the Emerald City.

He's not the only one. Sacred Scripture is full of those who were afraid. Afraid of whom? Of God; of answering God's call. Full of those who doubted, who felt emptiness and experienced brokenness. In this reflection we are going to look at precisely such figures. Oddly enough we will find all four—the doubtful, the fearful, the sterile, and the broken—in one pivotal tableau, the one that begins the Jesus story, celebrated during the time we now call Advent.

In the Advent story we find in each character a threefold movement of encounter, reaction, and life lessons learned for the spiritual journey. Here we discern a well-formed triple pattern: a call, initial negative reactions, and finally, submission. So let's take a reflective look at the four principal figures of Advent; namely, John the Baptist, his parents, Zechariah and Elizabeth, and his relative, Mary.

John the Baptist

John received a call. And he answered it. Matthew's gospel at the beginning of Advent (Cycle A) starts off: In those days John the Baptist appeared in the wilderness of Judea, proclaiming, "Repent, for the kingdom of heaven has come near." But when he saw many Pharisees and Sadducees coming for baptism, he said to them, "You brood of vipers! Who warned you to flee from the wrath to come? Bear fruit worthy of repentance.... Even now the ax is lying at the root of the trees; every tree therefore that does not bear good fruit is cut down and thrown into the fire" (Mt 3:1–2, 7–10). This obviously is not a man unsure of himself. On the contrary, this is a man on fire with purpose. This is God's prophet aiming for the jugular, a strong, confident man. When he was called he reacted without hesitation. He accepted and began his mission.

But somewhere along the way—we don't know when or where— doubt began to creep in. Was he right? Was he called by God or was it all self-delusion? Was all this fervent preaching for naught? Was his cousin Jesus the one he was paving the way for? John was not so sure anymore. Maybe after so many years, he was at a low point. Things were not working out well. After all, he was no longer to be found along the Jordan but languishing in jail, detained in Machaerus, Herod's fortress, situated on the lonely desert heights overlooking the Dead Sea, awaiting who knows what.

Now John had time to think. Maybe he had been all wrong, chosen the wrong path, bet on the wrong Messiah. Doubts made for troubled dreams, and he decided to act: When John heard in prison what the Messiah was doing, he sent word by his disciples and said to him, "Are you the one who is to come, or are we to wait for another?" (Mt 11:2–3). There it was, plain, simple, and direct. Jesus answered the delegation the best way he could: "Go and tell John what you hear and see: the blind receive their sight, the lame walk, the lepers are cleansed, the deaf hear, the dead are raised, and the poor have good news brought to them." And then he pointedly added with softness and compassion, "And blessed is anyone who takes no offense at me" (Mt 11:4–5). After John's disciples left, Jesus says to the crowd:

"Truly I tell you, among those born of women no one has arisen greater than John the Baptist..." (Mt 11:11).

John of Advent is like many people throughout the ages, those who say "yes" but then have second thoughts. Their words sound like this: "I have been faithful to God. I have kept trust. I have prayed. I have been active in ministry. I read all the right books, faithfully go to Mass, give to the poor. And things have not turned out all right." I recently received letters from two John the Baptist-type people. One woman started out by filling me in on her family, noting that her boys were doing fine. But the girls? One is living with a man and is planning to marry him outside the church. The other married a Jewish man and had the children baptized Catholic, but is now converting to Judaism and is going to raise the kids—her grandchildren!— in the Jewish faith.

My other correspondent's daughter had just given birth six months ago. The doctors recently removed a tumor the size of a grapefruit from her daughter who is very sick now with chemotherapy. The baby was born with a hole in her heart, and a thumb that is dangling and will have to be removed.

"Are you the one who is to come or shall we wait for another?"

Throughout the ages how many of us have asked this question with grief or bitterness or disappointment? "Have I been wrong to be so faithful? Worse, have I been a fool? People prayed for my son, we had a prayer chain going, we believe in healing, pleaded for a miracle. He died anyway. Some whispered it was because I didn't have enough faith. If I had only believed more firmly!" To help come to terms with these feelings, (this is especially true for those of a charismatic bent), I invite you to listen to the words of a fine and insightful Southern Baptist minister named Al Staggs:

> My wife died in April of this year following a twelve-year battle with cancer, a particularly malignant melanoma. Comments from well-meaning but misguided friends about the healing power of faith have compelled me once again to rethink my theology of healing. I confess that I have extremely low tolerance for the so-called faith healers or for the peddlers of heal-

ing. I'm aghast that anyone would dare to claim to understand the mind of God about any particular person or any particular illness. What these folks do to people is to hold out hope for a complete reversal of a person's physical condition. When the miracle does not occur, the lack of miraculous action can be attributed to a person's lack of faith, which only compounds the person's problems. Not only are these people terminally ill, but they are also being taught that they are not good Christians. In my weaker moments, I am reminded of the passage from Matthew 7:22–23 where Jesus says, "Many will say to me on that day, 'Lord, Lord, did we not prophesy in your name, and in your name drive out demons and perform miracles?' Then I will tell them plainly, 'I never knew you. Away from me, you evil-doers!'"

A few weeks prior to my wife's death, visiting friends recounted story after story of "miraculous" answers to their prayers. After hearing a steady diet of incidents in which people were healed of their infirmities or found better paying jobs, my wife looked over at these people and said simply, "It hasn't worked that way for us."

Sometimes I just want to ask these people who become so excited about miraculous healing, "Has your vaunted prayer program yet kept anyone alive forever?" Eventually we all die, including those who were healed of their particular disease. No one has yet managed to avoid the grim reaper. So why save our success stories for just those precious few who have been allowed a few months or years longer than they would otherwise have had? There needs to be a major emphasis on God's grace and sufficiency for every illness and every situation. The Christian community should talk just as loud and long about God's presence in the most hopeless situations as we do about the "miraculous healings."

[Henri] Nouwen had this to say about death: "Death does not have to be our final failure, our final defeat in the struggle of life, our unavoidable fate. If our deepest human desire is indeed to give ourselves to others, then we can make our death into a final gift. It is so wonderful to see how fruitful death is when it is a free gift." Nouwen's words and his own approach to his life and to his recent death are a counterbalance against those whose "healing" hit-and-run ministries suggest that death is a defeat and that only miraculous cure is a victory.

Stories of miraculous healings have their place. The miracle of a believer's faith, however, in the face of terminal illness, and the faith of a loving family, is just as important as any story of a miraculous cure of an illness. Very few people experience a total reversal of illness. Most people diagnosed with terminal illness struggle through it to the very end. So let us hear the stories of the miraculous presence of God in the lives of these saints who are faithful to the end.

There is our key: holding onto the faithful presence of God in our worst moments, clinging to belief in our moments of doubt in the ultimate victory of his love which "will make all things new again."

"Are you the one who is supposed to come or shall we look for another?" No one is free of second thoughts, especially in times of crisis. Not even John the Baptist. Not even Jesus: "Father, if it is possible, remove this cup from me." "My God, my God, why have you forsaken me?" But there is the response and life lesson: "Nevertheless, not my will but thine be done....Into your hands I commend my spirit, my gift." In other words, as Staggs said, be assured of and hold on to the miraculous presence of God in times of seeming abandonment, in times when we are tempted to look for another.

There was a very moving article in the September 19, 1998 issue of *America* magazine by a woman whose pen name is Anne Donovan. The title of the article is "The Painful Effort to Believe," and it is the account of the birth of her stillborn daughter and her desperate attempt to come to terms with holding onto faith in such tragedy. She writes:

Those things I had relied on—modern science, women's intuition, God's mercy—had failed, and I had nothing to hold on to. Medical staff, family members, my husband; they all shifted around me as I was induced and slowly dissolved into labor. There was nothing anyone could do except help me deliver the baby. When a chaplain forced herself into the room to talk about God, I yelled at a nurse to get her away from me.

All my multilayered, carefully constructed faith was stripped away as I focused on one thing: the injustice that our little girl didn't have a chance to take even a single breath. It never occurred to me to pray, not from the moment we first heard the news, not when I was in labor, and not a month later as I sat at home sorting through my emotions and preparing for a memorial Mass of the Angels.

Prayer seemed so futile, even unnecessary, like throwing a glass of water on a burning house. I had prayed my entire pregnancy for the baby to be healthy and she was. Carly was perfect but she wasn't alive, cooing in my arms. How could I not feel betrayed? My mother, who has attended daily Mass for as long I can remember, encouraged me to join her, to help ease my mind. As much as I admire the strength of her devotion and the real comfort she receives from the ritual of Mass, I could not face going.

It wasn't that I was angry at God. It was, and still is, more a sense that I have to be alone and focused to work through this spiritual crisis. My grief is so intimate. I carried Carly; I gave birth to her; I endured aching arms and breasts for month afterwards whenever I heard an infant cry. As much as others tried to comfort me, their words only succeeded in alienating me more. I remember telling my husband that I felt like I was on a ship pulling away from a dock where our friends and family stood waving good-bye.

In the weeks following Carly's death, well meaning friends and relatives called and sent hundreds of cards and letters offering helpless words of condolence. Most of their efforts said the same thing: "It was God's will. We cannot understand God's will." Those words kept me up at night for months, spinning through my frantic mind, tying me in philosophical knots.

I know they were trying to help, but every time the issue of

God's will sprang up, I was miserable. It got to the point where I couldn't even numbly smile or nod any more when the phrase inevitably popped up. I just clenched my teeth to keep from saying something I'd regret....

What worries me about all of this is that I realize only a few people are willing to have a dialogue with me that explores the tangled, dark, and frightening mess of our doubts and fears and anger over Carly's death. Many of my friends and family lapse into embarrassed silence when I mention her name, as if I have just told a distasteful joke.

I started to notice a distinct difference between most of the letters from our Christian friends and those from our Jewish friends. The letters of Jewish friends expressed a genuine exploration of the sense of injustice and pain that the news of Carly's death stirred in them. They acknowledged their confusion and wished that time would be kind to us. They did not try to placate us with the idea that someday we would understand why this happened. They spoke from the heart, telling us only: "This is unfair, it is so painful, it is so tragic, we are thinking of you." We grew to treasure their honesty and their willingness to explore.

I have been told some remarkable things in the interest of consolation. I have been told to rejoice that my daughter went to heaven unmarked by sin, her soul clean and pure, perfect, that God has a special place reserved for her. I have been told that I should feel privileged: I have my very own baby angel, my own divine connection. To me, these are cartoonish images. They are about as comforting as imagining God as a robed elderly man with a long white beard, floating around on a cloud. These are images used to reassure a child, and they feel frozen in time....

There is an excerpt from a letter Harriet Beecher Stowe wrote to a friend that eloquently captures the essence of my struggle: "When the heart strings are suddenly cut, it is, I believe, a physical impossibility to feel faith or resignation; there is a revolt of the instinctive and animal system, and though we may submit to God, it is rather by constant painful effort than sweet attraction."

In the article, Donovan's final words are these: "Some may wonder why, after our experience, I still want to make the painful effort to believe. I can only respond that, despite my doubts, having seen the breathtaking perfection of my daughter's peaceful face, it is impossible to think God was not there."

The questions in time of tragedy always come back to this: "Are you the one who is to come or shall we look elsewhere?" Where is the miracle, the cure, the answer to our prayers? Where are you, God? And the only response in a time of tragedy and doubt, as Anne Donovan experienced, is clinging to the presence of God.

Perhaps the story of John the Baptist—who turned into John the Perplexed—is found in the story of one distraught woman. She cried to the priest: "Where was God when my son died?" The priest answered softly: "The same place as when his Son died." If John received the call, reacted with certainty, and then lapsed into doubt, he is legion. But John came around and gave his life as a final gift to the One Who Is to Come. God was present in his fidelity and in the loyalty of his followers, despite his doubt. Truly, no greater man was born of a woman.

And so, too, for us. Yes, pray for a miracle, the sudden cure. It does happen. But also pray to discern the divine presence in pain, suffering, and death. Offer all of these as gift, a gift which will be forever accepted by a Love that never falters in a place where there are no more tears.

Mary

Mary is the next Advent figure whom we will consider. Not, be it noted, the mythological Mary who was perfect, but the Mary of the gospel who was afraid. Notice that when we first meet Mary, in the story of the Annunciation, there is a familiar pattern evolving. First, there is a call from Gabriel, God's messenger: "Hail, O highly favored one!" Immediately, Mary experiences misgivings and fear. As Luke writes in his gospel: "She was much perplexed by his words and pondered what sort of greeting this might be." The angel responds quickly: "Do not be afraid, Mary, for you have found favor with God." For Mary was afraid—it's right there at the beginning of the story. But what provoked her fear? Was Gabriel a fearsome-looking creature, like a Klingon from Star Trek? No, it was his greeting, his message, the invitation to a new consciousness that provoked the fear.

In this greeting Gabriel addressed Mary as something more than she thought she was: "Greetings, favored one! The Lord is with you" (Lk 1:28). Up to this point, Mary, like Eliza Doolittle in *My Fair Lady*, could sing: "I'm just an ordinary woman." She knew who she was—or thought she did. She was a little backwoods girl, a minority figure, someone of little social or economic standing, the Eliza Doolittle of Nazareth. As Kathleen Norris writes in her book, *Amazing Grace: A Vocabulary of Faith*, "Gabriel addresses his majestic words in an unlikely setting to an unlikely person, someone poor and powerless, extremely vulnerable in her place and time, a young peasant woman about to find herself pregnant before her wedding." Suddenly, this heavenly messenger declares that she, in fact, is highly favored by God, a loved self who has been given a mission from God. What can this mean? It is true? Little Mary is troubled with such big exalted language. The image which the angel conveys is unnerving, and she retreats in fear.

Put yourself in Mary's place—which, of course, is the intent of the story. Think about it, imagine it. You are in the kitchen when the classic process begins. You get the call: "Greetings, highly favored one, O deeply loved one with a mission from God!" You then offer a quick response, and even quicker retreat: "You must be mistaken." The truth is, you see, that we are used to identifying ourselves in much more modest ways—by our genes, our job, our roles, our psychic makeup, and our relationships. We say, for instance, "I am the daughter of Ralph and Anna, and I work in health care. I like Italian food. I'm 5'8". I am basically shy but this year I am going to become more assertive. I am an American, I enjoying reading and skiing..." and so on.

Back to "the call": "Naw...it can't be," we say to ourselves. And immediately we duck the implications of our call by making light of it. "*Moi?*" as Miss Piggy would ask. O highly favored one? "Highly favored," when I am so obviously in need of redemption? As the comedian Bert Lahr, who played the Cowardly Lion, was wont to say, "It is to laugh." Hey, Gabriel, the real address should be, "O messed up one!" That at least would be more accurate. "Gabriel, my fine-feathered friend, you have made a mistake and knocked on the wrong door." But Gabriel has knocked on the right door. The trouble is that he is talking to someone whom we seldom identify with: our deeper selves.

In her book, *Gift of the Red Bird*, Paula D'Arcy wrestles with this same issue:

> I see that in the last few years I lost myself in the roles I was playing. Mother. Author. Speaker. Friend. Counselor. Rather than these roles being channels for God to use in certain seasons of my life, they became my life. They became my security and my identity. They were how I saw myself, and who I thought I was. When I was stripped of them, I felt like nothing. Instead of being a facet of me, these roles became my worth. As they moved, changed, disappeared, I did, too.
>
> Now I am working hard to find and love the person behind the roles. The real me. The child of God. When I know her my roles can return to being roles, expendable and fleeting. I filled some of these roles so that others would approve of me. Now I am learning to approve of myself. It leaves room for my god to be God, and not the voices and approval of others. The power of this insight is worth all the months in bed.
>
> I think about my early prayers for strength, health, and peace of mind. I wanted it to fall from the bedroom ceiling. I didn't want to work for it. I wanted an instant cure. I prayed for my body to be well as I was simultaneously misusing it. I begged to find peace while I pressed my nervous system to the bone. I am pretty funny.
>
> Today I am making a list: "Who has my life belonged to?"
>> the telephone
>> my child
>> appointments

> my career
> my church
> my friends
> the television
> my need for approval
> my guilt

Writing it down feels like casting my own lots. Written down, in black and white, many of my owners seem insane. Why have I given anyone permission to run my life? How did I wind up responsible to so many things, but not to myself? It has taken a lot to get me to think these thoughts. And even if I'd written this list several months ago and had listed God, it would have been a lie. I talked about him a lot, but hardly knew him at all. It was more comfortable to have ideas and theories about him, than to have a real ongoing encounter.

This evening I sit on my deck, enjoying the moon. I look again at my list. It would be easy to criticize myself, but that won't solve anything. Only waking up will change things. I take a sharp black marker and remake the inventory. I write God at the top, and me second. My child is third. I scratch out the television. The noise it creates is half of the reason I am seldom quiet. It pretends to fill an emptiness. But it only fills space. The emptiness doesn't go away.

Like D'Arcy, we have adopted many identities—except the one that counts: "O highly favored one." But, of course, we're not sure we want that identity tapped. We're not so sure we want to know our deeper selves. After all, what would that mean to our lives if we really believed that we are so incredibly favored, so profoundly loved, unmistakedly entrusted with a mission?

You may be familiar with the Sufi tale about an orphaned eagle who is raised by chickens. The eagle thinks he is a chicken forever to be pecking at the ground, until another eagle flying overhead sees him and reveals to him who he really is. But the eagle who thinks he is a chicken resists the notice. He is fearful and denies who he really is. He goes back to pecking on the ground even when the other eagle is showing him how he can soar through the blue skies above him. "There is no 'deeper self,'" he tells himself.

That is the sad truth about us: we have been told we are eagles but we have opted to stay chickens. It's so much more—comfortable! Or, to put it directly, we settle for and even prefer our present state and resist the call to be more than we appear. And we have our strategies for staying this way, don't we? One of them is always showing and advertising our surface selves. We speak on the surface, saying only what the culture will accept and not the deeper things of faith that occupy our hearts. We speak a language that belies our real sensitivity, and stick to the cultural image of what a "regular" guy or gal should look like, dress like, and sound like. Thus doing, we bury our gift, our status as highly favored.

Sooner or later we forget our call, our story, and eagles that we really are, we never soar: we stay with the chickens. We remain ordinary, decent Christians. No wonder we react in fear when someone has the nerve to come along and tell us who we really are, and invite us to a new consciousness as highly favored ones, as saints.

Former Congressman Tip O'Neill tells a story of a man named "Honest Jake":

> Honest Jake became well known in the Boston area because of his assistance to three generations of immigrant families. He owned a little variety store and would extend credit to the poor immigrants to help them get started in their new land. As Honest Jake neared his sixtieth birthday, a group of people he had helped decided to give him a party and a generous gift of money. Jake received the money gratefully and began to use it for his own makeover. He had his teeth capped. He bought a hairpiece. He invested in a diet and exercise program and lost a lot of weight. He purchased a whole new wardrobe.
>
> Finally, he boarded a plane and a few hours later the new Honest Jake hit the beach at Miami. He met a beautiful young woman, asked her for a date, and she accepted. But before they could go out on the date, a thunderstorm came up. Honest Jake was struck by a lightning bolt and died instantly. In heav-

en, he said to God, "After all those years of hard work, I was just trying to enjoy myself a little. Why? Why me?" And God said to him, "Oh, is that you, Jake? I'm sorry, I didn't recognize you."

Like Honest Jake, we're overlaid with the images the world wants. By appearing worse than we are, we don't have to be better than we are. And there it is. Once we convince ourselves that we are not highly favored—only chickens, not really eagles—then we can settle for just being "basically good people," which means we can be minimal, bland, closet disciples of Jesus Christ. That's why Mary's story is important. She too was fearful of self-discovery. She too resisted the notion that there was something more, something deeper to be evoked by God. Her virtue, her nobility, her heroism, her "glamour," if you will, was to overcome her fear and accept God's estimate of her. Her response, "Be it done unto me according to your will," is the turning point for all spiritual Cowardly Lions.

In her beautiful prayer, the *Magnificat,* Mary sings about God's subversion. She sings about how God reverses all plans and designs. God chooses the little instead of the big, the weak instead of the strong. God lifts up the lowly and puts down the mighty. And God makes fruitful both a young virgin and an elderly woman.

Mary sings about God and how God has plumbed her depths. Her song says that if God could break into the life of an ignorant, fearful, small-town peasant girl, God could and would do the same for all lonely, lowly, broken, and insignificant people such as you and me. More than that, it is what God desires. After all, what was it that Mary called herself? "Behold, look at the handmaid, the servant, the slave-girl of the Lord." Then she added words to this effect: "But he who is mighty has said that I am something more and so has done great things for the likes of me, and he can do the same for you." Mary's message and meaning? Say "yes" to the more that you are.

Elizabeth

Moving in and out of Mary's story is Elizabeth. We immediately note that Elizabeth is cousin to Mary: cousin through blood but also, a cousin through fear. Elizabeth has been dealt a bad hand in a society that, for women, prizes childbearing above all else: she is sterile. "Cursed" is the word of her day. This is Elizabeth: a woman, a Jew, childless, old—what else could be stacked against her? A tattered woman with no issue. Could anyone love her besides her husband, away in Jerusalem at the temple talking to an angel while she stayed in the hill country talking to herself?

And who is Elizabeth today? She is everyone who is sterile, everyone in a loveless marriage, everyone with ungrateful and hurtful children, everyone in a dead-end job, everyone in an unresolved, uncommitted relationship. We can see her in those who walk in spiritual dryness, who can no longer believe in God, who cannot pray, who are without hope, simply going through the motions of living; those who see no way out, who are stuck, who are empty. She is anyone who, like the Lion, is fearful of life itself.

Do these Elizabeths, these seemingly unlovable, ungifted, untalented, unwanted, empty, sterile people, have a story to show the way out of their dilemma? Yes. It is the story of a king, who, like Elizabeth, was sterile:

He was a powerful king, loved by the queen and feared by his enemies. He had everything, except what he wanted most: he had no child. "Who will carry on my work?" he cried. "Who will inherit my power, my memory? I must have an heir!" And so a reward was offered to anyone who could help the royal couple fulfill their dream and overcome their sterility. Many tried and many died as the king and queen remained bitter and childless.

One day an old woman, wise and virtuous, came to the king and queen. Shown into the throne room, she told them then and there that a child could be theirs if the king would but do one thing. "And what is that?" the king asked anxiously, filled with hope.

The Wise One spoke: "Your majesty, because there is no system in your kingdom for washing away human waste, there is much sickness in the land. All waters are the same. Use your army, therefore, to dig canals through the cities and villages so that the waste water may go to one place while the water for drinking and cooking will go to another."

The king was skeptical. "And this will bring me a child?"

The Wise One smiled, "It is assured, your majesty."

It was done. The pestilence that had attacked the people for generations was eventually gone, but after many months there was still no sign of pregnancy. So the Wise One was summoned back before the throne.

"You have lied to me. I did as you said and yet no child is ours. Prepare to die."

But the Wise One spoke quickly. "Oh, but my good king, you have fulfilled only a part of the requirement. You must now parcel out the land to the serfs and peasants, allowing each a lot large enough for both sustenance and sale."

"Why," roared the king, "should I give away what is mine?"

"So that you might have one with your name to follow," she said softly. The mention of the "one" spoke so deeply to the king that he did as the old woman had instructed. Every able-bodied peasant and serf was given his own lot. For the first time in memory, they could feed their families and guests with ease. Then the king and queen waited. But still no child grew between them. The king was furious and demanded that the old woman be brought before him, and he condemned her to death.

"Your majesty may kill me, but then you will never know if the last requirement will bring fruit."

"The last?" the kind asked with suspicion and hope.

"Yes, your majesty, one last thing will ensure you an heir. Of this I am sure."

"If it does not," said the king with menace in his quivering voice, "your heirs will be denied their mother."

"Have no fear. The last thing you must do is dismantle your army. For the last two decades our kingdom has fought war after war. Make lasting treaties with your neighbors and dissolve that force which once protected your aggression."

"But my army!" exclaimed the king.

"I give you no choice, your majesty."

And so it was done. For the first time in the memory of many, young men remained home behind plow and anvil, and children danced safely by the borders. The king, having sacrificed so much, was sure that now he would receive his heart's desire. But the days turned into months and as the months turned into a year, the king had a scaffold erected in the throne room. The old woman was sent for.

"Now you will die. Do you have anything to say?"

The old woman's eyes looked toward a window and she spoke quietly. "Your Majesty, your wife was barren, as was the land. Your people died of sickness, starvation, and war, and now look at your land. You have given your people health, wealth, and the security of peace. You have given them a better life and your name is spoken with reverence. It is bestowed upon the children of your subjects and will be passed down to their children, and their children's children. Yours will always be a name spoken with honor. You, through acts of loving kindness, will be the father of and remembered by all the children of this land."

The king, whose eyes had followed the old woman's, gazed at the new landscape he had created. Taking her hand, he knew she was right. His children now would number with the stars and he would be remembered forever.

What is the lesson here for the Elizabeths of this world? "Sterile" people find life through charity. "Cowardly" people find courage through giving—just as the Cowardly Lion did.

Zechariah

Finally, there is Elizabeth's husband, Zechariah. When the invitation to a new life, a new way of being, was foretold by the angel, he doubted. He disbelieved. As a result he was given a severe punishment: he was left without a voice. Thus, in the dynamics of storytelling, he could not tell his—or anyone else's—story. He could not pass on his story to his son; he no longer had a heritage. He was struck dumb, a man without a story—and so without a journey, without a life, without hope. An outcast. A sinner.

Zechariah feared that his sin would always remain with him, would always render him dumb, would always label him, always identify him as a failure, as unworthy. But the Advent story reclaims Zechariah, and once more he speaks. He becomes brokenness reclaimed, dryness watered, silence released, the dark night of the soul abated. Subsequently in the gospels, Zechariah will wear the face of Zacchaeus, the Samaritan woman, the found sheep, and the good thief. His story will be told as memory reclaimed, dumbness loosened, forgiveness rendered.

Zechariah finds his counterpart in this story:

On the day the Baal Shem Tov was dying, he assigned each of his disciples a task to carry on in his name, to do some of his work. When he came to the last disciple he gave him this task: to go all over Europe and retell the stories he remembered from the Master. The disciple was very disappointed. This was hardly a prestigious job. But the Baal Shem Tov told him that he would not have to do this forever; he would receive a sign when he should stop, and then he could live out the rest of his life in ease.

So off he went, and days and months turned into years and years of telling stories, until he felt he had told them in every part of the world. Then he heard of a man in Italy, a nobleman in fact, who would pay a gold ducat for each new story told. So the disciple went to Italy to the nobleman's castle. But to his absolute horror he discovered that he had forgotten all the Baal Shem Tov stories! He couldn't remember a single story. He was mortified. But the nobleman was kind and urged him to stay a few days anyway, in the hope that he would eventually remember something. But the next day and the next, he remembered nothing. Finally, on the third day, out of sheer embarrassment, the disciple protested that he must go.

But as he was about to leave, oh, yes, suddenly he remembered one story. This would prove that he indeed did know the great Baal Shem Tov, for the disciple was the only one there when this story took place. This is the story he remembered:

Once the Baal Shem Tov told the disciple to harness the

horses, for they were about to take a trip to Turkey where, at this time of the year, the streets were decorated for the Christians' Easter festival. The disciple was upset, for it was well known that Jews were not safe during the Christian Holy Week and Easter. They were fair game for the Christians, who shouted, "God killers!" In fact, it was then the custom during the Easter festival to kill one Jew in reparation.

Still, they went. They went into the city and then into the Jewish quarter where the Jews were all huddled behind their shutters out of fear. They were secluded, waiting until the festival was over and they could go out on the streets again in safety. So imagine how startled and surprised they were when the Baal Shem Tov stood up and opened all the windows of the house where they were staying. And furthermore, he stood there in full view. Looking through the window he saw the bishop leading the procession. He was arrayed like a prince with gold vestments, silver miter, and a diamond-studded staff.

The Baal Shem Tov told his disciple, "Go tell the bishop I want to see him." Was he out of his mind? Did he want to die? But nothing could deter this order, so the disciple went out, approached the bishop, and told him that the Baal Shem Tov wanted to see him. The bishop seemed frightened and agitated, but he went. He went and was secluded for three hours with the Baal Shem Tov. Then the Master came out, and without saying anything else, told his disciples that they were ready to go back home.

As the disciple finished the story, he was about to apologize to the nobleman for the insignificance of the story when he suddenly noticed the enormous impact the story had on the nobleman. He had dissolved into tears and finally, when he could speak, he said, "Oh disciple, your story has just saved my soul! You see, I was there that day. I was that bishop. I had descended from a long line of distinguished rabbis, but one day during a period of great persecution, I had abandoned the faith and converted to Christianity.

"The Christians, of course, were so pleased that in time they even made me a bishop. And I had accepted everything, even went along with the killing of the Jews each year until that one year. The night before the festival I had a terrible dream of the Day of Judgment and the danger to my soul. So when you came the very next day with a message from the Baal Shem Tov, I knew that I had to go with you. For three hours he and I talked. He told me that there might still be hope for my soul. He told me to sell my goods and retire on what was left and live a life of good deeds and holiness. There might still be hope. And his last words to me were these: 'When a man comes to you and tells you your own story, you will know that your sins are forgiven.'

"So I have been asking everyone I know for stories from the Baal Shem Tov. And I recognized you immediately when you came, and I was happy. But when I saw that all the stories had been taken from you, I recognized God's judgment. Yet now you have remembered one story, my story, and I know now that the Baal Shem Tov has interceded on my behalf and that God has forgiven me."

When a man comes to you and tells you your own story, you know that your sins are forgiven. Whenever the story of Zechariah is told, you know that you can be forgiven, fear can be overcome, and your tongue can be loosened to sing of the marvels of God. And whenever the stories of John the Baptist, Mary, and Elizabeth are told you know that inadequacy, smallness, and emptiness are no barriers to the call of God.

So there is our Advent foursome. When Advent next comes around, perhaps take one of the quartet to walk with each week of the holy season. The first week, walk with John and his doubts; the second week with Mary and her fear; the third week, with Elizabeth and her emptiness; and the fourth week, with Zechariah and his brokenness. Remember that each one was touched by Christ in one way or another; each one was redeemed by his love. Each one finally came to know victory. Each one is us.

Back to the Cowardly Lion, who is a kind of composite of our Advent folk. In the end he got his medal of courage signifying—

what? As the clever though now-debunked Wizard put it, the medal signified that the Lion's courage was there all the time. All he needed to recognize his worth and overcome his fear was a good deed. Not that the Lion would *always* be sure of himself, or that being courageous was easy; but ultimately, being faithful earned victory for the Cowardly Lion. Our faithfulness will yield the same.

Questions for reflection

1. Do I feel as if God has abandoned me? If so, do I feel bitter about this because I have been faithful to God?

2. Am I angry, disappointed, when my prayers seem to go unanswered?

3. God seldom comes in the miracle. Can I learn to see God in the patient, faithful, ministering lives of those who remain constant in adversity?

4. "Are you the one who is to come, or are we to wait for another?" When have I, like John, asked this question of God?

5. Like Mary, am I afraid of my identity as a "highly favored one"? Do I settle for being a chicken rather than an eagle, simply because being a chicken is less demanding?

6. Am I like Elizabeth, and work at charity as a means to overcome my spiritual sterility, my barrenness?

7. Have I been struck speechless, as was Zechariah? Do I have the faith to speak again?

THE FLYING MONKEYS

Capital Sins

The Wicked Witch had her minions: the mindless, lockstepping soldiers and, even better, the monkeys. I say better, because they had wings and could fly off in pursuit of the fleeing fivesome: Dorothy, Toto, the Scarecrow, the Tin Man, and the Cowardly Lion. They found the group, de-strawed the Scarecrow, scared off the Lion, knocked down the Tin Man, and carried off Dorothy and Toto. It is hard to avoid flying monkeys, especially when there are so many of them.

The devil is just as resourceful. He has his minions, his elite corps of "flying monkeys" to harass us on our spiritual journey. And, truth to tell, they are quite effective. We call them sins. And there are not many of them—seven, in fact. We call them the seven capital sins. Can you name all seven? (For the record, they are pride, envy, greed, anger, lust, gluttony, and sloth.) The capital sins are so named, as the *Catechism of the Catholic Church* reminds us, because they are the font, or "capital," or source of so many other sins.

When used to describe human feelings, pride, envy, anger, greed, lust, gluttony, and sloth are sinless. Everyone has such feelings, and they remain neutral unless they are acted upon in an excessive, hurtful manner. Then they become sinful and quickly run into other sins. They are very effective at de-strawing us, knocking us down, scaring us, and carrying us off.

And so this chapter is another series of reflections like chapter nine, consisting mostly of stories. Each requires very slow reading, a long pause after each story, reflection, and self-examination. You must sit back and read carefully in order to experience the truism of the storyteller's creed: the story begins when the storyteller stops. I will pick only five of the seven sins: pride, envy, greed (avarice)— "Pride, envy, avarice, these are the sparks/ Have set on fire the hearts of all men" (Dante, *The Inferno*, Canto 6)—sloth, and anger.

Pride

> Farewell! a long farewell, to all my greatness!
> This is the state of man: to-day he puts forth
> The tender leaves of hope; to-morrow blossoms,
> And bears his blushing honors thick upon him;
> The third day comes a frost, a killing frost,
> And, when he thinks, good easy man, full surely
> His greatness is a-ripening, nips his root,
> And then he falls, as I do. I have ventur'd,
> Like little wanton boys that swim on bladders,
> This many summers in a sea of glory;
> But far beyond my depth. My high-blown pride
> At length broke under me, and now has left me,
> Weary and old with service, to the mercy
> Of a rude stream that must for ever hide me.
> Vain pomp and glory of this world, I hate ye;
> I feel my heart new open'd. O, how wretched
> Is that poor man that hangs on princes' favors!
> There is betwixt that smile we would aspire to,
> That sweet aspect of princes, and their ruin,
> More pangs and fears than wars or women have;
> And when he falls, he falls like Lucifer,
> Never to hope again.
>
> —Shakespeare, *Henry VIII*

O God of earth and altar,
Bow down and hear our cry,

> Our earthly rulers falter,
> Our people drift and die;
> The walls of gold entomb us,
> The swords of scorn divide,
> Take not Thy thunder from us,
> But take away our pride.
>
> —G.K. Chesterton, *A Hymn*

These two bits of wisdom serve to introduce our stories on pride. Since even Lucifer fell by pride, it's been his own most potent weapon, the one he resorts to after trying all others. Remember this story from chapter two?

> When the devil saw a seeker of truth enter the house of the Master, he was determined to do everything in his power to turn him back from his quest. So he subjected him to every form of temptation—wealth, lust, prestige—but the seeker was able to fight off these temptations quite easily.
>
> But that changed when he actually got to the Master's house, There he was somewhat taken aback to see the Master sitting in an upholstered chair with his disciples at his feet. "That man certainly lacks humility, the principal virtue of saints," he thought to himself. Then he observed other things about the Master he did not like. For one thing, the Master took little notice of him. "I suppose that's because I do not fawn over him like the others do," he said to himself. He also disliked the kind of clothes the Master wore and the somewhat conceited way that he spoke. And all this led him to the conclusion that he had come to the wrong place and must continue his quest elsewhere.
>
> As he walked out of the room the Master, who had seen the devil seated in the corner of the room, said, "You need not have worried, tempter. He was yours from the very first, you know."

Here is a wonderful tale which illustrates a very common type of pride. It concerns the people of Gubbio, and a troublesome wolf:

> In thirteenth-century Italy, there was a small city nestled in the foothills of a great mountain. It was a city of considerable beau-

ty and the people were very proud of it. They had piazzas with
wonderful fountains, restaurants with wonderful food, churches
with wonderful spires, and civic buildings with wonderful sculp-
tures. Whenever anyone from this city traveled to Florence or
Venice or Rome, their dress would stand out, for in those days
people from different places wore slightly different clothing.
People would say to them, "Strangers, where are you from?"
They would raise themselves to full stature, stand their ground,
and say, "We? We are from Gubbio." That is the way they
answered, proud and defiant, and that is the way they were.

Now it came to pass that one night, out of the woods on one
side of Gubbio, out of the deep and dark woods of Gubbio,
there came a shadow. The shadow moved through the streets of
Gubbio, going up this street and prowling down that alley until
the shadow found someone, and then it pounced. In the morning the people of Gubbio found a mangled, gnawed body; the
bones broken, the clothing in shreds. That was all that was left.
They gathered around the remains. Many could not look.

One man spoke in anger, "How could this happen in
Gubbio?" A reply was quick in coming, "It must have been a
stranger, someone passing through, who did this horrible
thing." Everyone nodded their heads. That was most surely it.
Nevertheless, that night the people of Gubbio locked their
doors and stayed inside. No one left their homes to walk the
beautiful streets of Gubbio—no one, that is, except one
woman. In the morning they found her body, mangled,
gnawed, the bones broken, the clothing in shreds.

The people gathered around the remains, their anguished
voices going back and forth. "How could this happen?" was followed quickly by, "It must have been a stranger." Then an old
woman spoke up, "I saw it." All went silent. "It was late last
night. I could not sleep. I went to my window and pushed back
the curtain. In the dim light that the moon provided, I saw lop-
ing down the street, blood dripping from his mouth, a wolf. A
large, lean, gray wolf."

All day long this was the talk—in the piazza, in the fields, in the shops, in the restaurants, in the churches, in the homes: "There is a wolf in Gubbio." Two young men heard it and formed a plan. One said, "Those who kill the wolf will make a name for themselves." "You are right, my friend," replied the other. "And the people will be grateful." "We have swords, do we not?" They smiled. So that night they prowled the streets of Gubbio to find the wolf. But the wolf found them before they found the wolf. In the morning their bodies were found on the street, mangled, gnawed, the bones broken, the clothing in shreds.

Now the people of Gubbio were terrified. They gathered in the piazza in the center of the city. Many were shouting, their voices climbing over one another. "How could this be?" exclaimed someone. "This is what we must do..." schemed others. Finally, one man was loud enough to silence the others. "We must bring in the soldiers. They have numbers and experience. They will be able to rid us of this wolf." The voice of a merchant immediately countered, "Never! If we bring in the army, everyone will know we have a wolf in Gubbio. Our prestige, our commerce, our tourism will be hurt." Everyone recognized the wisdom of this, and they were silent.

In the silence a small girl spoke. She said that she had heard of a holy man in a neighboring city who spoke to animals. Perhaps he could come here and speak to the wolf. The people laughed. An old man waited for their laughter to stop, then said that he, too, had heard of a holy man who spoke to animals. He thought it would be a good idea to see what that man could do. "Besides," he finished, "does anyone have a better idea?" A delegation was quickly formed and commissioned to go to the neighboring city and find this holy man and tell him...tell him...tell him what?

"Tell him," said one person, "to tell the wolf to keep the commandments, especially the commandment that says, 'Thou shalt not kill.'" "No," said another, "it is not enough to tell the wolf what not to do. You must appeal to the best in him. Tell him to keep the great commandments, the ones Christ taught, to love God and neighbor." "My friends," said the butcher, "a wolf is a wolf is a wolf. There will be no change. Tell the holy man to tell the wolf to go someplace else."

The people applauded this suggestion and began to shout out names of places where the wolf might go. "Tell the wolf to go to Perugia. They deserve a wolf in Perugia. Or Spoleto. In Spoleto they would not even know the wolf was there." There was no shortage of suggestions; most of the cities of Italy were named. Finally, the delegation said that they must be on their way. They would tell the holy man of everyone's concerns. They left immediately, but they did not go the short way past the woods where the wolf lived. They took the long way.

When they arrived at the city of the holy man, everyone was at the noon market, milling around the piazza. They asked a man if there was a holy man in the city who had the reputation of talking to animals. The man said, matter-of-factly, that there was and that you could find him on the outskirts, where he and some of his friends were fixing up an old church. The man then said that he would take them there.

So the delegation from Gubbio followed the man to the edge of the city. He pointed to a group of brown-robed men wrestling with brick and mortar and said, "There, the one in the middle, laughing, that's him." The delegation saw a man in a soiled brown robe, a young man, much too young to be a holy man. Worse yet, he was short, much too short to be a holy man. But the people from Gubbio had come this far.

They approached him and told him their tale of terror. They pleaded with him to come to Gubbio and tell the wolf to keep the commandments, especially the one that says, "Thou shalt not kill." They asked him to tell the wolf to keep Christ's great commandments to love God and neighbor, and then to send the wolf to Perugia. (The delegation had settled on Perugia.)

The holy man listened and told them to go home. He would see what he could do. The delegation left immediately. But they did not take the short way, past the woods where the wolf lived. They took the long way and arrived home just as the sun was beginning to set. They locked their doors.

As the last rays of the sun left the sky, the holy man stood at the edge of the wood. When there was no sun at all, he entered the woods. The floor of the forest cracked and broke under his steps, and soon he found himself deep in the heart of the woods. There was no light there, and since he could not see he simply closed his eyes and went forward. Finally he stopped. He knew that if he put out his hand, he would touch the wolf. He said, "Brother Wolf."

In the morning when the people awoke and went into the piazza they found the holy man standing next to the fountain. They quickly gathered around him and began to shout, "Did you tell the wolf to keep God's commandments, especially the one that says, 'Thou shalt not kill?' Did you tell him to keep Christ's great commandments to love God and neighbor? And did you tell him to go to Perugia?"

The people so surrounded the holy man that no one could see him, for he was very short. So he climbed the three steps of the fountain, and with the water springing up behind him, he said nothing, only smiled. Finally the people quieted down and he spoke. "My good people of Gubbio, the answer is very simple. You must feed your wolf." With that he descended the fountain steps, the people parted, he walked through their midst, and he returned to his own city.

The people of Gubbio were furious. They shouted to one another, "What does he mean 'our wolf'? This is not our wolf! We did not ask this wolf to come to Gubbio." All day long on the streets, in the churches, in the fields, in the shops, in the restaurants, in the homes people asked, "What does he mean, 'We must feed our wolf'?" When night came, they went home and locked their doors.

That night, out of the woods came the shadow. It prowled down this street and up that alley. It loped across a square and disappeared through an archway. Then it turned down a narrow street. Suddenly a door opened. Light streamed out from the inside. It illumined the dark street, and a hand pushed a platter of food into the light. The shadow came to the offering, looked up into the light with burning eyes, and ate the food.

The next night out of the woods came the shadow. It prowled down this street and up that alley. It loped across a square and disappeared through an archway. Then it turned down a narrow street. Suddenly a door opened. Light streamed out from the inside. It illumined the dark street, and a hand pushed a platter of food into the light. The shadow came to the offering, looked up into the light with burning eyes, and ate the food. It was not long before every man, woman, and child in Gubbio had fed their wolf.

Now the people of Gubbio still traveled from city to city in Italy. Their distinctive dress still called attention to themselves, and the people would ask, "Strangers, I do not know your clothes. Where are you from?" They would reply simply, "We are from Gubbio." The response was quick in coming and often accompanied by a sneer. "Gubbio? Gubbio? We hear you have a wolf in Gubbio." They would smile and say, "Yes, we have a wolf in Gubbio. And we feed our wolf."

Envy

For when the foul sore of envy corrupts the vanquished hearts, the very exterior itself shows how forcibly the mind is urged by madness.

—Pope St. Gregory I, *Morals*

If pride, the first capital sin, is as old as Adam and Eve, the second capital sin, envy, can be considered as old as their children, Cain and Abel. Envy is a sin which contracts the heart and sours the soul—and often leads to murder. Fiction and fable are full of such tales. Remember the Wicked Queen and Snow White, the three stepsisters and Cinderella, the Man in the Iron Mask, Bette Davis in *A Stolen Life*? Closer to home, remember the mother of a cheerleader who had her daughter's rival slain? Remember James Michener's story from chapter ten? Now contemplate this story:

The phone rang just as I was relaxing with a glass of iced tea after a long day of doing laundry, cleaning house, and shopping for groceries. "Guess what?" Dad asked before I could say hello. "David is being inducted into the Tascosa High School Hall of Fame!" I felt my whole body tighten. "Gee," I managed, "That's great, Dad." "Your mother and I are so proud of your brother! He's coming back to Amarillo just for the ceremony—though the Good Lord only knows where that boy finds the time."

I watched a bead of moisture trickle down the side of my glass. Yes, my younger brother David certainly led a busy, distinguished life. "Cindy, are you still there?" "Yes, Dad. When's the big day?" "April sixteenth. The school will be giving David an award for graduates who have gone on to big things. Mark your calendar. This is an honor for the whole family!"

After assuring Dad I wouldn't miss the ceremony for the world, I hung up. Then I threw myself on the couch. You really couldn't call it sibling rivalry, because when it came right down to it there was no contest between David and me. I knew that better than anyone. I was proud of David. It was other people who got under my skin.

"What's it like having a brother like him?" they would inevitably inquire, skipping even an obligatory question about my life. I was a working mom trying to make ends meet. I shopped at Wal-Mart and balanced my checkbook carefully. My husband was a good man who worked hard for the Texas Highway Department. But I had nothing to brag about, certainly no hall-of-fame achievements.

While growing up I never felt like the leader. David, five years younger, was always out in front, collecting awards by the armful. He was valedictorian at Tascosa High, making up for all the As I hadn't got. That's when I first began hearing it: "You must be proud to have a brother like that, Cindy." I was. David and I got along great. As kids we had a make-believe restaurant. He was the maître d' and I was the chef, whipping up gourmet meals out of clay. In summertime we got people to pay us for painting their addresses on the curb. When David gave organ recitals, I was beside him, turning the pages of music and basking in his amply reflected glory. We drifted apart a little when I went to high school. I finished a couple of semesters of college, then got married and started a family. Meanwhile, David's life took off like a moonshot.

I got up off the couch and poured the rest of my iced tea down the sink. Oh, well, I thought, I should be used to David getting all the attention.

A few days later I was picking up some dry cleaning when a friend of my parents came rushing up to me. "I heard about David. Isn't that just the neatest thing?" she asked. I allowed it was, then made an excuse why I couldn't stand around and gab.

It crossed my mind that I might feel better if I talked to somebody about my feelings, maybe even give David a call. But he was so busy with his law practice in California. He's probably caught up with an important case, I thought, with that sour note of self-pity I always hated. The fact was, our lives had diverged and he had taken the high road. While he was acing his courses at Rice University and graduating magna cum laude, I was having babies and taking aerobics classes, trying desperately to get back in shape. When he was an editor of the Harvard Law Review, I was struggling over Bible study lessons. On my way home an acquaintance came up alongside me at a red light, rolled down his window and shouted, "You say 'Hi!' to that brother of yours for me, you hear?"

April 16 was only a month away, but something told me it was going to be the longest month of my life. Right there at that light I prayed: Lord, just get me through to the other side of this hall-of-fame ceremony. I'm sorry, maybe I'm just having some sort of midlife blues, but this is one of those times you're going to have to carry me.

The big day came. David accepted his award with characteristic grace and humility, giving a speech that sent goose bumps down my arms. Afterward we all crowded into a reception hall—relatives, old friends, former teachers, and ministers. I tried to melt into the scenery. Our family doctor was kind enough to make small talk with me until he saw David shake free of a throng of admirers. "Oh, 'scuse me, Cindy," he interrupted. "I want to say hello to David." Something inside me snapped. The last thing I wanted to do was burst into tears in front of all these people. I slipped away and drove home. The kids were out and my husband was working. I sat down on the couch and buried my head in my hands. "Why, Lord, why do I feel this way? I thought you were going to help me!"

A moment later I heard the crunch of gravel in the driveway and the thud of a car door. Then the bell rang. "Cindy, what's wrong?" David asked, stepping inside.

"Oh, just a headache. You shouldn't have left all those people back there."

"I was worried when I couldn't find you."

"Don't worry about me. It's your day."

David sat down next to me. "It's not much of a day without you."

It was no use holding back. I let go of the feelings I had held in for years. I poured out my heart to David, telling him all of my petty, shameful resentments. "I've convinced myself no one is interested in me," I said, sobbing.

David took my hand. "Remember when we painted addresses on curbs?" he said. "Whenever it was my turn to ring a doorbell I was afraid I might flub our sales pitch and disappoint you. None of this means as much to me if you don't feel part of it. The other morning," he said, "when I was getting dressed before a big client meeting, I couldn't decide on a tie to wear. I found myself thinking, 'Which one would Cindy pick?' You're my big sister. I've always wanted to make you proud of me."

I threw my arms around him. "Cindy, I've always looked up to you, the way you've raised your family and lived your life. Don't you understand?" David didn't go back to the reception right away. He stayed and we talked about old times, good times we had growing up.

Growing up, I learned that day, is something we never stop doing, and God is there to help us. As St. Paul writes: "Now there are varieties of gifts, but the same Spirit; and there are varieties of services, but the same Lord; and there are varieties of activities, but it is the same God who activates all of them in everyone. To each is given the manifestation of the Spirit for the common good." Among the many gifts God gave me is a wonderful brother. I remember that when people ask me about him these days.

Greed

> So for a good old-gentlemanly vice,
> I think I must take up with avarice.
>
> —Byron

> I preach for nothing but for greed of gain
> And use the same old text, as bold as brass.
>
> —Chaucer, "The Pardoner's Tale"

The third capital sin we will consider is avarice or greed. The chief effect of greed, as everyone knows, is spiritual blindness.

Two men were sitting in a cafe in old Baghdad. A camel went by. The man asked his friend, "What does that camel make you think of?" The friend replied, "Food." His friend exclaimed, "Food? Food? We don't eat camels! Since when did we start eating camels?" "Oh," said the man, "everything I see makes me think of food."

Or try this one:

Once there was a man who dreamed of nothing but gold. He was obsessed with it. Morning, noon and night he dreamed of gold. One day he got up from his desk and ran to the marketplace. He ran through the crowd to the table where the man was selling gold coins. He swept them all into his little bag and ran away.

A policeman was standing right next to the table and he nabbed him. He took him to the police station and as he was locking him up he said to the man, "I can't understand it. There you are, me right next to the merchant's table and at least one hundred witnesses, and you steal something right in front of them!"

The man replied, "I never saw any of them. I only saw the gold."

These are Sufi tales. But now see how the theme translates to our culture: a while back I was watching one of those TV magazine shows. The reporter was exposing a rather sordid type of crime that has become relatively common of late. It seems there are some doctors and lawyers who hire people to rear-end cars and then coach the "victims" into faking symptoms in order to bilk the insurance companies out of millions of dollars.

The reporter was interviewing one of the perpetrators about a young father and his child who were crushed to death in one of these "accidents." The scam artist was asked about the deaths of these two people, as well as the widow and family left behind: didn't it bother him? He shook his head no. What was in your mind? was a further question. The money. When the man was asked if he was so focused on the money that he didn't care if people died, he merely shrugged his shoulders.

Greed blinds.

To lighten up a bit on a very serious sin, I have a story to tell you about greed and pride both mixed together. This is from Italian folklore:

Once upon a time it so happened that the Lord Jesus and St. Peter had had a long day preaching and teaching and traveling all over the land with the Good News. Now it was dusk and they were tired, very tired, and hungry, very hungry. They struggled into a little village. In it was a very large house and a little hovel. The Lord Jesus was heading for the little hovel when St. Peter grabbed his arm and swung him around and said to the Lord Jesus, "Ah, Lord, let us go and knock on this large house with many rooms and see if we can find food and lodging for the night." And the Lord Jesus, being very tired and very acquiescent to St. Peter said, "All right."

And so they went to the door and they knocked on the door and the door opened and a woman stood in the door and St.

Peter said: "We are good people—we've been about good things all day. But we are very tired. And we need some food and we need sleep for the night. And we saw your house and its many rooms and we thought you could accommodate us."

And the woman put her hands on her hips and she said, "What does this look like, an inn? What do I look like, an innkeeper's wife?" And when the door slammed, it came very close to St. Peter's nose. He was flabbergasted and sputtered, "But...but...." But the Lord Jesus put his hand on St. Peter's shoulders and said, "There's another house. We could ask there."

And so across the road they went to the small hovel and the Lord Jesus knocked on the door. The door opened just a crack and a nose and eyes appeared in the crack and a voice said, "Yes?" And the Lord Jesus said, "We are hungry. We need food. And we are tired and we need a place to sleep." And the door opened just a little bit wider. And with it came the full face of a woman and she said, "I have very little food. And you'll have to sleep in the only one room we have. I am a widow and there are four children here and so it might be noisy and your sleep might be anything but restful, but you are most welcomed."

And the Lord Jesus said, "That would be fine." And they went in, and while the Lord Jesus played with the children and St. Peter sulked in a corner, the woman cooked up the simplest meal that she could possibly cook and they ate it very quickly. And then the Lord Jesus and St. Peter curled up in a corner as the others were curled up, since there was only one room in that house. And there they fell asleep.

They woke in the morning and the woman cooked up some bread in a skillet that had fat in it from many, many, many times before and the bread was soaked in the little fat so that it tasted very well. Before the Lord Jesus and St. Peter went on their way, she gave them both an apple, telling them that wherever they were going she was sure it would be a long journey and they would need something to eat. The Lord Jesus thanked her and said to her, "Do you know what I do? I give blessings. And so I would like to give you a blessing." He said, "My blessing for you is 'What you start now, may it continue all day.'" The woman said, "Thank you very much."

And St. Peter said to the woman, "You know, we may be coming back this same way another time. Perhaps...." And the Lord Jesus stared at St. Peter and thought this was inappropriate. And Peter was quiet and the Lord Jesus and St. Peter left. And the woman sat down and began to weave at her loom. But magically, the weaving seemed to take on tremendous power. From her loom came the most beautiful cloth in the world. And it seemed to come so effortlessly, so easily, so without strain her fingers and her feet moved in such magical rhythms that pretty soon almost her entire house was filled with the most wonderful cloth and what she started continued all day just as easily and effortlessly.

Late in the afternoon, the woman from the house across the street walked down, and she knocked on the door and as was her custom before anyone could even say, "Come in," she had pushed in and said, "Were you bothered by those two beggars...!" And she looked around and the house was filled with the most beautiful cloth. She said, "What is this? What is this? What is this wonderful cloth that fills your house? How did this happen?" And the woman said she did not know how it had happened. But, yes, those two men had stayed the night and one of them, before he left, had given her a blessing. He said, "What you start now, may it continue all day." And, lo and behold, this continued and she did not know how this had happened exactly. Only she knew it was very, very easy to do.

And the woman said, "Oh! They came to my house first. It was the same two guys. All this beautiful cloth could have been mine. I pushed them away. What a mistake! What a mistake! What a mistake! If I had just let them in they would have given me their blessing and I could have had all this beautiful, beautiful cloth instead of you having this beautiful cloth. Your house is even too small for this cloth. This cloth would fit wonderfully in my house. Your house is so small it's so crowded now with all this beautiful cloth. And I could have had all this just by inviting them in. Oh...!" Then the woman said, "Wait a minute!

Are they coming back?"

The other woman said, "Well, one of them said they might come back this way."

The woman said, "Your house is much too small, crowded with your children. You do not have enough food for yourself and your children. They are growing. They are growing. And they need this food. My house is large. I have rooms to spare and food to spare. It would be better if they stayed at my house rather than your house. They would be more comfortable and better off."

And the woman said, "You're right. They would be, for my house is very small and my children make it very noisy and the food I have is very little and even to divide it up is not enough for two grown men like that. And so you are right. If they come back, I will send them across to your house. Thank you," she said. And the first woman left and went back to her house.

Sure enough, two weeks later, along came the Lord Jesus and St. Peter, and the Lord Jesus knocked on the door and the crack in the door opened and there were two eyes and a nose and when she saw them she smiled and the door opened. And the Lord Jesus said, "We are back. And it's been a long day and we are hungry and we would like some food. We are tired and we would like a place to sleep."

And the woman said, "I would love to feed you and you are always welcomed here and there is always a place for you to sleep. But my neighbor came by and she regretted having turned you away the first time. And she has a large house. You would be so much more comfortable there. The rooms are better. The beds are better. The food is better. And I know you are very hungry and that you are very tired and certainly you will be more comfortable there. She is waiting for you so why don't you go across the street and she will welcome you."

And the Lord Jesus said, "That is fine, whatever you want." They closed the door. And as Lord Jesus was walking across the street St. Peter said to him, "She just wants a blessing! She heard about the blessing. That's all she wants. She doesn't care about us. She just knows you give blessings and she wants a blessing. And that's why. Don't you give her a blessing! Let's take the food and let's sleep but let's get out in the morning. Don't give a blessing." And the Lord Jesus said, "All I have in my purse is a blessing and I have to give what I have." And Peter said, "No, no, not to her! Not to her! This is the only reason she's doing this, to get the blessing. She heard about the blessing and this is what she is trying to do." And the Lord Jesus said, "Peter, calm down. I give blessings. I can't help it. I'll give her a blessing." St. Peter said, "Not fair. It's not fair."

And the Lord Jesus knocked on the door and the woman opened the door and said "Helllooo. Come innnnn...." And in they came. And she turned around and called to her husband, "Harry!" And food appeared, massive amounts of food, and the Lord Jesus ate a little bit and St. Peter ate way too much and belched. And when they were done, the woman said, "We have two beds for you in different rooms. Let me take you to them." And up they went to the beds and they were deep beds and they slept soundly and well all night long.

And in the morning when they came down she had packed for them both a hamper full of food to take on the road and a wooden basket full of fruits and meats and cheeses and wine gourds. And St. Peter smiled just a little bit. And the Lord Jesus said, "Thank you very much. This has been a wonderful hospitality. And, you know what I do, I give blessings."

And St. Peter leaned over and said, "Don't give her a blessing!" And the Lord Jesus leaned back to St. Peter and said, "Take it easy."

And the Lord Jesus said to the woman, "I give blessings and for your wonderful hospitality, I would like to give you a blessing. I would like to give you this blessing: 'What you start now, may you continue all day.'" She said, "Thank you very much. Thank you very much for that blessing."

"We must go now," said the Lord Jesus. And so out the door they went, on their way, on their mission. And the woman closed the door and leaned back against it and knew that all day long she would be at the loom and from her loom would come the most beautiful cloth and so before she began, knowing she would be busy all day, she went to the outhouse to relieve herself....

Greed displaces.

Greed not only blinds us to other realities of life but it has one other evil effect: it displaces real values. You know, when you fill the glass with water, you displace the air. Greed is like that. It displaces other values. The fundamental question to ask of greed is this: "What is greed keeping me from?" First, it keeps us from self-knowledge. All the energy and time spent in acquiring things; all our bowing to wants and declaring them needs: all our efforts to turn luxuries into necessities eventually leads us to believe that we are only what we have. In fact, our faith tells us quite the opposite, that we are always more than we have.

The comedian Mort Sahl used to say that if you ask a Californian who he is he would point to his car. This type of identification, that of ourselves with our possessions, and a general lack of self-knowledge make us ever more pliable to the incessant advertisers who are in the business of creating needs and selling their product to satisfy them. Soon we have no center. We have become what the marketplace has hoped for: the ongoing, shop-till-you-drop consumer. Deep down, we know we are more than that; but greed doesn't allow us the time to find out until it is too late.

Furthermore, greed displaces the only thing in life that ever, ever really counts: relationships. Ben Stein captures it best when he says: "No corporate title can replace the times when your son leans his head on your chest and falls asleep. No limousine or private jet makes up for being there when your son is growing from a child into a young man. Time spent with your child isn't a distraction from the main event. It is the main event."

Greed puts children and spouses at the bottom of the list as parents subcontract out the raising of their children, while they go off and "build for their future." Modern parents can afford to give their children many luxuries; and yet the only luxury that children really want is the parents themselves. Greed displaces. Every added room, every additional car, every extra television set displaces. True enough, people need a certain amount of material goods and money to live a decent life and provide for the future. But the question is: when does a legitimate desire to meet present needs exceed reasonable limits? Greed is present in the desire to accumulate more even when one already has what is sufficient and reasonable. With that accumulation comes separation, separation from the very ones we profess to love.

Consider this story:

> A tycoon had not yet made a contribution to the local hospital fund drive. The chairman of the drive paid him a personal visit saying, "Our records show you have not yet donated to our drive."
>
> The tycoon said, "And do your records show my mother died penniless? Do they show that my only brother is disabled? Do they show that my sister was abandoned and left to support four kids?"
>
> The chairman felt ashamed of his approach. He apologized, "No, they don't. I'm sorry."
>
> "Well," said the tycoon, "if I didn't help my own family, why should I help you?"

How has greed kept us so busy acquiring, working, making money, and building egos through possessions that we no longer really care for, bond with, or know our family and friends? Many of us no longer eat together, no longer spend time together, no longer are there when tears need to be dried and bodies hugged. Why? We are busy working toward a "better life" down the road instead of capturing the irretrievable, never-to-be repeated moments of closeness and love here and now. Greed displaces genuine values.

Sloth

> Weariness
> Can snore upon flint, when rusty sloth
> finds the down pillow hard.
>
> —Shakespeare, *Hamlet*

The fourth capital sin we will consider is sloth. Sloth? When people think of sloth they usually think of someone who lolls around on a couch all day popping bonbons into their mouths. Today's besetting sin is anything but sloth! For heaven's sake, most of us run around all day like maniacs. There is never enough time: busy, busy, busy. Nobody could accuse us of sloth. We are exhausted.

But sloth is not physical laziness or indolence. Rather, the capital sin of sloth, a kind of "living death," has three divisions: moral sloth, spiritual sloth, and intellectual sloth. Let us first look at moral sloth.

Bruno Bettelheim, the psychoanalyst, lived in Germany as a child. At that time the Nazi terror was starting to move through Germany, and the signs were clear that it was going to engulf Bettelheim and his Jewish family. In his book, *The Informed Heart*, he tells how he and his peers pleaded with the elderly people of the family to flee Germany, run away, because this terror was at their door. But the more they pleaded the more the old people said: "No, we can't leave our possessions, we can't leave our homes, we're settled here." And this went on week after week until finally the young people left and the Nazi terror came and swallowed up those Jews and killed them.

That is an example of moral sloth, and it yields a definition that applies to many of us. Moral sloth can be defined as knowing that one is set upon a damaging or deadly course and somehow cannot muster the courage, the hope, and the faith to do something different. The man who detests his job but continues along in it for a lifetime is guilty of moral sloth. The woman who sees herself as a martyr to her family; the grownup child who never makes a break with his or her parents; the married couple whose marriage is a lifelong hell; the teenager whose crowd is leading him or her to drugs or drink or premarital sex; the sexually or chemically addicted who claim victimhood: all of these people are guilty of moral sloth.

These people all know they are on a damaging course. They know they are going to suffer or die from their behavior. They know what they are doing is utterly hurtful and destructive for themselves and everybody else, but they can't bring themselves to change. As a matter of fact, the one thing that the slothful have in common is the perfect alibi. If you should mention, as I have done to some of these people, that they might possibly have other options, whether a different reaction or another way of life, they come at you with a ton of excuses and anger.

The man who is in a terrible job he hates, which is going to shorten his life by twenty years, will say: "But I've gotta support my family!" The liar, the cheat, the sexual predator, the unfaithful, the dishonest—all will claim they are victims and cannot help their behavior. The martyred housewife will say: "But how can my kids do without me if I'm not there every moment? How will they make the bed? How will they find the refrigerator? How will they work the microwave oven? How will they have clean clothes?" And you say, "Well, at some point they have to be on their own. How old is your little boy?" "Well, twenty-eight."

Do you see what's happening here? The grownup child says, "Well, I can't leave because my parents need me." Teenagers know that they are going to destroy themselves with the drugs or the drink, but the need for popularity and acceptance is so great that they don't have the courage to move away from destructive behavior. And that is moral sloth.

How do we know if we are guilty of moral sloth? We know we are guilty when we find ourselves continually depressed or in pain or giving pain and can produce excellent moral and practical reasons why we can't improve our lot.

Let's move on to the second division, spiritual sloth. This kind of sloth is called "acedia," or apathy, in the old religious manuals. Apathy was considered the worst of sins. We might describe it today as the "whatever" syndrome, or the "cool" syndrome.

"Do you want coffee or juice with your breakfast?" Whatever.
"Do you want a thick crust, thin crust, stuffed crust, or no crust pizza?" Whatever.
"I'm leaving you for someone else." Whatever.
Scandals abound among public figures and in public places. Whatever.
Every night in the United States a million children go to bed homeless and hungry. Whatever.

Soft money continues to corrupt our political system. Whatever.

Apathy is the indifference we display to things of the moment. Whatever. We don't know, don't care to know. We play it cool, and to be cool is the height of hip. Perhaps, to give it a benign spin, it is all the result of the society in which we live, where we get dunned with tons and tons of information and commercials. Saturated, we easily slip into overload and shut down for protection. Dumbed down, we become immune to shock TV and shock radio and normalize pathology. Another child killed a child? Whatever.

We are "whatever-ing" our lives away, and this is spiritual sloth. It keeps us uninvolved, isolated: don't disturb my little world. We need to be aware of this kind of sloth and move on. Writer Jonathan Kozol speaks of his own journey out of academic detachment and apathy toward belief:

> Well, I had a religious upbringing. I'm Jewish, and my mom and grandma were religious, but, as happens to many people who go on to places like Harvard College, that got washed out of me very quickly. At Harvard, you didn't talk about religion. Even if you believed in God, you didn't mention it, because people would make fun of you.
>
> I went on from Harvard to Oxford, where I had a Rhodes scholarship. And then after a few years I came back to the States, in 1964, to Boston, my hometown. I probably would have done something normal like go to medical school or law school if it hadn't been for the civil rights movement. In the summer of '64, you'll remember, those three young men were killed in Mississippi—two white, one black. One of them happened to be Jewish, from New York. And I identified with him.
>
> One day I just got on the subway. The end of the line was Harvard Square. I went to the other end, which was the ghetto of Boston, and signed up and became a teacher of little kids— black kids in a segregated school. And, in a sense, that was my formative decision. I didn't think of it that way. But, in a sense, that twenty-minute ride took me to a place from which I've never returned.

Reading the gospels and the lives of the saints will help dispel the "whatever" soul sickness. Prayer will keep you open to the Spirit. Dag Hammarskjöld, who was an author as well as a much-respected Secretary General of the United Nations, writes:

> I don't know who—or what—put the question. I don't know when it was put. I don't even remember answering. But at some moment I did answer yes to Someone—or Something—and from that hour I was certain that existence was meaningful and that, therefore, my life in self-surrender had a goal. From that moment I have known what it means "not to look back" and "to take no thought for the morrow."

Finally, intellectual sloth is apathy toward that which makes life worth living. It is a spiritual dryness, a deadness of the soul, intellectual laziness. This is at least partly due to the philosophy of relativism that dominates our educational system. A year or two ago, the *Chronicle of Higher Education* had several articles by professors alarmed at the attitude of students toward the Holocaust. The students agreed that Hitler was a nasty man but could not bring themselves to condemn him. After all, in his time and place, who is to say he was wrong? Everything is relative. One era's vices are another era's virtues, and vice versa. People construct their own morality. Whatever.

The result? As Jesuit professor Joseph Linehard says: "A generation of college students has been so anesthetized by relativism that they cannot say that Shakespeare was the greatest master of the English language for fear of offending someone who thinks Danielle Steel is. But if they can never say, 'You are wrong,' they can never say, 'I am right,' either. So we take no stands, bear no witness, flee evangelization, and dub heroism as pathological and useless, for nothing really matters anyway."

It's a good thing the signers of the Declaration of Independence didn't suffer from apathy. Have you ever wondered what happened to them?

> Five signers were captured by the British as traitors and tortured before they died. Twelve had their homes ransacked and

burned. Two lost their sons in the Revolutionary Army, another had two sons captured. Nine of the fifty-six fought and died from wounds or the hardships of the Revolutionary War.

What kind of men were they? Twenty-four were lawyers and jurists. Eleven were merchants, nine were farmers and large plantation owners, men of means, well educated. But they signed the Declaration of Independence knowing full well that the penalty would be death if they were captured. They signed and they pledged their lives, their fortunes, and their sacred honor. Carter Braxton of Virginia, a wealthy planter and trader, saw his ships swept from the seas by the British navy. He sold his home and properties to pay his debts and died in rags. Thomas McKeam was so hounded by the British that he was forced to move his family almost constantly. He served in the Congress without pay, and his family was kept in hiding. His possessions were taken from him, and poverty was his reward. Vandals or soldiers or both looted the properties of Ellery, Clymer, Hall, Walton, Gwinnett, Heyward, Rutledge and Middleton.

At the Battle of Yorktown, Thomas Nelson, Jr. noted that the British general Cornwallis had taken over the Nelson home for his headquarters. The owner quietly urged General George Washington to open fire, which was done. The home was destroyed, and Nelson died bankrupt. Francis Lewis had his home and properties destroyed. The enemy jailed his wife, and she died within a few months. John Hart was driven from his wife's bedside as she was dying. Their thirteen children fled for their lives. His fields and his grist mill were laid waste. For more than a year he lived in forests and caves, returning home after to find his wife dead, his children vanished. A few weeks later he died from exhaustion and a broken heart. Lewis Morris and Philip Livingston suffered similar fates.

Such were the stories and sacrifices of the American Revolution. These were not wild-eyed rabble-rousing ruffians. They were soft-spoken men of means and education. Standing tall, straight, and unwavering, they pledged: "For the support of this declaration, with a firm reliance on the protection of the

Divine Providence, we mutually pledge to each other, our lives, our fortunes, and our sacred honor."

Sloth was not part of the vocabulary of the signers of the Declaration of Independence.

If we want a sign of intellectual sloth in our lives, look at the newspapers and magazines we read and the TV shows we watch: all commercial enterprises, filled with celebrities and ways to consume. Do we read good Catholic magazines that challenge us and give us a gospel perspective, as well as values to live by and get excited over?

Sloth—with its spin-off, apathy—is one of the deadliest of sins evident in our lives today. Moral, spiritual, and intellectual sloth run rampant. As we have suggested before, a life of prayer and reflection, pious devotions and spiritual reading, can liberate us.

Anger

> Anger is a short madness.
> —Horace

Anger is indeed a short madness, although it can sometimes be a long one which blossoms into hatred. Johnny Lee Clary knows that. He was the Grand Dragon of the Ku Klux Klan in Oklahoma. He was once invited to speak on a Tulsa radio station along with his "opponent," the Reverend Wade Watts, a black minister and state president of the National Association for the Advancement of Colored People (NAACP). When the minister held out his hand for a handshake, no way was this Grand Dragon going to take it. Clary hated Watts.

Clary says his hatred was honed by his father, who taught him at the age of five to hurl racial slurs out the car window, and his uncle, who regaled him with stories about shooting black men. The only one not filled with hatred was his grandmother, who read to him from the Bible. When Johnny Lee went to Sunday School and came home singing, "Jesus loves the little children,/ All the children of the world;/ Red and yellow, black and white,/ They are precious in his sight," his father scolded him, forbade him to sing it, and removed him from Sunday School.

When Clary was eleven, he came home one day to see his father standing with a gun to his head and pull the trigger. What a horrendous sight for a child to witness. Johnny Lee was sent to California to live with his older sister and, as a lonely lad, he began to watch TV. One day he saw David Duke, the Grand Wizard of the Ku Klux Klan, on a talk show and was fascinated. He wanted to get in touch with the Klan, to belong to something. So he made contact, joined, and soon became Duke's bodyguard.

At the age of twenty, Johnny Lee Clary became a Grand Dragon. He was a tireless recruiter for the Klan and a fiery speaker; that was how he wound up on the radio station with the Reverend Watts. It was to be a debate. The minister said, "Hello, Mr. Clary. I'm Reverend Watts. Before we go in, I just want you to know that I love you and Jesus loves you." The debate went on but the Reverend's calm so rattled him that he stormed out. Clary tells the rest:

> I gathered my things and was heading through the lobby when the Reverend appeared. I would have gladly pushed him out of my way except that he was holding a baby in his arms. "Mr. Clary, this is my daughter, Tia," he said. "And I have one last question for you." He held out a little girl with shining dark eyes and skin, and one of the sweetest expressions I had ever seen. "You say you hate all black people, Mr. Clary. Just tell me—how can you hate this child?" Stunned, I turned and almost ran. I heard the Reverend call after me: "I'm going to love you and pray for you, Mr. Clary, whether you like it or not!"
> I didn't like it. Over the next ten years I had two burning goals. One was to climb the Klan's national ranks to the position of Imperial Wizard. The second was to make Reverend Wade Watts pay for what he had done. I would make him hate me.
> But as ferociously as the Oklahoma Klan continued its campaign, just as firmly Reverend Wade Watts worked for justice and equality. Klansmen barraged his family with threatening phone calls. His windows were broken; effigies were torched on his lawn. His church was burned to the ground. The thirteen Watts children—a number of whom were adopted—were threatened and had to be escorted to school by the highway

patrol. Once or twice I found myself thinking about that baby,
little Tia. I drove the thought away with hate. Still, nothing the
Klan did stopped the Reverend, nothing shut him up. When he
joined ranks with an Oklahoma senator to outlaw the telephone hot lines we used for recruiting, we called an emergency
meeting. Klan members crowded around me as I dialed the
Watts home.

"I want you to know we're coming to get you," I hissed when
the Reverend answered. "And this time we mean business...."

"Hello, Johnny Lee!" he said, as though hearing from a long-
lost relative. "You don't have to come for me, I'll meet you. How
about at a nice little restaurant I know out on Highway 270? I'm
buying."

"This isn't a joke, old man. We're coming over, and when
we're finished, you'll wish you'd never crossed us."

"This place has the best home cooking you ever tasted.
Apple pie that'll make you long for more. Fluffy mashed potatoes. Iced tea in mason jars...."

I slammed down the phone. "He wants to take us out to dinner," I said in disbelief. "Talked about apple pie and iced tea."

"The old man's gone crazy," someone said. "Let's forget
about him."

We left Reverend Wade Watts alone after that. I turned my
energies to solidifying my position in my "family," and in 1981
was appointed Imperial Wizard. I had just gone through a
divorce and lost custody of my baby daughter, and in despera-
tion I focused on a new goal. I wanted to unify all hate groups—
from skinheads to neo-Nazis—under the umbrella of the Klan.
I arranged a national meeting where those groups would meet
and, I hoped, unite in strength.

This was to be the culmination of my efforts. But on the day
of the gathering, the Klan, skinheads, and neo-Nazis all started
fighting, accusing one another of stealing their members and
mailing lists. By the time I arrived, my unity meeting was in
shambles. As I looked out over the stormy proceedings, I realized that these groups wanted to "purify" the world and have it

all be like them—but they hated one another. Did I really want
to live in a world of people like that? Were those the people I
wanted to be my family? A family whose hate extended to all
colors, backgrounds, and ages? Even babies like Reverend
Wade Watts's little daughter Tia? "How can you hate this child?"
he had asked. How far I had come from the days when I sang
those words: "Jesus loves the little children,/ All the children of
the world;/ Red and yellow, black and white,/ They are precious in his sight...."

Suddenly I was repulsed by the poison that swirled around
me. I felt sick to my stomach. I turned in disgust and walked out
the door. Eventually I told the other Klan officials I was giving
up my position and leaving the group forever.

My life was a wreck. As the weeks passed, filled by a sense of
shame and worthlessness, I fell into deep depression—and the
stultifying numbness of alcohol. Then came the terrible day I
found myself in my shabby apartment raising a loaded gun to
my head. "Daddy, I'm following in your footsteps," I thought.
"There's no other way to go...." I was about to pull the trigger
when I saw sunlight break through the partially closed blinds
and onto a Bible that lay gathering dust on my bookshelf, an
old Bible like the one Reverend Wade Watts carried that day at
the radio station. A Bible like the one I had seen my grandmother read so many times. Maybe there is another way. I put
down the gun and picked up the Bible. It fell open to Luke 15,
the parable of the prodigal son. I read the story three times,
then fell on my knees and wept.

I quietly joined a church—whose congregation was multira-
cial—and kept a low profile, studying the Scripture, getting
grounded in God's Word. Two years passed. And finally, in
1991, I made a phone call I had to make. "Reverend Watts?" I
asked when he picked up. He knew my voice right away. "Hello,
Johnny Lee," he said warmly. "Reverend Watts, I...I want you to
know that I resigned from the KKK two years ago. I gave my
heart to Jesus and I'm a member of an interracial church."
"Praise the Lord!" he shouted. "I've never stopped praying for

you! Would you do me the honor of speaking at my church?" How could he forgive me? How could he have cared about me all those years?

When I stepped to the podium at his church and looked out over the congregation of mostly black faces, I told my story simply, not hiding from the past or sugarcoating the depth and bitter consciousness of my involvement. Then I told them how God had changed all the hate in my heart to love. There was silence when I finished. A teenage girl got to her feet and ran down the aisle toward me, arms open. I started to move in front of the altar, to pray with her. As I passed the Reverend, I realized he was weeping. "Don't you know who that is, Johnny Lee?" he asked quietly. "That's Tia. That's my baby." Yes, what I needed was a real family. And there had been one waiting to open its arms to me all along.

Another poisonous blossom of anger is revenge, a disturbingly popular vice in our society. "Don't get mad, get even" is the mantra. Jesus dealt with revenge in Luke's gospel (9:51–56), when he and his disciples were on their way to Jerusalem. The journey involved going through enemy Samaritan territory to get there, but Jesus and the disciples were not allowed passage. In contemporary slang, they were "dissed," given disrespect. Revenge was called for, and James and John had the answer: "Lord, would you have us call down fire from heaven to destroy them?" The gospel says: "But he turned and rebuked them. Then they went on to another village," another route.

It is lamentable that national anger seems to be a tradition in many parts of the world: the animosity between Arabs and Jews, the Irish and the English, Turks and Greeks, blacks and whites, their-side/our-side-of-the-tracks. Jesus' teaching is clear on this point: anger, revenge, and violence are not the way to go. "Put your sword back into its place; for all who take the sword will perish by the sword" (Mt 26:52), Jesus tells Peter at Gethsemane. Let me bring this point to our time. A woman who recalls her childhood in Germany during the war, at a time when that country was being mercilessly bombed by American and British pilots, tells a true story:

One day, not long before the end of the war, I saw two airmen parachuting out of an enemy plane that had been shot down. Like many others who had seen the parachutists falling through the afternoon sky, I went to the city's central square to wait for the police to arrive with the prisoners of war. Eventually two policemen arrived with two British prisoners in tow. They would wait there in the city square for a car that would take the British airmen to a prison in a neighboring city where prisoners of war were kept. When the crowd saw the prisoners, there were angry shouts of "Kill them! Kill them!" No doubt the crowd was thinking of the heavy bombings their city had suffered at the hands of the British and their allies. Nor did the crowd lack the means to carry out their intent. Many of the people had been gardening when they saw the enemy fall from the sky and had brought their pitchforks, shovels, and other gardening implements with them.

I looked at the faces of the British prisoners. They were very young, maybe nineteen or twenty years old. I could see that they were extremely frightened, and that the two policemen, whose duty it was to protect the prisoners of war, were no match for the angry crowd with its pitchforks and shovels. Something had to be done: but what?

Then, in horror, I saw my fourteen-year-old brother run and place himself between the prisoners and the crowd, turning to face the crowd and shouting for them to stop. Not wanting to hurt him—the townsfolk all knew him—the crowd held back for a moment, long enough for my brother to say: "Look at these prisoners. They are young! They are no different from your own sons. They are only doing what your own sons are doing—fighting for their country. If your sons were shot down in a foreign country and became prisoners of war, you wouldn't want the people there to kill your sons. So please don't hurt them."

The townspeople listened in amazement, and then shame. Finally, a woman said, "It took a young lad to tell us what is right and what is wrong." The crowd began to disperse. I will never forget the look of tremendous relief and gratitude on the faces of the young British airmen. I hope they have had long, happy lives, and that they haven't forgotten the young boy, my brother, who saved them.

This crowd was acting just like the disciples in the gospel: they were ready not only to call down God's wrath on these pilots, but to take matters into their own hands right then and there. It took a teenage boy to set them straight, a boy who asked them for an act of love and kindness—not revenge.

Another blossom on the tree of anger is quarreling or dissension. People's egos get in the way and everyone in the family, the group, the parish, suffers. Read on:

Once upon a time, a flock of quail lived near a marsh. Every day they would fly to the nearby fields to feed. But the only problem was a Bird Hunter who lived nearby; of late, he had snared many quail in his net and taken them to market to be sold. He had grown so successful in catching them because he had learned to imitate perfectly the call of the leader. The Bird Hunter gave the call, and the quail, thinking it was the leader, flew to his area where he tossed his net over them and captured them.

One day the leader called all the quail together for a conference. He said, "We are being decimated! Soon none of us will be left. The Bird Hunter is catching us all. But I have found out how he does it. He learned my call and deceives you. I have a plan. The next time you hear what you think is my call and fly to the area, and the Bird Hunter throws his net on top of you, here is what you are to do: all together, stick your heads through the openings in the net, and in one motion fly up with the net and land on the thornbush. The net will stick there, you can extricate yourselves, and the Bird Hunter will have to spend all day freeing his net."

And this is what they did. The Bird Hunter came with his imitation call, and the quail came. When the net was thrown over them, as one body they stuck their heads through the openings, and flew away to the thornbush. They left a frustrated Hunter trying all day to get his net loose. This went on for some time until the Hunter's wife bitterly complained that her husband was bringing home no quail to bring to market. They were becoming poor. The Bird Hunter listened to his wife, told her of the actions of the quail, and with his hand on his chin, added, "But be patient, dear wife. Just wait till they quarrel. Then we shall catch them again."

Well, it so happened that one day when the Bird Hunter made his call, all the quail rose up and flew to the area where he was. But as they were landing, one quail accidentally brushed against another. "Will you watch where you're going, you clumsy ox!" cried the one quail.

The other said hastily, "Oh, I'm sorry. I really am. I didn't mean to do it. It was an accident."

"An accident, was it?" cried the first quail. "If you'd watch where you're going instead of peering all about, you wouldn't be so clumsy."

"Well," said the second quail, "I don't know why you take that attitude. I said I was sorry, and if you can't accept that...." And they got to quarreling. Soon the others, perceiving the argument, gathered around and took sides, one for the first quail and the other for the second.

Meanwhile, the Bird Hunter had his net ready and threw it over the birds. They began to cry to one another, "Come, let us stop arguing and hurry or else we'll be caught. Let's fly over that way!" But the other quail responded, "No, we're always flying over that way. We're always doing what you people want. Come, let us fly this way!" And while they were arguing which way to go, the Bird Hunter, with a smile on his face, gathered them up in the net, brought them to market, and that day made a fine penny.

Summing up

So there you have it: pride, envy, greed, sloth, and anger, five of the seven capital sins. In this chapter, our reflections, for the most part, have consisted of light stories with heavy messages. So let's end our reflection with a teaching to children. How would you tell them about the seven capital sins? You could do no better than to turn to British author Joan Windham's delightful treatment. Here it is:

Once upon a time there was a forest in Rumania (it is still there for all I know). Anyway, at the time that I am talking about there lived in the forest a man called Alexander, whom people sometimes called Alex for short. Alexander was a Charcoal Burner. He used to collect little twigs and thin branches from the trees in the forest, and he made little fires and burned the sticks very slowly so that they turned into black sticks called Charcoal. (If he was in too much of a hurry they turned into White Ashes instead and he would have to begin all over again.) People use Charcoal for quite a lot of things. They draw with it, and make fires with it, and use it for medicine, and make shoe polish with it. So you can see what a useful job Alexander had.

Alexander looked after his little fires by himself all day and he learned to be very patient because if he was impatient his Charcoal would turn into Ashes. In a quiet job like that the birds and the animals get used to the person who is working, and take no notice. Alexander saw baby squirrels playing, and mother foxes taking their cubs to roll in the sun, and all kinds of things that we never see. It made him think how quiet and patient God must be. "Here is this enormous forest," he thought to himself, "and it is full of living things: plants and animals and birds and insects. They all lead busy lives; not one of them is lazy. And yet very few people even know that they are here! There must be hundreds of them that are too shy even for me to see. And yet God knows all about them and what they do all day. He never frightens them however near he is because he is so still."

While Alexander was quietly living in the forest and burning his Charcoal and thinking about God and watching the birds and animals, there were great Goings On in the town where he sold his Charcoal. And this is what was happening. At first there had been very few Christians in the town, but as time went on there were more and more. At last the priest said that they really ought to have a Bishop of their own instead of belonging to a Bishop called Gregory who lived a very long way off and scarcely ever had time to come and see them. So it was decided that Bishop Gregory should come, and that everybody should say which priest they wanted to be the new Bishop. Well, some wanted This priest and some wanted That priest and some didn't know whom they wanted but they didn't want either of Those. At last they collected seven priests who wanted to be the Bishop, and they wrote and told Gregory that they wanted him to come and choose.

The Town Hall was all ready with a Throne at the end of it for Bishop Gregory and chairs and seats for all the people. When everyone was settled, the First man who wanted to be the Bishop came in. He was tall and thin with a big nose and a very Grand expression. He looked at the crowds of people as if they were too Common for Words. The people who wanted him to be the Bishop clapped and cheered as he went and stood in front of Gregory. "Do you think that you would be a good Bishop?" asked Gregory. "I am sure I would," said the man. "I think that you are too Proud," said Gregory. "Next, please!"

The Second man had silk clothes and a jeweled crucifix, and he had a rosary made of real rubies in his hand. "Would you keep all those lovely things for yourself, if you were the Bishop?" asked Gregory. "Of course I would. They are my own property," said the man, and he held them a little tighter. "You are too Covetous, I think," said Gregory. (Covetous means selfish and miserly.) "Next, please!" said Gregory.

The Third man had the most brightly colored clothes and a smiling face and beautiful curly hair. He winked at all the people, and the ladies clapped their hands because he was so handsome. "Do you want people to go on thinking that you are handsome and clever when you are the Bishop?" asked Gregory. "But of course!" said the man, and he looked quickly at the people to see if they were listening. "Even a Bishop must have his bit of fun." "I think that you are too fond of Pretty

Ladies," said Gregory. "Next, please!"

The Fourth man had black hair and a frowning face. He stared at the people angrily and then went and stood in front of Gregory. The people who wanted him clapped for him, but he shook his head at them and they stopped. "If you were the bishop, would you be Strict with the people and punish them severely if they broke the rules?" asked Gregory. "I would," said the man. "They are a lazy, sinful lot, but I'd not put up with any of their nonsense!" And he glared at Gregory. "You get Angry too easily," said Gregory. "Next, please!"

The Fifth man was very fat indeed, but he looked kindly at the people, and he waved his hand at the ones who wanted him. As he stood in front of Gregory, he pulled a buttered bun out of his pocket and began to eat it. "Excuse me!" he said. "Couldn't you have waited until after the Choosing to eat your bun?" asked Gregory. "Not me!" said the man, "I wouldn't miss my tea for anyone on earth. It keeps a man good tempered to be fat." "I think that you are too Greedy," said Gregory. "Next, please!"

The Sixth man was thin and mean-looking; he did not look happy. He stared at all the priests who had already seen Gregory. (They were standing at the back of the Throne, waiting to see who would be Chosen.) "Well," said Gregory, "what is the matter? Aren't you happy? Don't you want to be Bishop after all?" "No good my wanting it," said the man. "I've no good looks like that man over there, or riches like that one, or a nice house like that one, or a kind family like that one. I never get the things that Other People have." "You are too Envious to be happy," said Gregory. (Envious means being so jealous of other people's things that you haven't time to see what nice things you have yourself.) "Next, please!" said Gregory. But no one came.

"Next, please!" said Gregory, looking around. "I thought you said that there were seven people who wanted to be Bishop," he whispered to the Mayor who was standing beside him. "I've only, seen six." "NEXT, PLEASE!!" shouted the Mayor, and all the people laughed. Then the door banged, and in came an untidy man with ruffled hair and shoes undone. He was yawning and rubbing his eyes. "Sorry, my Lord," he said to Gregory. "As I was the last one, I thought that I'd have a nap while I was waiting, and I didn't hear you call." "Do you always have naps when you can?" asked Gregory. "Always, my Lord," said the man solemnly. "A man can't have too much sleep, I always say." "I think that you are too Lazy," said Gregory.

All the people rustled and coughed and sat up and shuffled their feet. They stared at Gregory and waited for him to say which of the seven priests would be the Bishop. "Well," said Gregory, and he looked around at all the people, "I am sorry, but I don't think that any of them would do for a Bishop."

The people started talking among themselves, then someone shouted: "But we must have one of them! There isn't anyone else!" "No," said Gregory. "They may not be bad as ordinary people go, but they would not be good as Bishops. You couldn't have a Bishop who was Proud or Greedy or Lazy or any of the other Seven Deadly Sins, now could you?" "You're too Choosy," said the people. "You can't have a Perfect man." "No," said Gregory, "but he ought to try to be Perfect, and these men don't."

All the people started arguing again, and in the noise Gregory said to God: "Please, God, if you really want a Bishop here, will you choose one for yourself? It is very difficult for me with all these seven, and the people are getting so cross." Just then someone shouted: "You'd better have Alexander the Charcoal Burner if you can't think of anyone better!"

All the people laughed because they couldn't imagine having sooty, raggy Alexander for a Bishop! But Gregory knew that this was God's answer to his prayer, so he held up his hand for the people to stop laughing, and said: "Who is this Alexander?" "I was only joking," said the man who had shouted. "He is a Charcoal Burner and he lives in the forest." "Will somebody please go and get him?" said Gregory. The people all stared. What was Gregory thinking? Did he really mean to see if Alexander would do? Yes, he did.

So Alexander was brought along. First he washed the black marks off his face and hands, then he went to Bishop Gregory and knelt and kissed his ring. Then he stood up and waited to see why the Bishop had sent for him. "Alexander," said Gregory, "do you think that you would be a good Bishop?"

"Me, my Lord?" said Alexander. "No, I have no learning. I don't know anything at all."

"Would you like a Rosary made of Rubies?"

"Why no, thank you, my Lord," said Alexander. "I have a very nice wooden one; it will last me a lifetime."

"Do you like Parties and Pretty Ladies?" "I don't know any," said Alexander. "I've never been asked to a Party myself, but a bit of fun now and then is good for everybody." He wondered why Gregory was asking him all these questions in front of the townspeople.

"Do you think that the Townspeople are a lazy, sinful lot?" asked Gregory. "Oh no, my Lord, please don't think that! There's good in everyone if you look for it." Alexander had quite forgotten how mean the people were in paying for their Charcoal.

"Have you had your Tea yet?" asked Gregory. "I don't have it as a rule," said Alexander, "only when it is raining and I can't burn my charcoal. I eat when I am hungry, and that does me nicely." "Are you happy?" asked Gregory. "Have you everything that you want?" "I'm very happy, my Lord," said Alexander. "I love my work, I have enough to eat, I have my own little house, and God is good to me."

"Would you change your work for something quite different?" asked Gregory.

"I would if God wished it," said Alexander.

Gregory stood up. He walked down the steps of his throne and put his arm round Alexander's shoulders. "Here is your new Bishop," he said to the people. At first they all sat with their mouths open. Surely it could not be true! Surely the Bishop was having a joke with them! Then, as they began to think, they saw that Alexander was just the opposite of all the other seven, and they looked at Alexander. And looking at him they loved him.

So Alexander the Charcoal Burner became a Bishop, and he was one for years and years.

Questions for reflection

1. Pride: can I claim my wolf and stop looking down on Perugia, on others? Or, as Jesus put it, can I see first the beam in my own eye before I spot the speck in another's?

2. Envy: of what or whom am I envious? Not just feeling envy; that's natural. But do I focus on the other to the detriment of my own gifts? Does envy constrict my life?

3. Greed: what passion colors the way I see the world, other people? How does greed affect my relationships? How do I use greed to manipulate my neighbor? How does seeing only gold make me look past people?

4. Sloth: what behavior in my life is self-destructive, no matter how many practical "excuses" I may have? What are the tired old reasons I keep giving as to why I can't change? Is spiritual apathy a part of my life? Am I passionate about God and God's justice? Do I study my faith? Can I justify it, defend it, understand it?

5. Anger: what makes me angry? Is my anger directed toward the injustices, prejudices, and cruelty of the world? Or is my anger petty and selfish, emanating from my own wants and desires?

THIRTEEN

DOROTHY

Priorities

Dorothy clicks the heels of the magic red shoes and closes her eyes. She opens them to wake up in her bed surrounded by Auntie Em and Uncle Henry, who are soon joined by Professor Marvel at the window and the three farmhands. She tries to explain her adventures in the land of Oz but they all just smile and chalk it up to a bump on the head she received during the storm. Dorothy resigns herself to their disbelief and seizes on the wisdom that sustains her. "This is my room and you are all here…I love you all. Oh, Auntie Em, there's no place like home!"

When all is said and done, she's found What Really Matters, and that's the theme of this reflection. We are asked to take time to ponder the essential question, what really matters, and its correlative, what really doesn't. What is important and what is primary—or should be—in our human lives, our spiritual lives? Remember Ben Stein's words from a previous chapter? Modern folks might frame their reply in his words: "No corporate title can replace the times when your son leans his head on your chest and falls asleep. No limousine or private jet makes up for being there when your son is growing from a child into a young man. Time spent with your child isn't a distraction from the main event. It is the main event."

But for some, getting their "main events" straightened out is a challenge. They struggle with the biblical Martha-Mary story:

"Martha, Martha, you are worried and distracted by many things; there is need of only one thing. Mary has chosen the better part, which will not be taken away from her" (Lk 10:41–42). Mary has chosen what really matters.

In Shakespeare's play *Henry VIII*, as the worldly Cardinal Wolsey lies dying, he speaks to his aide, Cromwell, and laments:

"Cromwell," he said, "I did not think to shed a tear
In all my miseries, but thou hast forced me,
Out of honest truth, to play the woman.
Let's dry our eyes and thus far hear me, Cromwell,
And when I am forgotten, as I shall be,
And sleep in dull, cold marble where no mention
Of me must more be heard of, say I taught thee.
Say 'Wolsey, that once trod the ways of glory

And sounded all the depths and shoals of honor,
Found thee a way out of his reck to rise in,
A sure and safe one, 'though thy master missed it....'

There take an inventory of all that I have,
To the last penny, 'tis the king's. My robe
And my integrity to heaven is all
I dare now call my own. O, Cromwell, Cromwell,
Had I but served my God with half the zeal
I serve my king, He would not, in mine age,
Have left me naked to mine enemies."

The worldly cardinal: he, above all people, missed what really mattered.

The wonderful film *The Dead Poet's Society*, tells the story of a remarkable teacher's influence on his students in a prestigious boys' boarding school. The teacher, Mr. Keating, brilliantly played by Robin Williams, invites the boys to jump up and stand on his desk as he has done in his teaching, so they can see things from a different perspective, a wider view, and in so doing, discover what really matters.

This reflection is that kind of invitation. It asks you to stand up on the desk, above the clutter and above the noise, to see a different horizon—then seize it. Mr. Keating constantly shouted out to his students, "*Carpe diem!*" Seize the day! Seize the truth of what really matters. So, through the medium of the stories that follow, I will attempt to do what Mr. Keating did with his students: to stop and pause and insist that you ask within your hearts: "what really matters?" A lot of things matter, but what really matters in your pursuit of wholeness and holiness on your life's journey?

Considering the question

Years ago, when I was an associate at St. Benedict's parish, I spent a lot of time in the school with the children. Two memories from that time spring to mind. The first is irrelevant to this reflection, but it sticks with me.

One day, in the school corridor, I met a little first-grade boy who seemed fascinated with my Roman collar, the little white plastic strip that fits into a clerical shirt. He stopped and pointed at the collar and asked, "Do you have a boo-boo?" "No," I laughed, "that's not a band-aid. It's a special collar that tells everyone I'm a priest." I removed it and said, "Do you want to look at it?" The boy nodded yes. As I handed it to him, I pointed to the raised letters on the inside of the collar, which spelled out the name of the company that made the collar. Knowing that he was not reading yet, I asked, "Do you know what this says?" Without skipping a beat, he replied, "Yes." Calling his bluff, I said, "All right, what does it say?" Looking at the letters as if he could read them, he replied, "Kills fleas and ticks for six months!"

Beyond that fun one, it's the other memory I'm after. I was going around visiting all the classrooms at report card time. (That was something the priest often did, as you might recollect if you went to parochial school.) For those who got a good report card, it was a positive joy. They bounced right up to the priest knowing they were winners who were going to get a lot of praise when they got home. And then there were those who had less to cheer about. They would come up with kind of a hangdog look and almost surreptitiously grab the report card and slink back to their seats. And you can imagine what the reactions at home would be.

Report cards are important; there's no question about that. They are a kind of measurement for the teacher and the student, and a really great help for the parents. But I remember one particular day, when I went home after handing out the report cards and picked up the morning paper. On the front page was a story about a grammar school in the Midwest which had been blown away during a storm. According to the account, the roof had fallen in on some of the students and killed them. The paper listed their ages and names: seven, eight, nine year olds. How little of life had they seen, these dead children? I thought: did they, too, get their report cards that day? Perhaps. Again, report cards are an important measurement of learning and progress. But reading those names and looking at the photos of those dead children, I had to ask myself: what really matters? What is really important?

Unfortunately, it usually takes a tragedy to put things in perspective. We watch, for example, people devastated by the many floods and tornados and mudslides not only in this country, but throughout the world. A recent television documentary featured several people who had experienced some trauma or calamity which resulted in severe losses. One woman had looked on helplessly as her home was swallowed up by a mudslide and tumbled down the cliff into the bay below. An elderly couple had survived a tornado which ripped the roof off their home and flung all its contents into the air. Another person had returned from a trip to find his home and business in ashes. Yet another told of losing all he owned in a faulty investment. When asked how they had coped with their losses and what they had learned, every person interviewed shared a similar insight. "Yes, we've lost everything," as one responded, "but that's precisely the point: we lost things. What really matters is that we are alive!"

Some years ago I was invited to give a conference for clergy in another diocese. This type of conference has proliferated in recent years because priests are under increased stress as our numbers decrease and the burdens increase. And so many dioceses and religious orders are trying to help priests understand what their job is, as well as affirm them, raise morale, build camaraderie, and help them weather the storm. The day after I had participated in this particular conference, the news came out about the deaths of the six Jesuits, their housekeeper, and her daughter in El Salvador. These priests were murdered for nothing more than preaching the news of peace and justice to an oppressed people. When I heard this story I was caught up short: raising the morale of our American priests is important, but what really matters?

Listen to this woman's story:

They huddled inside the storm door, two children in ragged, outgrown coats. "Any old papers, lady?" I was busy. I wanted to say no—until I looked down at their feet. Thin little sandals, sopped with sleet. "Come in and I'll make you a cup of hot cocoa." There was no conversation. Their soggy sandals left marks upon the hearthstone. I served them cocoa and toast with jam to fortify against the chill outside. Then I went back to the kitchen and started again on my household budget....The silence in the front room struck through to me. I looked in.

The girl held the empty cup in her hands, looking at it. The boy asked in a flat voice, "Lady...are you rich?" "Am I rich? Mercy, no!" I looked at my shabby slipcovers. The girl put her cup back in its saucer—carefully. "Your cups match your saucers." Her voice was old, with a hunger that was not of the stomach. They left then, holding their bundles of papers against the wind. They hadn't said thank you. They didn't need to. They had done more than that.

Plain blue pottery cups and saucers. But they matched. I tested the potatoes and stirred the gravy. Potatoes and brown gravy, a roof over our heads, my man with a good steady job—these things matched, too. I moved the chairs back from the fire and tidied the living room. The muddy prints of small sandals were still wet upon my hearth. I let them be. I want them there in case I ever forget again how very rich I am. In case I ever forget what really matters.

Once, a missionary friend of mine told me of his ordeal in China:

At one time, myself and a family—a mother and father and two children—were living in the same quarters, all under house arrest. We had been under house arrest for several years and we were living somewhat comfortably. Well, one day a soldier came and told the family: "You can all return to America, but you may take only two hundred pounds of belongings with you, no more, no less."

Well, as I said, we had all been there for years. Two hundred pounds. So the family got out a scale, and then the arguments started between the husband and the wife and the two children: "I must have this vase." " I must take this typewriter; it's almost brand new." "I must have these books." "I must take this...I must take that." And so they weighed everything, took it off, weighed it, put it back. Back and forth, back and forth, until finally they got it just precisely on the dot: two hundred pounds.

The soldier came in the next day and said, "Ready to go?" The parents said, "Yes." He said, "Did you weigh everything?" They said, "Yes." "Did you weigh your kids?" "No, we didn't." "Weigh the kids," he said. And in a moment, off went the typewriter, off went the vase, off went the books, into the trash. All the things that they thought they could not do without—into the trash.

What really matters? Here's a provocative little fable about a man and his garden and a gift from the flower lady:

One evening a workman was wearily plodding his way home, when he stopped to rest by the side of the road. A woman came by the place, hauling a cart filled with flowers. The smell of her blossoms so perfumed the air with sweetness that just the smell of them seemed to take away the weariness from his bones and lighten his spirit. He had never experienced such a wonder from the many blooms of his own garden. "How much must I pay or what must I do to have some of your wonderful flowers?" he asked the woman. "Good sir," she said, "take what you wish." "What return must I make for them?" he questioned. "Your gratitude is enough," she said.

So the man filled his arms with blossoms and hastened joyfully home. His wife and children rejoiced with him over the remarkable flowers for they, too, discovered that the sight of them delighted the eye, and the smell of them refreshed the soul. So as not to lose his treasure when the blossoms died, the man planted them in a small plot of land behind his house.

Sunlight and water kept the amazing flowers alive, still performing their marvelous magic. When his children came to play in the yard, the man cautioned them against carelessness and wild play lest they trample the flowers and damage them. But the flowers remained hardy and strong so long as there was enough sun and moisture to nourish them. Nowhere else could the man and his wife and children find such remarkable solace from weariness, such comfort in sadness, such spiritual nourishment as these remarkable flowers provided. Here was a treasure beyond value.

As the family grew and more children came to play in the garden, the man became even more concerned over his remarkable flowers. He must protect them. He built a high wall around them. In time, because of numerous children, he would allow them entrance to the small sanctuary only sparingly and with utmost care. Unfortunately, this began to cause consternation among the family members. If the children caused their father stress or anguish, he would refuse them access to the flowers. Eventually he set up rules as to who may enter the sanctuary, how they must enter and what they must do while they were there. For his part, he continued to see that his treasure received enough sunlight and water so that the flowers could continue to perform their wondrous magic.

As grandchildren began to appear, the man felt even greater need to safeguard his treasure. Access to the flowers must be open to all members of his family, but not without certain precautions. Requirements must be met and standards upheld. Offices were established to judge worthiness and to determine accessibility. It was even necessary to have lawyers to defend, judges to weigh, guards to safeguard, caretakers to upkeep, and so on and so on. The man's family, however, saw less and less of the flowers and experienced less and less of their magical powers. In the meantime, many of them went out in search of the flower lady. Well, she was still out there, giving away her amazing flowers.

Sounds like so much of our experience, doesn't it? An educational system awash in vested interests and regulations that leave little time or money for the children themselves. A medical profession strangled by insurance paperwork and bureaucratic demands that leave little time or care for the patient. The friendship that moved from spontaneity to "if you invite me then I feel obliged to invite you." The marriage that is all rights and no obligations. The Church that suffocates the Spirit with overbearing authority, guilt, and rules. What really matters, of course, is the free gift of the flower lady— God. But what have we done to our gift? We have boxed it in with rules and regulations, permissions and procedures. We have lost what really matters.

Well, you get the drift. This hits home for all of us. We have lost sight of what is important, the basics. You know the symptoms: the front room whose furniture you cannot sit on lest you soil it; the carpet you can't walk on; the Lenox dishes you're saving for the pope's visit. We see it in the agonizing that goes on all the time with career parents who struggle to balance out who or what comes first.

The famed baseball player of yesteryear, Harmon Killebrew, tells a story of his childhood. Almost every day his father would take him and his brother out to the front lawn to practice baseball. He tells of his mother standing on the porch shouting to her husband that all this base running was ruining the lawn. He remembers his father's reply: "Martha, we're not raising grass here. We're raising boys!" What really matters?

Basic questions

One of the reasons we go away on retreat or observe special practices during Lent is to address the fact that we have let the extraneous become central, the peripheral become important, the trivial become suffocating, and the accidental become the essential. Our pursuit of material things has put a distance between us and those we love. We tend to let go of the things that really matter, and often it is not until it's too late—when health fails us or when death intrudes—that we suddenly make our Shakespearean lament: "O Cromwell, Cromwell, had I but served my God with half the zeal I serve my king...."

I have talked to widows, who, when their husbands were living, good-naturedly but quite sincerely would complain about their husbands' snoring. Now they say, "How I wish he were here to disturb me with that snoring!" as they achingly reach over to hug an empty space. What really matters? "If only I had reconciled with my children, my neighbor, my friend, before I had this heart attack. Even if they would not reconcile with me, I could have made the gesture and said, 'You are forgiven,' even though they may have rejected me. Now it's too late; they're gone, or I'm going. Was it worth all those years of rancor, all those years of venom, all those years of negative thinking?"

What really matters? Look at the stereotype of the businessman on his deathbed—yet I have seen this happen often enough in real life—regretting the time away from his family, making money, admitting at last the emptiness of his rationale. Listen to the mothers and fathers who say, "Well, I did this so that I could buy them all the things they needed," while knowing in their hearts that their children wanted them more than anything in this world. And now it's too late; the children are grown. What really matters?

Let me give you an example of what really matters by relaying this homily I gave shortly after the death of Frank Sinatra, Ol' Blue Eyes:

On May 14, 1998, as the whole world knows, Ol' Blue Eyes, the Chairman of the Board, the leader of the Rat Pack, Francis Albert Sinatra, died. For fifty years he was a star. No one could wrap himself around a song like Sinatra, the master of intimate popular singing. He was, as Frank Rich of the *New York Times* wrote, "one of the greatest artists of any kind this country has produced." Just listen to his 1955 masterpiece, "In the Wee Small Hours," and you'll know why. But as Frank Rich continues: "In death, though, it's abundantly clear that Sinatra creates a national problem for American sensibilities...[for] as a human being, he not infrequently resembled a thug."

We all know what happened in Sinatra's life. He went from being the skinny singer in the bow tie to the hard-drinking sophis-

ticate who personified the new modern mood which was, according to critic Stephen Holden, "the golden age of bad behavior
without consequences." He hung around with mobsters from
Lucky Luciano to Sam Giancana, and bedded and abused women
by the score. He had those he disliked beat up or he did it himself. He was vindictive and insulting, calling Barbara Walters "the
ugliest broad on television," and getting one of his critics, the
famed musicologist Jonathan Schwartz, fired from his job.

Committing public adultery with Ava Gardner while married
to his first wife, Nancy, then marrying Ava as well as two more
women after her, Francis Albert Sinatra can hardly be called an
exemplary Catholic—even though his first marriage was
annulled, his second and third marriages were declared invalid,
and his fourth marriage was validated in a private ceremony at
St. Patrick's Cathedral in 1979. Yes, he was a Catholic, for he
met the sole minimal requirement for that position: he was baptized in the same Church as the pope. When he died, people
came from all over to view his body, including the Catholic
Cardinal Archbishop of Los Angeles. And he was given a
Catholic burial following a Catholic Mass.

Some sneer at this. They say, "Money talks." How can they—
"they" meaning the Cardinal, the Church as a whole—give a
Catholic Mass to an obvious public sinner, who was in his lifetime and in his conduct no more "Catholic" than the man in
the moon? Let it turn out, for example, that Sinatra leaves the
archdiocese a couple of million dollars (although I doubt it),
and the sneering will broaden.

These cynics have a point. And here is where we must rise
above the knee-jerk reactions and tabloid thinking, and pause as
a Catholic community to ask, "Why?" Listen now, for your own
personal spiritual benefit, to two reasons why Francis Albert
Sinatra was given a Catholic burial—and should have been.

The first reason can be found in the parish policy from our
own parish manual. It reads: "With few extraordinary exceptions, everyone shall receive a Christian burial. No one, no matter how poor or indifferent a Catholic, no matter how evil or

how a person died, whether naturally or by his own hand or another's, will be denied a Christian burial. The gospel imperative is that when a person is dead, all is over and the only final obligation the Christian community has in charity is to pray for the deceased and to demonstrate by its liturgy that wideness and kindness which Christ himself showed. For a Christian community to deny its ritual of prayer and worship to even a public sinner is not to imitate our Master, who prayed for those who crucified him."

What this policy is saying is that the focus is never on the deceased—whether saint or sinner—but on the faith community, which takes to heart these words of Jesus: "You have heard that it was said, 'You shall love your neighbor and hate your enemy.' But I say to you, Love your enemies and pray for those who persecute you, so that you may be children of your Father in heaven; for he makes his sun rise on the evil and on the good, and sends rain on the righteous and on the unrighteous. For if you love those who love you, what reward do you have? Do not even the tax collectors do the same? And if you greet only your brothers and sisters, what more are you doing than others? Do not even the Gentiles do the same? Be perfect, therefore, as your heavenly Father is perfect" (Mt 5:43–48; cf. Lk 6:27).

"Love your enemies and pray for those who persecute you." Frank Sinatra—as well as other people, both known and unknown, who are Catholic yet live apart from the values of their faith—are "enemies" in that they do not practice or uphold or exemplify Catholic life. In fact, they embarrass and shame us; they have persecuted us by their lifestyles and scandals. There's no denying that. But remember this: they are not the point. We are. Under the imperative imposed by Jesus in the words we just heard, we are to pray for those who persecute us. Therefore, giving Christian burial and a Mass to the unworthy and scandalous says nothing about them but everything about us and our obedience to Christ's words. Giving Christian burial to the unworthy does not endorse their life. It endorses ours.

Do you see what is at stake here? Oh, I know that in this imperfect world money and celebrity talk and both the famous and infamous get what they want, even in death. But, once more, the point is this: how seriously do we want to be disciples, even to practicing the hard sayings of Jesus?

So, how come Frank Sinatra got a Catholic burial and Mass? Is it because money and fame talk loudly? As I said, some will say that. They always do. But now you know better. Sinatra got a Catholic burial and Mass because, as much as we might like to, we will not "hate the enemy." We will not love only those who love us; we will not greet only our brothers and sisters in the practice of the faith; but we will try hard to love our enemies and, in our public liturgy, pray for those of our own who have persecuted us. We refuse to let them determine who we are.

The Catholic burial and Mass, you see, lets Jesus determine who we are, that is, his followers who show public love to the "enemy" and who go beyond the pagan rejection of them. The Catholic burial Mass for the scandalous is one way the faith community lives out the gospel. It has, I repeat, nothing to do with the scandalous or their status as public sinners. It has everything to do with us and our status as public disciples.

There is, as I said before, a second reason for giving a Catholic burial to those who might be deemed unworthy. And this is that we dare not confine the Spirit or define the limits of what the Spirit can do—or give any kind of public notice that we do. We dare not pronounce on the compassion and grace and the action of God. We are in no position to make a final judgment on anyone's soul. Allowing a ritual Catholic burial to be performed leaves open the question of God's mercy.

In today's second reading, young Stephen is stoned to death (Acts 7:58—8:2), a painful and horrible way to die. Another young man named Saul is there, approving and holding the coats of the stone-throwers to make their dreadful task easier. Imagine that Stephen's mother has heard about the commotion and comes upon the scene. Sobbing, she runs over and cradles the broken body of her son in her arms and rocks him back and forth as if trying to return life to that dead body. Finally, she senses the other young man standing there and she looks up with anguish and hatred and screams at him: "Damn you! May your soul rot in hell for this!" and she collapses in grief.

Who would not sympathize with her? Who would not say the same, wish the same? Saul and Nazi torturers and Saddam Hussein—may they all rot in hell for what they did, and do. But after the understandable anger and hurt and pain something else must remain for the disciple of Jesus. Because we know that Jesus never closed the final door, never said "no" forever. That damned young man, Saul, became St. Paul. Stephen's mother may have written him off—we can understand that—but not God. The Spirit went beyond the limits of her grief in a way she could never have imagined—or he.

On Calvary, a despicable young man who admitted to terrible deeds and accepted his punishment as fair was promised Paradise at the last minute. His was a deathbed conversion known only to him and Jesus—a conversion that may well have been the result of years and years of his parents' tears and prayers.

The publican, the prodigal son, the woman caught in adultery, Peter, the Samaritan woman at the well, Zacchaeus, Augustine, Ignatius, Malcolm Muggeridge, Thomas Merton, and Dorothy Day: all are testimony to the fact that we never have the last word, but God does. Granting a Catholic burial Mass to one seemingly unworthy says that we don't know what happens within the secrets of the heart at the last moment.

We are in no position to judge. We have no right to weigh what went on between the divine God and the human heart of a wretched sinner. The Mass of Christian Burial for the public sinner simply proclaims the faith community's humility before this issue and its refusal either to dictate to or second-guess the Spirit. In other words, the Catholic service proclaims the sovereignty of God, the everlasting possibility of a mercy we are not privy to.

So, there we are. People like Francis Albert Sinatra—many before him and many to come after him—will, with few exceptions, be given a Christian burial in the Catholic Church. This is not because of their position, but because of ours, a position derived from Jesus himself: our obligation to publicly pray for our very own who have persecuted us, our obligation to allow the good thief scenario its full play.

As I said before, we must rise above the knee-jerk reaction of cynicism and tabloid gossip and the accusations of church politics. Rather, we must look to ourselves as serious Christians who try hard to practice the teachings of Jesus. Thus, we must realize that the question, for believers, is never about Frank Sinatra—or any of the scandalous, the sinners, the seemingly unworthy. The question, remind your interrogators, is always this: what are *we* all about?

Now ask yourself: what was your reaction to the death of Frank Sinatra, or to any other unsavory celebrity who has been buried from the Church? What matters to you: the "scandal" or the mercy, the gossip or the sign, the "talk of the town" or the sovereignty of God and your recognition of it? Are you among the complainers sulking that the same pay was given to the latecomers as was to the first? "Take what belongs to you and go; I choose to give to this last the same as I give to you. Am I not allowed to do what I choose with what belongs to me? Or are you envious because I am generous?" (Mt 20:14–15). When all is said and done, what really matters?

Motivation

Along the path of our spiritual journey, what unexamined, unarticulated, "spiritual" actions are really self-serving and unworthy of the kingdom? The good deeds, the noble gestures, the generous service: sooner or later, does the "what really matters" get subverted in secret, unworthy motives, thus causing us to fall into the worst deceit? As T.S. Eliot puts it, of "doing the right thing for the wrong reason"?

The word "bribe" now suggests a shoddy and despicable deed, but it once had a very different meaning. This word originally meant "a

252 • THE YELLOW BRICK ROAD

piece of bread." If you look it up in the dictionary you'll find precisely that definition: "bribe" is Old French for "a piece of bread, scraps." A "briber" was one who begged for bread. And that brings me to a story of how the word got its present meaning.

> Once upon a time, hundreds of years ago in France, Antoinette was busy cleaning up her maisonette when she heard the familiar cry of a wandering holy man. "Alms...alms for the poor," he cried as he walked with effort down the narrow cobblestone street. Since, as you know, monks had no worldly goods and did not work for a living, it was not unusual for these holy men to walk the streets begging for whatever people would give them.
>
> Antoinette therefore went to her cupboard and cut a bribe—a piece of bread—from a fresh loaf and she sliced a wedge of cheese and dipped a cool drink from an urn down under the pantry floor. These she gave to the monk who by habit had paused at her curb in expectation of this mid-morning meal. He was most grateful and thanked her profusely. "I will pray for you," said the holy man. "I will pray to God that your kindness will be rewarded with life everlasting. And I will pray the same for your husband and mother," he promised, as he humbled himself and took his leave. She smiled graciously and returned to the house.
>
> But I must tell you this. The act of charity I just described wasn't what it seemed. The truth was that, for one thing, it was neither spontaneous nor unexpected, even though it may have been at one time in the past. Generosity, you see, had become a habit with the mistress and the monk, a ritual in which appearance and flattery played a larger role than the kindness it portrayed. In a word, the mistress and the monk had forgotten what really mattered. They were faking it even though maybe neither of them realized it fully. They may not have realized that they had fallen into empty routine, that they had assumed acting roles in this small drama which they performed with regularity before a neighborhood audience, an audience whose acknowledgment the lady of the house held in high regard.

You see, the monk would come by in the mid-morning of every third day without fail, publicly announce himself while still a ways off, chanting "Alms...alms for the poor," and then post himself at her dooryard for her to see—and the neighborhood as well. For her part, the mistress would expect him to come by in the mid-morning of every third day and would, without fail, have ready a refreshing drink, a wedge of cheese, and a bribe of fresh bread, given with greetings and well-wishes to the holy beggar who stood most visibly three paces past the bush nearest to her door. Neither had rehearsed this well-crafted script, but each knew it by heart. Its lines and gestures had become second nature. The mistress and the monk were faking being nice to each other and they didn't even know they were faking. They were playing to an audience.

That is, until the day Abner appeared at her door.

Now, this happened to be the mid-morning of the third day, but the voice chanting, "Alms...alms for the poor," just didn't sound right to the mistress's ear. Yet there was the familiar robed figure in her dooryard and at the appointed time, head bowed above his folded hands as was usual. So the mistress could do no less than prepare the bribe and bring it to him. But when the holy man raised his hands to accept the bribe—the piece of bread—the mistress was taken aback. These were different hands. This wasn't a monk. Or rather, it wasn't her monk, and instinctively she withdrew the tray with the bribe on it.

"Another holy man prays for me," she said quickly. "I don't need your prayers. Another prays for me." But the monk answered simply, "I am Abner, a name, Mistress, which means light and brightness. I wish only alms," he said, touching her wrist lightly. "Nothing more," he continued. "Please, Mistress, I call upon your gentle kindness...alms for the poor." But the mistress couldn't move. Although the hand touching her wrist had no power of grasp, it held her fast nonetheless. "I only wish alms," he had said, and was it not alms she had to offer? Why then had instinct withdrawn her bribe? This holy man was also deserving of her gentle kindness, was he not? Was it kindness, after all? His face she never saw, downcast as it was beneath the fold of his monk's hood, but Abner of light and brightness had surely stared into her very soul; in that flash of truth, it was all revealed.

All the while, all these years, her bribe had not been offered freely from an overflowing, grateful heart. Instead, it had been selfishly given in exchange for flattery and favor, and now she knew it. In that moment she knew it. The touch upon her wrist had undeniably exposed her bribe for what it was, and not only her own pious pretense, but that of so many others in her village and across the land who also conspired with these wandering holy men to be seen as the "righteous" they wished others to think them.

So it was: the word which originally stood for hospitality and kindness of the highest order—giving a piece of bread in the Lord's name—lost its good name and fell into disrepute and disuse. Today, we say a "piece of bread" instead of a "bribe." Once a bribe was the symbol of open generosity and genuine good will. Now the word bribe stands for ill-mannered fakery and the worst kind of human insincerity—because two people forgot what really mattered.

Our response

Because we have let things that didn't matter get into the way of what really matters; because we have topsy-turveyed our priorities; because we have never jumped up on the teacher's desk; because our horizons have been so narrow and self-centered; because *carpe diem*, seize the day, instead let it go by and slip through our hands; because of all this we have taken a bad detour along our spiritual journey.

We must get back on track by asking ourselves: what do we spend too much time on, carping over? What are some of the things we could let go by the board? In the larger scheme of life, they're not that important, are they? Report cards are surely important, but when you look at dead seven year olds; well, in relation to that, they're not all that important. What matters is whether or not the mother and father of that dead seven year old hugged and kissed him as much as they possibly could throughout his life. The report card really didn't matter when they went to the funeral, did it? The hugs unhugged, the kisses ungiven, the time unspent—these are the things that cry out for repentance. The love of God and the love of neighbor put aside because we were too busy—these cry out for repentance. Human relationships, friendships, kindnesses: how do they figure in our lives?

We pause a bit now and reflect on our life's priorities. Our actions, our choices, our decisions: have they fostered what we say really matters to us? Or have we subverted the things that matter, put them on the back burner, failed to cultivate them? What decisions ought we make to recover what is important in our lives, what really matters, before it is too late?

If you are alone as you read this, let me invite you to kneel down on the floor. I ask you in your heart to recite and respond to this very brief litany. For the first part of the litany, the response is, "Lord, have mercy":

> For putting second things first... Lord, have mercy.
> For not rejoicing in your love...R.
> For forgetting the one thing necessary...R.
> For neglecting to stand on high tables...R.
> For getting lost in what doesn't matter...R.
> For cluttering my life, and the lives of those dear to me...R.
> For collecting things at the expense of people...R.
> For discovering almost too late what really matters...R.
> For loving bricks more than bricklayers...R.

> *To these next petitions, the response is, "I thank you, Lord":*
> For simple gifts... I thank you, Lord.
> For your presence in my life...R.
> For affirming touches...R.
> For my parish community...R.
> For prayers that ground me...R.
> For friends that support me...R.
> For my gifts...R.
> For this reflection...R.
> For helping me to seize the day...R.

For your call...R.
For your love...R.
For knowing my name...R.
For reminding me what really matters...R.
Amen.

Questions for reflection

1. Am I anxious over so many things that I forget what really matters?

2. Do I set so many rules and regulations that I stifle the very things which are meant to give joy?

3. Have I become so obsessed with formulas and conventions that I have lost my sense of soul?

4. Are my religious practices more for show than out of love for the "Father who sees in secret"?

5. Can I make the litany at the end of this chapter my own daily, heartfelt prayer?

FOURTEEN

UNCLE HENRY & AUNTIE EM

Old Age

Uncle Henry and Auntie Em don't appear much in the movie version of *The Wizard of Oz*. They appear at the beginning and then again at the end. They are important but peripheral to the main story and to the front-and-center characters.

Just like old people. They are not given much respect, although their number is growing considerably as a segment of our population. By the year 2040, for example, one in five Americans will be over sixty-five. We will have massive numbers of elderly people supported by the decreasing young. As we seniors lose our place in a market-driven society, we are at the mercy of our needs. We find ourselves in places we never dreamed of. Like Abraham:

> Now the Lord said to Abram, "Go from your country and your kindred and your father's house to the land that I will show you. I will make of you a great nation, and I will bless you, and make your name great, so that you will be a blessing. I will bless those who bless you, and the one who curses you I will curse; and in you all the families of the earth shall be blessed" (Gn 12:1–3).

It is worthwhile to remember that both Abraham and his wife Sarah were very senior citizens when this call came to uproot themselves and go to a place they never heard of before. They too were asked to leave their relatives, their old neighborhood, their friends, and a way of life they were familiar with. Like all older people who become settled, they must have found it extremely difficult to make a change at that point in their lives, to leave the land they knew and loved for a land which they did not. But they obeyed God's word and set out.

It was a perilous journey and a long one, but through it all, God kept the promise made to Abraham at the start of the journey: "I will establish my covenant between me and you, and your offspring after you throughout their generations, for an everlasting covenant, to be God to you and to your offspring after you. And I will give to you, and to your offspring after you, the land where you are now an alien, all the land of Canaan, for a perpetual holding; and I will be their God" (Gn 17:7–8).

I see this ancient story repeated over and over again today. Senior citizens, as they call us (notice, I said "us"), are today's Abraham and Sarah. Many of us have been summoned to leave our ancestral home, something we may not have wanted to do. And we set out…to where? Well, some are in senior citizens' high-rise apartments, some are in nursing homes, some are living with one of their children or rotating among several of them. Some live alone.

Yes, many of us have left our old neighborhood, old friends, old ways. And, too, like Abraham, we have known loss during our long journey, haven't we? Many are widows and widowers, their spouses deceased like Sarah before Abraham. Perhaps they are buried "back home," wherever that is, making it hard to visit the cemetery. Most of us have lost friends and acquaintances as each year goes by; we see our old circle contract. We go to too many funerals for our contemporaries.

Along the way, some have lost grown children through death, a never-ending ache. Some have lost children through distance: they live so far away from us, we hardly see them or the grandchildren. And although some people's children are the delight of their lives, others have lost children through divorce, disagreements, addictions, or other forms of alienation and estrangement. Some children adopt lifestyles that embarrass us. Some have joined another faith or have simply stopped practicing any religion; we worry about the grandchildren being raised with nothing.

Some of us have experienced the loss of diminished faculties and health. We fiddle with our hearing aids, adjust our glasses, reset our wigs, compare our operations, line up our medications, pop our pills, sneak our Scotch, drink our Ensure, and visit our doctors. We keep Medicare and Medicaid awash in paperwork. And, more and more, we forget things: as they say, "You know you're getting old when you take a stroll down memory lane and you get lost." We stand before the open refrigerator door, unwittingly to ask life's most profound theological question: "What am I here for?"

An elderly couple in their late eighties were both becoming extremely forgetful. He would forget where he put his eyeglasses. Then, as he went from room to room searching for them, he would forget what he was looking for. She would announce she was going to the store for butter, but when she got there she would forget what she was shopping for.

One evening, as they watched TV, the husband stood up and the following dialogue took place:

She: Where are you going?

He: To get snacks. It's my turn.

She: I want a hot fudge sundae. Write it down!

He: I don't have to write it down.

She: And put nuts on it. Write it down!

He: I don't have to write it down.

She: And whipped cream. Write it down!

He: I don't have to write it down.

The husband left to get the snacks. When he returned, he presented his wife with a plate of bacon and eggs.

She: Where's the toast?

To all these trials and tribulations, we can add a loss of respect. I don't mean the normal generation gap thing. (Remember when you were in the second grade, and when your mother asked about your teacher, you told her that she was really old—but she was really only twenty-eight?)

Here's a delight:

The grandmother of a sharp little girl was slightly taken aback when her granddaughter asked, "Grandma, how old are you?" Grandma replied, "Well, honey, when you're my age you don't share that information with anybody. I will never tell anyone my age."

"That's OK," said the little girl, "I already know. I saw your driver's license on the dresser in your bedroom. It had the color of your eyes and a lot of other things about you on it, like your date of birth. So I subtracted that year from this year and the answer was seventy-six. You're seventy-six years old."

"That's right, sweetheart," grandma replied, "I am seventy-six."

There was a pause, then the little girl said sadly, "I'm sorry you got an F in sex."

An elderly college professor a while back found himself listening to a graduate student discussing some issue in his life. The student mentioned that he had had a long talk with his mother about the problem.

"Your mother?" the professor asked. "I like a young man who still discusses problems with his mother."

"Oh," he said, "I wouldn't think of making any major decision without consulting her. She always has wise counsel."

The professor was touched. Then the student added, "After all, you can't have lived forty-six years without learning something, right?"

"Forty-six years?" the professor asked.

"Yeah, she's forty-six," the student answered.

"My, forty-six. Is your mother still able to get out and about?"

"Sure," he said.

"Isn't that wonderful! Forty-six, having lived all those years, and still able to move without assistance. How inspiring!"

There's a loss of respect in the ways we are frequently patronized, even by well-meaning family members. We are seen as people to be spoken down to (some even use baby talk with us) taken care of, and distracted like children. When I was in the hospital recently, the young nurses and staff members would call me "dear" or "honey," as if I were in the early stages of senility. Worst of all, when I left, some of the young ones kissed me! What's wrong with that, you say? What's wrong with being kissed by lovely young nurses? What's wrong is that they clearly thought it was safe to kiss me!

People see us as if we were beyond feelings and dreams, as if we didn't have a rich inner life or current passions and desires and a taste for romance and a craving for arms around us. But like every other living thing, we still need to be touched. In Donna Swanson's moving poem, "Minnie Remembers," she has Minnie say:

> How long has it been since someone touched me
> Twenty years?
> Twenty years I've been a widow.
> Respected.
> Smiled at.
> But never touched.
> Never held so close that loneliness
> was blotted out.

There's more to us than meets the eye: more dreams and desires and passions, more memories, wit, and intelligence. We resent being categorized as formless "senior citizens," to be distracted like children and not engaged as persons. But in a market-driven society, where we are no longer "useful" for production or reproduction, we are patronized and not revered for who we are. We could cry out Shylock's complaint in *The Merchant of Venice*, exchanging the words "senior citizen" for "Jew" every time we read it:

> Hath not a Jew eyes? Hath not a Jew hands, organs, dimensions, senses, affections, passions? Fed with the same food, hurt with the same weapons, subject to the same diseases, healed by the same means, warmed and cooled by the same winter and sum-

mer as a Christian is? If you prick us, do we not bleed? If you tickle us, do we not laugh? If you poison us, do we not die?

Indeed, like Abraham and Sarah, we have made a journey—perhaps lots of them—and along the way, have experienced loss. "Go from your country and your kindred and your father's house to the land that I will show you" (Gn 12:1). Like Abraham and Sarah, we have been called to a foreign land and have made a difficult journey. Along the way, we have lost some things, and we have gained some things—life and love and adventure and achievement—but most of all, we have journeyed with the promise. For remember, God made a covenant with us: "I will be your God, and you shall be my people" (Jer 7:23).

God has been and will be faithful. How do we know that? Let me suggest that one sign of this fidelity, the covenant kept, is that you are reading these pages. You have made your journey, left your ancestral home, heeded the call, settled into a "foreign land," and here you are. And God has been with you through all the ups and downs. God is your God, and you are one of God's people. You have joined the caravan with Abraham and Sarah, perhaps unwillingly. Nevertheless, God has brought you to the place where you are today. And again, God has been with you: this is the one underlying, sustaining truth that should reassure you. You are part of a biblical people who have confronted challenge and change. You have laughed and cried on the journey. You are God's chosen. And someday, as we well know, the journey will be completed.

But I must share something with you. It has been my experience that before the journey is ended, while there is still time, there are five challenges to be met before we face the four last things (death, judgment, heaven, hell).

What are these remaining challenges? We can poetically describe them as: share, flair, repair, despair, and fear. These are the five frontiers that must be reached before salvation.

Share

In her book *Gift of the Red Bird*, Paula D'Arcy, who lost her husband and her baby in a car crash, reflects on many things. Here is one of them:

The obvious persons to question about life passages are those who have gone ahead of us. Our grandparents, great-grandparents, the elders. I never knew my paternal grandfather, and my paternal grandmother spoke no English. My maternal grandfather was said to be as fine a person as anyone knew. But he died when I was barely four years old, and all my memories of him are sketchy. It is only my maternal grandmother whom I remember, and with whom we even lived for the first four years of my life.

Throughout my childhood she visited us often, and I have vivid memories of seeing her at her place of work. She ran a small city tea room at a time when women hardly worked at all, let alone managed a business. She was spitfire, and I admired her initiative. But when she died in her eighty-third year and the family met to capture her essence for the minister's benefit, I was stunned with an awareness that we barely knew her at all. We knew, of course, names, dates, and places. We knew amusing anecdotes and significant moments. But we didn't know her. She hadn't let us in. She died with her story. No one could say what her true feelings, needs, and loves were.

That impacted me like a blow to my person. To have lived and died and to never have been deeply known. To have always been proper and right, but to never have shared your dreams, hopes, and hurts. Your acquired wisdom. So in June of 1986 when my late husband's family announced a large family reunion, I was particularly eager to attend. It would be wonderful for Beth to find her roots and meet relatives face to face. But good for me also. I wanted to hear the stories told by those with the experience of years.

Do you recognize yourself here? Do people really know you? Have you shared yourself? We all have a rich heritage behind us. There are memories and stories, follies and triumphs, sin and virtue, successes and failures to be shared. In these days when the young are programmed early on into the artificial commercial images of the media, it is more important than ever to share your stories with them, your own journey, to be known for the person you are and not the image you project. You may be hiding away what ought to be shared, waiting until it is too late to share it. Enter into this story:

My brother-in-law opened the bottom drawer of my sister's bureau and lifted out a tissue-wrapped package. "This," he said, "is not a slip. This is lingerie." He discarded the tissue and handed me the slip. It was exquisite: silk, handmade, and trimmed with a cobweb of lace. The price tag with an astronomical figure on it was still attached. "Jan bought this the first time we went to New York, at least eight or nine years ago. She never wore it. She was saving it for a special occasion.

"Well, I guess this is the occasion." He took the slip from me and put it on the bed with the other clothes we were taking to the mortician. His hands lingered on the soft material for a moment, then he slammed the drawer shut and turned to me. "Don't ever save anything for a special occasion. Every day you're alive is a special occasion."

I remembered those words through the funeral and the days that followed when I helped him and my niece attend to all the sad chores that follow an unexpected death. I thought about them on the plane returning to California from the Midwestern town where my sister's family lives. I thought about all the things that she hadn't seen or heard or done. I thought about the things that she had done without realizing that they were special.

I'm still thinking about his words, and they've changed my life. I'm reading more and dusting less. I'm sitting on the deck and admiring the view without fussing about the weeds in the garden. I'm spending more time with my family and friends and less time in committee meetings.

Whenever possible, life should be a pattern of experiences to savor, not endure. I'm trying to recognize these moments now and cherish them. I'm not "saving" anything; we use our good china and crystal for every special event, such as losing a pound, getting the sink unstopped, or the first camellia blossom. I wear my good blazer to the market if I feel like it. My theory is if I look prosperous, I can shell out $28.49 for one small bag of groceries without wincing. I'm not saving my good perfume for special parties; clerks in hardware stores and tellers in banks have noses that function as well as my party-going friends. "Someday" and "one of these days" are losing their grip on my vocabulary. If it's worth seeing or hearing or doing, I want to see and hear and do it now.

I'm not sure what my sister would have done had she known that she wouldn't be here for the tomorrow we all take for granted. I think she would have called family members and a few close friends. She might have called a few former friends to apologize and mend fences for past squabbles. I like to think she would have gone out for a Chinese dinner, her favorite food. I'm guessing—I'll never know.

It's those little things left undone that would make me angry if I knew that my hours were limited. Angry because I put off seeing good friends whom I was going to get in touch with— someday. Angry because I hadn't written certain letters that I intended to write—one of these days. Angry and sorry that I didn't tell my husband and daughter often enough how much I truly love them.

I'm trying very hard not to put off, hold back, or save anything that would add laughter and luster to our lives. And every morning when I open my eyes, I tell myself that it is special. Every day, every minute, every breath truly is a gift from God.

While there is time, share. Give away your possessions, your gifts and your love now. Don't wait until someone else does it after you are dead.

Flair

When you reach a certain age, you should have acquired a certain wisdom that helps you see beyond the social pressures and conventions of daily life. For a faith-filled person, there is an acceptance of aging and its limitations—as well as its freedoms. One of those freedoms is to be yourself, at last. Yet this can be difficult because the ever-prevalent media puts so much emphasis on the outside, on one's image, one's looks.

Take, for example, the phrase "aging gracefully." In former times it meant that one had acquired enough life experiences and wisdom to have mellowed and formed into a mature person with a rich interior life. Nowadays, in a society that has all but abandoned value on any internal qualities and resonates only with body image and "personality" (in place of character), "aging gracefully" refers to one's external looks: "She's fifty but (with a little cosmetic surgery) she looks wonderful!" (Here, too, I want to mention the must-read book *Venus Envy*, by Elizabeth Haiken). Thus, all too often, we become enslaved to external props and conformities and never really become ourselves.

But at a certain age, you should be able and ready to say and do things that you want and break a bit out of the old molds. You have to have flair. You don't have to become a swinging Auntie Mame, but you can occasionally do some wild things. Consider Jenny Joseph's delightful "Warning":

When I am an old woman I shall wear purple
With a red hat which doesn't go, which doesn't quite suit me.
And I shall spend my pension on brandy and summer gloves
And satin sandals, and say we have no money for butter.
I shall sit down on the pavement when I am tired
And gobble up samples in shops and press alarm bells
And run my stick along public railings
And make up for the sobriety of my youth.
I shall go out in my slippers in the rain
And pick the flowers in other people's gardens
And learn to spit.

You can wear terrible shirts and grow more fat
And eat three pounds of sausage at a go
Or only bread and pickles for a week
And hoard pens and pencils and beermats and things in boxes.

But now we must have clothes that keep us dry

And pay our rent and not swear in the street
And set a good example for the children.
We must have friends to dinner and read the papers.

But maybe I ought to practice a little now?
So people who know me are not too shocked and surprised
When suddenly I am old and start to wear purple.

Being a senior citizen brings its limitations. But it brings its freedoms, too, the freedom to be yourself, more beholden to your repressed impulses, your creativity, knowing that the social tyrants of your life will come and go, and that ultimately you are answerable only to yourself and to God. On with the purple!

Repair

Next, repair—repairing broken relationships and hurts. In short, forgiveness. We must forgive those who have wronged us, and we must be forgiven by those whom we have hurt, perhaps badly.

There is a book by Simon Weisenthal, called *The Sunflower*. The book is somewhat biographical, about an incident during the two years that Weisenthal spent in a Nazi concentration camp. Let me review it for you.

Like so many others, Weisenthal's pain was extremely intense. Eighty-nine members of his family had died in these Nazi concentration camps. He had watched helplessly while his mother was shoved into one of those boxcars, never to be seen again, as she rode off to her death. He saw his mother-in-law machine-gunned right in front of him, so he had reason to have great pain.

One day when he was in the concentration camp, a nurse came out to where he was working, tapped him on the shoulder, and told him to follow her. He was taken to a makeshift hospital, to a very small room. In that room there was a single bed, and on this bed was a person almost completely wrapped in bandages, who looked very much like a mummy. It was obvious that this person would soon die. The nurse left Weisenthal alone in the room with the bandaged body, and the dying person began to speak. The bandaged body belonged to a very young man, twenty-one years old, a member of the dreaded

SS troops. The young man told his story:

He had been raised a Catholic, but in his teens he had joined the Hitler youth. He had abandoned his Catholicism in favor of his new religion, which demanded all he could give: total obedience and reverence to a new god called Adolph Hitler. When the war broke out, he volunteered immediately for the elite SS troops. He wanted to be a part of the easy and the quick victory that the Nazi propaganda had promised him. While he was in the eastern zone, he was given the assignment of dealing with the Jews in the local area. To "deal with the Jews" in the local area meant just one thing. And so his unit gathered up all the Jews and herded them into a building. They doused the building with gasoline, set up machine guns to take care of those who tried to escape, and they set it on fire, which was the common procedure.

This incident troubled the young SS trooper. Some of the Catholic teachings he had received while a child began to be stimulated. He began to be preoccupied with what he had done. In fact, his preoccupation led him to such distraction that he grew careless; the result of his carelessness was that in a skirmish, he was riddled with bullets. And here he was, lying bandaged in an isolated room in a makeshift hospital. One of the things that was on his mind was that above all, he wanted forgiveness.

And so he had requested that a Jew be sent in—any Jew. Male Jew, female Jew, a representative Jew—he wanted one of them there. And just by circumstance, the nurse tapped Simon Weisenthal, who went into this room and listened to the story and heard this man's plea. This young man, this boy, said he was not born a murderer and he didn't want to die a murderer; and he begged Simon, on behalf of his people, for forgiveness. And Weisenthal says that the only response he could give was to get up and leave the room without saying a word, without granting forgiveness.

So, there are two main characters in this story: Weisenthal, who could not forgive, and the young Nazi, who desperately wanted forgiveness before he died. I won't spend time comparing ourselves to Weisenthal. We, as disciples of the Christ who told the story of the prodigal son, who preached forgiveness and granted it to his enemies even from the cross, must model our lives on Christ's words.

Unforgiveness controls us, and keeps us chained to resentment and anger. It constricts our lives, our spirit. If we find it hard to forgive, we must ask Jesus to do it for us. But let me spend some time here comparing us to the unfortunate Nazi. Suppose we did something terrible or hurtful or betraying to someone in our lives; and now, like the dying soldier, we very much want forgiveness—but it is no longer possible for lots of reasons.

I can think of several examples: there is the parent who has been, who is, an alcoholic, who in his or her drinking days was abusive to the children, shamed and embarrassed them, poisoned their minds, turned their hearts, and left them with great scars. By this time, the children have left home. He or she has gone to A.A. and is in recovery, hasn't had a drink in years. Yet still the children, disgusted by long abuse, want no part of him or her. The parent, before he or she dies, is desperate for their forgiveness. They are either unwilling or unable to forgive. And so the alcoholic parent lives out the days in pain.

Or there is the wife who for many years has betrayed her husband with one, or many, affairs. Now she has come to her senses, but has left behind a great distrust, a chasm of miscommunication and misunderstanding, and a deep and abiding hurt. The husband doesn't know if he can forgive his wife. What does she do?

Or there is the boy who in his selfishness has exploited a girl, gotten her pregnant, and has either paid for or insisted upon an abortion so he would have no responsibility; or he has a son or daughter somewhere on this planet for whom he has not taken one iota of responsibility. And as the irresponsibility of his actions becomes evident to him, he wants to go and find his son or daughter, and get down on his knees and say, "I'm sorry. I love you. Forgive me!" But he doesn't even know who his child is.

Or there are brothers and sisters within the same family who say to me things like: "We haven't spoken to each other in fifteen years. Why have we been apart for so long over some petty disagreement?" They want forgiveness, and it's not forthcoming.

So what about the people whom we have hurt in the past, perhaps even the long-ago past? The people whom we have wounded who will not forgive us, who perhaps cannot forgive us: maybe they are already dead? Our guilt is heavy, very heavy. Like that young Nazi, we want forgiveness before we die; but the Simon Weisenthals of our lives—the ones whom we have injured and hurt—have simply disappeared. They are dead or we do not know where they are anymore or they have turned their backs and walked away a long, long time ago.

How do we handle situations like these? One answer is that we can turn to Mary, the Mother of God, in an imaginative intercessory prayer. If you are the young Nazi, and you so badly want forgiveness; and if the people of your life cannot or will not or are not able to forgive, then you can use the power of your imagination to heal through prayer. Here is how it works:

> Go alone to someplace quiet, like your bedroom. Sit down, breathe slowly, and close your eyes. In your mind's eye, see yourself where you are right now, sitting in the very chair you are in. You are alone. A knock comes on the door. You call, "Come in," and someone enters; it is precisely the person whom you have hurt or betrayed, whose forgiveness you want so badly. That person silently sits in a chair opposite you, eyes downcast, lips tight. There is silence, except for the aching desire of your heart to get up, rush over to that person, put your arms around him or her, and tell him or her how sorry you are. But you get no invitation, no signal—so you sit there in pain and guilt.
>
> Both of you sit there silently for a long time, until you sense another presence in your bedroom, a presence you had not noticed when you came in. Out of the shadows comes a lady, very beautiful and serene, with a concerned look on her face. It is Mary, the mother of Jesus, and our mother, too. She is sad because her children are angry and unforgiving toward one another. She goes over to the other person, and bending down, whispers something in his or her ear. The other person nods, and you notice a small tear trickling down his or her cheek.
>
> Then Mary, the compassionate, reconciling mother, silently comes over to you and holds out her hand for you to take. You take it and stand, and she leads you over to the other person. She takes that person's hand, and then lifts both hands up. You

are now standing face to face with the other person, with your mother Mary in between. She joins your hands together and steps back. Soon you and the other are embracing and weeping: the reconciliation is complete after these many years.

If you want or need forgiveness from someone in your past, try this prayer of imagination as often as you would like. Mary, to whom time and space are nothing, will always help you to reconcile, bring closure, repair. I am reminded here of Brennan Manning's story of an old man dying of cancer:

> The old man's daughter had asked the local priest to come and pray with her father. When the priest arrived he found the man lying in bed with his head propped up on two pillows and an empty chair beside his bed. The priest assumed that the old fellow had been informed of his visit. "I guess you were expecting me," he said.
>
> "No, who are you?"
>
> "I'm the new associate at your parish," the priest replied. "When I saw the empty chair, I figured you knew I was going to show up."
>
> "Oh, yeah, the chair," said the bedridden man. "Would you mind closing the door?"
>
> Puzzled, the priest shut the door.
>
> "I've never told anyone this, not even my daughter," said the man, "but all my life I have never known how to pray. At Sunday Mass I used to hear the pastor talk about prayer, but it always went right over my head. Finally I said to him one day in sheer frustration, 'I get nothing out of your homilies on prayer.'
>
> "'Here,' says my pastor, reaching into the bottom drawer of his desk. 'Read this book by Hans Urs von Balthasar. He's a Swiss theologian. It's the best book on contemplative prayer in the twentieth century.'"
>
> "Well, Father," said the man, "I took the book home and tried to read it. But in the first three pages I had to look up twelve words in the dictionary. I gave the book back to the pastor, thanked him, and under my breath whispered 'for nothin'.'

"I abandoned any attempt at prayer," he continued, "until one day about four years ago my best friend said to me, 'Joe, prayer is just a simple matter of having a conversation with Jesus. Here's what I suggest. Sit down on a chair, place an empty chair in front of you, and in faith see Jesus on the chair. It's not spooky because He promised, "I'll be with you all days." Then just speak to Him and listen the same way you're doing with me right now.'

"So, Padre, I tried it and I've liked it so much that I do it a couple of hours every day. I'm careful though. If my daughter saw me talking to an empty chair, she'd either have a nervous breakdown or send me off to the funny farm."

The priest was deeply moved by the story and encouraged the old guy to continue the journey. Then he prayed with him, anointed him with oil, and returned to the rectory.

Two nights later the daughter called to tell the priest that her daddy had died in that afternoon.

"Did he seem to die in peace?" he asked.

"Yes, when I left the house around two o'clock, he called me over to his bedside, told me one of his corny jokes, and kissed me on the cheek. When I got back from the store an hour later, I found him dead. But there was something strange, Father. In fact, beyond strange, kinda weird. Apparently just before Daddy died, he leaned over and rested his head on a chair beside his bed."

Coventry Patmore's moving poem, "The Toys," is worth pondering here, as well:

> My little son, who look'd from thoughtful eyes
> And moved and spoke in quiet grown up wise,
> Having my law the seventh time disobey'd,
> I struck him, and dismiss'd
> With hard words and unkiss'd,
> His mother, who was patient, being dead.
> Then, fearing lest his grief should hinder sleep,
> I visited his bed,

But found him slumbering deep,
With darken'd eyelids, and his lashes yet
From his late sobbing wet.
And I, with moan,
Kissing away his tears, left others of my own;
For on a table drawn beside his head
He had put, within his reach,
A box of counters and a red-veined stone,
A piece of glass abraided from the beach.
And six or seven shells
A bottle with bluebells
And two French copper coins,
Ranged there with careful art,
To comfort his sad heart.
So when that night I pray'd
To God, I wept, and said:
Ah, when we lie at last with tranced breath,
Not vexing Thee in death,
And Thou rememberest of what toys
We made our joys,
How weakly understood
Thy great commanded good,
Then, fatherly not less
Than I whom Thou has moulded from the clay,
Thou'lt leave Thy wrath, and say,
"I will be sorry for their childishness."

Despair

Despair can take on several forms during our golden years. For some, there may be a subtle, though real, sense of guilt that it is only lately we have turned to God. For some, there is the awareness that theirs has been a life of sin and evil, a fearful legacy to bring to the judgment seat. Others may be coping with a lifetime of little or no religious practice, a life of indifference to the faith; and only now, facing death, have they "got religion." Still others went to church on a reg-

ular basis, but God and the spiritual life were always left on the back
burner. Now each one wonders, with a touch of despair: is this
Johnny-come-lately faith good enough, found only now that we need
God? Will God see through the deception and condemn us?

Yet there is no need to despair. The simple truth is that last-minute
prayer is valid. We have to understand that we are not dealing with
human beings, like ourselves, who might naturally be cynical about
our new-found faith. We are dealing with God who, as we indicated
in chapter five, has been watching us, who has been pursuing us, for
a lifetime. As Francis Thompson writes in the poem, "The Hound of
Heaven":

> Whom wilt thou find to love ignoble thee,
> Save me, save only Me?
> All which I took from thee I did but take,
> Nor for thy harms,
> But just that thou might'st seek it in My arms.
> All which thy child's mistake
> Fancies as lost, I have stored for thee at home:
> Rise, clasp my hand, and come!
>
> "Ah, fondest, blindest, weakest,
> I am He Whom thou seekest!"

We are dealing with a God who has no pride, who washes feet, who
tells stories of a father running to his latecomer son, a woman who
sweeps the whole house just for a penny, and a simple-minded farmer
who leaves ninety-nine sheep to search for one little lost lamb. Most
strikingly, we are talking about a God who actually and shamelessly
accepted the last-ditch apology of the man next to him on the cross.
Simply put, there are no latecomers with God. Listen to the classic
prayer of another latecomer, St. Augustine:

> Late have I loved Thee, O Beauty so ancient and so new;
> Late have I loved Thee!
> For behold Thou wert within me, and I outside;
> and I sought Thee outside and in my loneliness
> fell upon those lovely things Thou hast made.

Thou wert with me and I was not with Thee.
I was kept from Thee by those things,
yet had they not been in Thee,
they would have not been at all.
Thou didst call and cry to me
and break open my deafness:
and Thou didst send forth Thy beams
and shine upon me
and chase away my blindness.
Thou didst breathe fragrance upon me,
and I drew in my breath
and now do pant for Thee:
I tasted Thee
and now hunger and thirst for Thee:
Thou didst touch me
and I have burned for thy peace.

For some, despair takes the form of hopelessness. All their lives they have lived in doubt, in darkness. All their lives they have wondered if they have done God's will. All their lives they have yearned for some sign that, in the end, God was with them. Will they ever be reassured? Will they ever see God seeing them?

For such people, Scripture tells the story of two senior citizens, Simeon and Anna (Lk 2:25–38). Here were two people in their eighties who also longed to sense some sign of God in their lives, some indication that God had been with them on their life's long journey; some sign that their lives, with all their glories and follies, had meant something, that God took notice; some indication that God would forgive their sins, some hint of God's presence; but they never seemed to have their longing satisfied. They were near despair.

Still, for some reason, they persevered. For some reason, perhaps out of habit, they prayed, even though their prayers never seemed to be answered. They kept faithful to their religion, even though often it was out of routine and formality and with heavy hearts—until one day. On that day, unexpectedly, Simeon and Anna each looked into the face of God. Not as they had expected—that is, not in a great epiphany or into a vision in the vast sky—but here and now, in a baby's face. There, in weakness, they saw the Almighty.

The stories of these two people tell us not to despair but to trust in God, who has been with us on our journey though often hidden. In our lives, there may have been times of disbelief, perhaps even a time when we left the Church, a time of flatness and anger. But Anna and Simeon tell us to trust. God's love is greater than our failures; God's love is stronger than death. Put aside despair and believe that God loves us with an unconditional love, and that God's word is true. We will someday gaze into God's face when and where we least expect it.

Fear

The final frontier to cross, the fifth challenge we must face, is fear. And there are two fears which are most prevalent among the elderly.

The first is the fear of dying with things left undone, unfinished. Some family members are still alienated from each other. We would like to see them reconciled before we depart from this world. Our adult son is still not settled; our divorced daughter is living with someone. The grandchildren are not baptized. We want to be around for our grandniece's graduation. In short, things are still incomplete, untidy, unresolved, and we would like to see them pulled together, resolved before we close our eyes. We want to finish well. Like all happy endings, we want the murderer found, the couple reunited, the children happy, grown, and settled. Then we can die in peace. And so we fear that we will die anxiously, with things still in a mess and the people dearest to us still floating in a limbo of unresolved lives.

But as believers, we need to remember that incompleteness here is built into our lives and will always remain that way. We were, after all, called into existence as the first step to Another. We are called at our baptism to be children of God. We are called to friendship with Jesus. "I do not call you servants any longer…but I have called you friends" (Jn 15:15). We were called to the beatific vision: "In my Father's house there are many dwelling places.…I go to prepare a place for you" (Jn 14:2). In other words, we were made for and called to union with God. That is the culmination of our lives. Yes, death is always an interruption to what we are doing in this world, to our

unfulfilled dreams; but it is also a call home to the One who started
it all. Death is not an interruption of our heavenly calling; it is, rather,
its climax.

The second fear is, of course, the fear of death itself. Listen to this
story:

A long time ago there lived a little boy whose parents had died.
He was taken in by an aunt who raised him as her own child.
Years later, after he had grown up and left his aunt, he received
a letter from her. She was in a terminal illness and, from the
tone of her letter, he knew she was afraid of death. This man
whom she had raised and touched wrote her a letter in which
he said:

"It is now thirty-five years since I, a little boy of six, was left
quite alone in the world. You sent me word that you would give
me a home and be a mother to me. I've never forgotten the day
when I made the long journey of ten miles to your house. I can
still recall my disappointment when, instead of coming for me
yourself, you sent your servant, Caesar, a dark man, to fetch me.
I well remember my tears and my anxiety as, perched high on
your horse and clinging tight to Caesar, I rode off to my new
home.

"Night fell before we finished the journey, and as it grew
dark, I became even more afraid. 'Do you think she'll go to bed
before I get there?' I asked Caesar anxiously. 'Oh, no,' said
Caesar, 'she'll sure to stay up for you. When we get out of these
woods, you'll see her light shining in the window.' Presently, we
did ride out into the clearing and there was your light. I
remember that you were waiting at the door; that you put your
arms tight around me; that you lifted me—a tired, frightened
little boy—down from the horse. You had a fire burning on the
hearth; a hot supper waiting on the stove. After supper you took
me to my new room. You heard me say my prayers. Then you
sat with me until I fell asleep.

"You probably realize why I am trying to recall this to your
memory now. Very soon, God is going to send for you and take

you to a new home. I'm trying to tell you that you needn't be afraid of the summons or of the strange journey or of the dark messenger of death. God can be trusted. God can be trusted to do as much for you as you did for me so many years ago.

"At the end of the road you'll find love and a welcome waiting. And you'll be safe in God's care. I'm going to watch and pray for you until you're out of sight. And I shall wait for the day when I make the same journey myself and find you waiting at the end of the road to greet me."

Someone is waiting for us. Jesus promised: "And if I go and prepare a place for you, I will come again and will take you to myself, so that where I am, there you may be also" (Jn 14:3). Vladimir Nabokov wrote: "Life is a great surprise. I do not see why death should not be an even greater one."

So, here we are: we are Abraham and Sarah, pilgrims from our homeland, journeyers with rich experiences, a people with triumphs and failures, gains and losses, full of story and history—what extraordinary biographies we have here! But always and everywhere, at all times and places, we are people of the covenant, whom God has called by name and from whom God has never been absent. Even though hidden at times, God loves us with an everlasting love.

Through it all, like precious stones being ground into a fine polish, we have become wisdom figures. In her book, *A Cloister Walk*, Kathleen Norris describes the "older folk" she visits in a monastery nursing home:

> There is little of the outwardly perfect among them. Their scapulars have taken on bits of crusts and odd stains. They sometimes seem to have one foot already in eternity, regarding the time, the date, and even the year as being of little consequence. But they also have a kind of polish, a gentle manner that has come from having been hard-scrubbed in the rough and tumble of communal living. Often, although their bodies daily betray them, they radiate an inner peace that nourishes the younger monks and nuns who care for them, or who come to them for guidance.

So, at our stage and age, we have to deal with five final obstacles, negotiate these last frontiers: we must learn to share, have a sense of flair, begin repair, fight despair, and face our fear. But we will accept the challenge because God will help us; God's love is greater than any obstacle. Our destiny is to live forever with God who, from the beginning, summons us to leave what we know for what we do not know. Yet this God has never abandoned us, and indeed, has become our way and our truth and our life. Let me leave you with this verse from a poem by Leonard Cohen:

> Ring the bells that still can ring,
> Forget your perfect offering.
> There is a crack in everything,
> That's how the light gets in.

Admit it: all of us are pretty well cracked. But think of all the light we let in! And think of the Light that awaits us when our journey is ended.

Questions for reflection

1. Am I saving my best china for the pope's visit? Do I hoard my things, saving them to pass on as an inheritance or for a "rainy day," or do I share them and enjoy them now, with others?

2. As I grow older, do I feel more freedom to become my own person, the one whom God intended me to be?

3. What relationship or situation needs to be repaired in my life? Have I ever used imaginative prayer? Is it appropriate now?

4. Do any past sins or mistakes cause me to feel despair? How can I begin to seek reconciliation with these persons or events?

5. Am I afraid that I will die with things unresolved? Can I accept the fact that I will never finish all there is to do with my life, and that death is a call from God to whom we have always been meant to return?

6. Can I see myself becoming a wisdom figure as I grow older? Who are the wisdom figures around me now?

FIFTEEN

AUTHOR! AUTHOR!

Seeing

In this chapter, we give a nod to the author of the Wizard of Oz stories, L. Frank Baum. (I gave a short sketch of his life in the introduction.) We owe him and all like him a great debt, for they are the writers, the artists, the poets, and the mystics who, each in his or her own way, give us life's greatest gift: the gift of seeing.

These extraordinary people have a way of seeing life that is different from the ordinary run of people. In turn, through their art and craft, they coax us with their visions, startle us with their insights, and may shock us with their images. They help lift our blindness if even for a moment and, if we are fortunate, we cherish what we glimpse. They give us a peek at the One who peeks at us, as we saw in the artistry of William Faulkner in chapter seven. And so people like L. Frank Baum invite us, teach us, to see in a new way. Significantly, this new way of seeing is at the very heart of Christianity. Recall Robert Barron's quote from chapter two:

> Christianity is, above all, a way of seeing. Everything else in Christian life flows from and circles around the transformation of vision. Christians see differently, and that is why their prayer, their worship, their action, their whole way of being in the world, has a distinctive accent and flavor. What unites figures as diverse as James Joyce, Caravaggio, John Milton, the architect

of Chartres, Dorothy Day, Dietrich Bonhoffer, and the later Bob Dylan is a peculiar and distinctive take on things, a style, a way, which flows finally from Jesus of Nazareth.

Origen of Alexandria once remarked that holiness is seeing with the eyes of Christ. Teilhard de Chardin said with great passion that his mission as a Christian thinker was to help people see, and Thomas Aquinas said that the ultimate goal of the Christian life is a "beatific vision," an act of seeing.

Likewise, recall the quote from Rabbi Harold Kushner in *Who Needs God*: "Religion is not primarily a set of beliefs, a collection of prayers or a series of rituals. Religion is first and foremost a way of seeing. It can't change the facts about the world we live in, but it can change the way we see those facts, and that in itself can often make a difference."

This teaching explains Jesus' urgent call to be alert, keep awake, be attentive. To what? To seeing that the kingdom of God is close at hand. Look and see what God is doing in and through Jesus and in the seeing, then "go and do likewise." Change your way of perception. What keeps us from seeing, however, is fear:

When we fear, we cling to who we are and what we have; when we are afraid, we see ourselves as the threatened center of a hostile universe. And fear—according to so many of the biblical authors and so many of the mystics and theologians of our tradition—is a function of living our lives at the surface level, a result of forgetting our deepest identity.

At the root and ground of our being, at the "center" of who we are, there is what Christianity calls "the image and likeness of God." This means that at the foundation of our existence, we are one with the divine power which continually creates and sustains the universe; we are held and cherished by the infinite love of God. When we rest in this center and realize its power, we know that in an ultimate sense we are safe, or in more classical religious language, "saved." And therefore we can let go of fear and live in radical trust.

But when we lose sight of this rootedness in God, we live

exclusively on the tiny island of the ego, and lives become dominated by fear. Fear is the "original sin" of which the church fathers speak; fear is the poison that was injected into human consciousness and human society from the beginning; fear is the debilitating and life-denying element which upsets the "chemical balance" of both psyche and society.

Bartimaeus, then and now

We see this fear operating in the Bartimaeus story. "Jesus, Son of David, have pity on me!" (Mk 10:47). In this cry he echoes what has been said from the beginning of time: the groaning of Bartimaeus is also our cry. "What do you want me to do for you?" Jesus asks. "Master, I want to see."

And this must be our constant prayer, as well: I want to see as you see. Recall here that the gospel accounts are designed not to give us answers or biographies, but to help us see, to catch the same vision which captivated the first disciples and the first Christians. But like Bartimaeus, we do succumb to fear and so remain blind. Can we recognize ourselves in any of the following voices?

"Jesus, son of David, have pity on me." I begin to clean the house and before I'm half-finished the dust is beginning to settle again. What's the use? I prepare a meal and while I'm doing it, I'm thinking of a menu for the next meal. The cycle continues and no one cares. I was considered important when I was raising the children, but now they are on their own. Oh, I know they love me, but the fact is they have gone, and they don't call me or visit me that much. I work and my husband works, but we don't seem to go anywhere. I feel useless and I don't see anything down the road. I am a blind beggar.

"Jesus, son of David, have pity on me." I go to work and the system is doing things I don't like. I disagree with the dog-eat-dog attitude and the ruthless methods that are used, but I feel stuck, powerless to do anything about it. My opinions don't seem to count; my job, like anybody's today, is not really secure. I'm too old to start somewhere else again and too young to retire. I have to protect my pension and my family's security. I take my paycheck and I go sit by the side of the road and don't see anything down that road. I am a blind beggar.

"Jesus, son of David, have pity on me." I spend most of my time in a senior citizen's apartment. The children don't call very often. I'm no longer able to work, no longer able to contribute anything useful to society. I feel worthless and don't see anything of value in my life. I am a blind beggar.

"Jesus, son of David, have pity on me." Our marriage is falling apart. He won't go for counseling. We don't believe in divorce and the children need us. But it's a dead end. I dread the years ahead of just coping, arguing, distancing, dying. I can't see any resolution. I am a blind beggar.

"Jesus, son of David have pity on me." My daughter began doing drugs at fourteen. By seventeen, she became pregnant with her first son. She later married and had a second son. She and her husband began using cocaine. There was never enough food for the children and they were taken away from her. We adopted the older boy. The other boy was adopted by relatives who won't let us see him. I close my eyes. I see myself as a blind beggar at the gate. I hear the noise of the crowd and call out.

These are the blind journeys of many of us. "Have pity on me. I can't see any way out." Fear has enveloped us. So let us now turn to Bartimaeus as our guide and see how this blind man overcame his fear and his blindness. (You can read the story for yourself in Mk 10:46–52.)

First, Bartimaeus hears about Jesus and calls out to him. And here it is, both for Bartimaeus and for all of us who are blind: the first step on the journey to seeing is hearing about Jesus. We must turn to the gospels. To learn trust, we must watch Jesus, listen to him in joy and in sorrow and in his utter reliance on Abba, the Father. Then from this acquaintance flows our cry, our plea: "Jesus, son of David, have pity on me!"

The next element worthy of note in the Bartimaeus story is that Bartimaeus was rebuked by his friends, by the crowd, by the cynics. Don't disturb the Master, Bartimaeus was told: he has better things to do than pay attention to you. Who do you think you are? But Bartimaeus pays no attention. On the contrary, he cries out all the louder.

We too are often rebuked, and often by well-meaning people: "What you need is a good psychiatrist"; "Forget it, you don't have what it takes"; "Religion is obsolete in this day and age"; "Everybody's doing it"; "You're wasting your time"; "Do you really think God cares about you? God has other things to care about." This ridicule, whether genial or strident, is hard to take; it will wear down our trust. But we must remember: we do count! The very hairs of our head are numbered. Jesus has come for the sick, not the well. He has invited all who labor and are heavily burdened to come to him for refreshment. Therefore, we must persevere in calling on the Lord; we must cry out ever louder.

And so blind Bartimaeus is told by Jesus to come to him. Bartimaeus hesitates; but finally, he casts aside his cloak and goes forward in his darkness. Why did he hesitate? To answer that let us look at the significance of his cloak. It was Bartimaeus' mat, his bed, his warmth, his security blanket—and his one possession. To let go of it was to let go of all he depended on. And that is exactly what the gospel is saying: let go of what you think is so critical and important and necessary, and risk all to run to Jesus. If you cling to your ego, to your self-made security, like Magdalene clinging to the feet of Jesus, the Spirit cannot come.

Discarding the cloak symbolizes the decision to discard the common cultural doctrine of self-salvation. New Age religions, a thousand humanistic psychologies, and all manner of advertisements preach self-salvation all the time. In this view, all guidelines rest in the self alone, from making moral decisions to choosing a lifestyle: no criteria other than that of the self is needed. The ego reigns supreme.

But at the heart of our faith is the notion of "other." There is something more outside ourselves, someone, like Jesus calling Bartimaeus, who beckons, calls, judges, heals, and saves. To know salvation is to accept the saving help that can come only from a power that stands outside of the mess we are in. We catch the truth of this in the old adage: "There are no atheists in foxholes." When terrible tragedy threatens, even nonbelievers will call on God, not only on the chance that God might be there, but perhaps because, when all is said and done, we know that we alone cannot save ourselves. No one of us can handle sickness and death, or the ultimate hollowness of a self-centered life, simply on our own. Only something—Someone—that breaks in from outside our closed system, our own egos, can give saving grace.

Thomas Merton discovered this. In his biography, *The Seven Storey Mountain*, he writes: "Free by nature, in the image of God, I was nevertheless the prisoner of my own violence and my own selfishness, in the image of the world into which I was born." A "prisoner" needs release.

The following words could describe Bartimaeus' plight—and Bartimaeus is us:

> In our very dependency and insufficiency, in our very fear and limitation, in the very threatened quality of our existence, we have within us an openness to the God who is neither dependent nor insufficient nor threatened. We carry about in our bodies the death of Christ, as Paul said, and in that very mortality we are orientated to the immortal source of being. When we sense how fragile and nonself-explanatory we are, we are forced, by a kind of inner compulsion, to kneel, to pray, to acknowledge the divine.

This is what blind Bartimaeus saw, and that is why he cried out beyond his own ego. That is why he discarded his cloak. We must all let go of the securities, the defenses, the devices which the world recommends. Our gain is in the loss.

Once upon a time there was an old man from the island of Crete. He loved his land with a deep intensity, so much so that when he knew he was about to die he had his sons bring him outside and lay him on the ground. As he was about to expire he reached down by his side and clutched some earth in his hands. He died a happy man.

He now appeared before heaven's gates. God, in the guise of an old, white-bearded man, came out to greet him. "Welcome," he said, "you've been a good man. Please come into the joys of heaven." But as the man was about to enter through the pearly gates, God said, "Please, you must let the soil go." "Never!" cried the old man, stepping back. "Never!" And so God sadly departed, leaving the old man outside the pearly gates.

A few eons went by and God came out again, this time in the guise of an old friend, an old drinking crony. They had a few drinks, told some stories, and then God said, "All right, time to enter heaven, friend. Let's go." And they started for the pearly gates. And once more God requested that the old man let go of his soil, and once more the old man refused.

More eons rolled by. God came out once more, this time in the guise of the old man's delightful and playful granddaughter. "Oh, granddaddy," she said, "you're so wonderful and we all miss you. Please come inside with me." The old man nodded as she helped him up, for by this time he had grown very old indeed and very arthritic. In fact, so arthritic was he that he had to prop up the right hand holding Crete's soil with his left hand.

They moved toward the pearly gates, and at this point his strength quite gave out. His gnarled fingers would no longer stay clenched, with the result that the soil sifted out between them until his hand was empty. Empty-handed, he entered heaven. The first thing he saw was his beloved island.

Bartimaeus, who let go and saw, would appreciate that story. Remember: Bartimaeus is a beggar with no resources of his own, no gift to give in return. The only thing he has to present to Jesus is his need. The gospel suggests that maybe this is just the way we too must be. Perhaps we should stop bargaining with Jesus and just offer him our need. No bribes, no false promises, no silly vows; just our emptiness, our need. Abandonment, as we saw in chapter six, is the way to overcome fear, and overcoming fear is the way to sight. That is the key to the dynamics of seeing.

The second time around

A very overweight man decided that it was time to shed a few pounds. He went on a diet and took it seriously. He even changed his usual driving route on the way to the office precisely in order to avoid passing his favorite bakery.

One morning, however, he arrived at the office carrying a large, sugar-coated, calorie-loaded coffee cake. For this he was roundly chided by his colleagues, but he only smiled, shrugged his shoulders and said, "What could I do? This is a very special cake. What happened is that, by force of habit, I accidentally drove by the bakery this morning and there in the window were trays full of the most scrumptious goodies. Well, I felt this was no accident that I happened to pass by this way, so I prayed, 'Lord, if you really want me to have one of those delicious coffee cakes, let me find a parking space right in front of the bakery.' And sure enough, on the ninth time around the block, there it was!"

Well, let's skip the ninth time around here. But on the other hand, let's talk about the second time around. Suppose we had a second time around, another chance to live our lives: what would we change and what would we not? Or, in terms of our theme, what would we see differently if in fact we were given sight? If we had the chance to have Bartimaeus' cry come true: "Lord, I want to see!" What would we want to see? I suggest it would be these four things:

First, we would want to see what our hearts have always told us, that the only thing in life that matters is our relationships with other people. How did we ever allow the blindness of individualism and consumerism to get in the way of that? Careers, jobs, entertainment, accumulation—all of us have sacrificed our relationships much too much in pursuit of these hollow gods. We don't eat meals together, don't have time for one another. We no longer see the other who stands right next to us.

Jay Leno has gained fame for his sharp wit. But in his recent book, *Leading with My Chin*, Jay shows a warmer side to his personality when he writes about his parents, who are now dead. Jay fondly recalls a certain incident from high school. He had finally saved up enough money to buy a raggedy, old pickup truck, and it became the apple of his eye. He spent long hours working on his new prized possession. His parents, noting his pride in the vehicle, bought brand-new upholstery for it. They must have known how disappointed Jay was the day he accidentally broke a window in the truck. He couldn't afford to get it fixed at the moment.

One day, Jay was sitting in class when it began raining heavily. He could see his truck out in the parking lot, and he knew that his upholstery was getting doused. Imagine Jay's surprise when his parents' car came flying into the school parking lot. Jay's mother and father came running out with a big piece of plastic, which they used to cover the broken window of the truck. As Jay watched them, he realized that they had left work and gone out to buy the plastic as soon as the rain began. And they had come speeding out to the school to cover their son's truck, because they knew it would be important to him. And Jay Leno reports that he sat there in his high school class and cried.

The second time around, would we see life and relationships differently? Would our memories be different? Relationships are what life is all about. They should come first. Do we see that? Can we see it now?

Second, this time around we would see the overlooked—you know, the needy, the poor, the troubled, the nonpersons who suffer because they feel they don't count in anyone's eyes.

Max DePree, a well-known guru of corporate leadership, tells of being at a hotel in Phoenix when his left knee gave out and he was unable to walk. So he was forced for a while to use a wheelchair. The next morning he and his wife Esther went to breakfast with her pushing him in his wheelchair. They had eaten several meals there before and each time the hostess had looked at DePree and politely asked the same question, "How many?"

But not this morning. She looked past him to Esther and said politely, "How many?" Then she led them to the dining room, and she turned again to Esther and asked, "Would he like to sit at the window?" Suddenly Max DePree realized that it was as if he, Max DePree, had disappeared. In a twinkling of an eye, this polite, well-meaning young woman had stripped him of identity and position. It made DePree realize that to be oppressed is wrong, but to be overlooked may be even worse.

Whom have we overlooked? Surely, the overlooked include the poor and needy. But perhaps we are overlooking something within ourselves. There are twelve-step programs for many problems these days: gambling, alcohol, narcotics, and sex addictions, to name a few. But the principle is the same in all these groups. One must first admit to having a problem before he or she is able to get on the road to recovery. How can we recover from something which we won't admit is a problem? No, we must first see the blind spots in our lives in order to seek recovery.

My next question is: what have we overlooked? In his book, *Say Yes to Life*, Rabbi Sidney Greenberg notes that when the Mona Lisa was stolen from the Louvre in Paris in 1911 and was missing for two years, more people went to stare at the blank space in the museum than had gone to look at the masterpiece in the twelve previous years it had hung there unmolested. Greenberg says this intriguing bit of information tells us something important about ourselves:

> It points to our all-too-human tendency to fail to take adequate note of precious things while we have them. But let one of them be taken from us and we become painfully aware of the "blank space" in our lives, and our attention is sharply focused on that "blank space."
>
> The walls of our lives are crowded with Mona Lisas, but we are unmindful of them. Countless blessings attend us daily and we are so insensitive to them. The more often and the more regularly we receive any blessing, the less likely we are to be aware of it. What is constantly granted is easily taken for granted..... [It was Helen Keller who wrote these words]: "I have often thought that it would be a blessing if each human being were stricken blind and deaf for a few days at some time during his adult life. Darkness would make him more appreciative of sight; silence would teach him the joys of sound."

Too often, it takes a serious threat to our blessings to make us aware of them. The newspapers reported a touching story of a mother who was taking her young son to Salt Lake City on a melancholy mission. The boy had lost the sight of one eye several years before, and in the intervening years doctors had tried valiantly to save his remaining eye. Now they had come to the reluctant conclusion that the eye could not be saved. Before the darkness set in, his mother wanted the boy to have a fond, lingering look at the majestic mountains of Utah so that he could take that splendid image with him into the sightless future. Can we read such a story without becoming acutely aware of the myriad Mona Lisas that constantly beckon to us and that we persistently overlook?

Whom and what have we overlooked that this time around we should see? "Lord, I want to see!"

The third thing we would want to see this time around is the love of God for us. In that, we would learn to discern the hints of God's divine care. A lawyer I know was browsing in a bookstore, where he picked up the biography of Jack Kerouac and discovered, to his surprise, that Kerouac was deeply moved by the story of St. Thérèse of Lisieux and her "shower of roses." Older Catholics might remember that St. Thérèse was a cloistered Carmelite nun of the last century and is known in popular piety as "The Little Flower." In her spiritual journal, Thérèse promised she would spend her heaven doing good on earth. She described this in a figure of speech by saying she would send a shower of roses to those who asked her help.

Well, the lawyer thought, surely, there is the intercession of the saints and the shower of roses is a nice figure of speech—or is it only that? The lawyer added, sometimes things happen that you can't explain, as he told this story:

> I remember during World War II that my father, a naval surgeon, was thought to have been a casualty during an amphibious landing in the Pacific. My mother gathered the family together and began a novena to St. Thérèse. The very next day, the doorbell rang and there stood a neighbor—it was winter, 1944—with a dozen long-stemmed roses. He hadn't heard that my father was missing, he knew nothing of our prayers, he just thought our family would like the flowers.
>
> Were the roses just a coincidence? Was the neighbor's gift a

fluke? My mother, who shortly afterwards learned that my father was alive, believed till the end of her days that the bouquet of roses did not happen by chance. It was, as she always described it, a sign. Are these things flukes or are these things brief glimpses behind the curtain of existence reminding us that we are awaited, that we are loved?

Would we see God's love for us, learn to better recognize the divine hints, more astutely the next time around?

Fourth and finally, we would see in one another—even the most despicable, the most disreputable—the image of God. In *Conjectures of a Guilty Bystander*, Thomas Merton recounts this now-famous revelation which occurred one day in Louisville, Kentucky. He was standing on the corner of Walnut and Fourth Streets, the busiest intersection in the shopping area, when he suddenly became aware that he loved all the people bustling about. He had a terrific insight of being connected to all of them through God. Beneath it all, Merton saw that they were all stamped with the image of God. He saw the divine spark beneath all the clutter, disfigurement, and sin. He saw the secret depth of each one, "where neither sin nor desire nor self-knowledge can reach," the point where we belong to God. He discovered that he was no longer a monk separated from them by life or place or calling. He was one with the whole human splendor whose core was God.

Merton was stunned and wrote: "There is no way of telling people that they are all walking around like the sun."

As we have mentioned before, spiritual blindness has always been a theme of the spiritual masters, and the gospels are as much about this as anything else. Bartimaeus' cry, "I want to see!" is the cry—must be the cry—of any person serious about the spiritual life, serious about being a disciple, about being truly human. I suggest that you take the story of Bartimaeus to heart; put yourself in his place and cry out to Jesus passing by: "I want to see!"

And if the Master asks, "What do you want to see?" you must answer: "I want to see the value and primacy of relationships. I want to see the people—the obnoxious, the poor, the disadvantaged—that

I normally overlook, along with my own faults and spiritual needs. I want to see much more readily the signs of your love for me, the little 'coincidences' in life that give hints of your presence. Finally, I want to see your image in everyone." In the spiritual life, seeing is not believing: rather, believing is seeing.

But such sight and insight only come after a time: they are the fruits of prayer and meditation. Thomas Merton's insight came only after years of prayer and spiritual discipline. His step into monasticism and away from the world was but preparation for eventually stepping back into the world with greater insight and compassion. Similarly, our steps away from the world and into prayer, retreats, and meditation are indispensable if we want to step back with new insight.

If we do not see with the eyes of Christ, perhaps it is because we have not spent time with him. This is why so many parish projects fail, so many well-intentioned programs falter. This is why so many pastoral ministers burn out. People no longer know why they do what they do: there is no spiritual foundation. They are no longer connected to the original vision. Consequently, their desire to do good wears down or becomes depleted; their efforts are no longer life-giving.

Sight and mission

Another great truism of the spiritual life is that our insights, our "visions," are never for the sake of themselves. They are inexorably linked to mission. In other words, seeing is never an end in itself, for we are given to see in order that others might see. Moses' experience with the burning bush occurs for the sake of his people's liberation. Isaiah is given a rapturous vision of God's glory only that he might hear the divine voice ask: "Whom shall I send?" Paul is given a terrifying vision of the Christ he was persecuting in order that he might be sent forth to the Gentiles. Peter sees Jesus as Messiah and is given the task of grounding the other apostles.

So the formula is this: prayer, insight, mission. Nowhere is this better revealed than in the gospel of Matthew (25:34–46): "Then the king will say to those at his right hand, 'Come, you that are blessed by my Father, inherit the kingdom prepared for you from the foundation of the world; for I was hungry and you gave me food....'"

And Joanne Zamorski of Lexington, surprised to be there, will speak and ask, "When did I ever see you hungry and feed you?" And Jesus will answer: "As long as you did it for Cecilia Bender, you did it for me." And Cecilia Bender, hearing her name, will step forward to speak: "I was born mentally retarded. And as I grew to be an adult, I had less and less place in the normal world: no friends, no job, no family. I was left a vegetable. And so I would have remained if Joanne Zamorski had not started Joanne's Deli. It was more than a place to eat. It was a place where people like me could find work. I found there a sense of my own worth. I was the sandwich maker there, and I was able to buy my own car and to learn to drive to work each day. Thanks, Joanne."

"Come, you that are blessed by my Father...for I was thirsty and you gave me something to drink...."

And Fr. Bob from Arizona will ask, "When did I see you thirsty?" And Jesus will answer, "As long as you did it for Arlene Williams, you did it for me." And a woman with a bright smile on her face will step forward. "For years I was a secret and compulsive drinker," she will say. "One Sunday morning at church we had a young visiting priest who began his homily with the words, 'I am Fr. Bob, and I am an alcoholic.' He told how he had come to depend on alcohol. After Mass I went home—and got as drunk as I had ever been. Later I came back and talked to Fr. Bob. He offered me a drink—coffee—and he offered me the understanding support I needed to begin the difficult journey to sobriety. It saved my marriage, certainly."

"Come, you that are blessed by my Father...for I was a stranger and you welcomed me...."

And Carl Simone of Seattle will ask, "But when did I welcome you, see you, a stranger?" And Jesus will answer, "When you did it for Steve Carroll, it was for me." And Steve will be there to tell his story. "On July 16, 1986, I was standing on the Raritan Bridge looking down into the dark, swirling water 180 feet below. Despondent over business losses I was about to jump—when a police officer came along. He talked me down gently and promised me help. In time and with professional counseling, I learned to handle my tensions and stresses better. That officer who saved my life was Carl Simone here. In his years with the police department he has talked hundreds of persons out of suicide. For my life, thanks, Carl."

"I was naked and you gave me clothing...."

And Dorothy Groll from Scarborough, Maine, will ask, "But when?" And Charlie Kelly will move beside her and take her hand. "I suffered from cerebral palsy," he will say. "I walked like a drunken man and slurred my speech. My parents had always been very protective. But after they died I was very much alone and afraid; yet I wanted some freedom. I found a job and moved into my own apartment, one designed for the handicapped. Dorothy Groll was seventy-three, and then a widow. She lived across the hall. Every day she came in and cooked for me and did my laundry and shaved me and, yes, dressed me. Without her help it would have taken me two hours to put on my clothes. Thanks, Dot." And he will kiss Dorothy standing there at his side.

"I was sick and you took care of me...."

Dr. Charles Hayne of Denver, Colorado will respond, "But I never treated you." And Jesus will answer, "Never?" And Bill Perdoni will speak up. "I lost my sight in a machine shop accident. For twenty-three years I saw nothing. When I was sixty-five, Dr. Hayne told me he thought a corneal transplant would partially restore my vision. He operated and when I opened my eyes, I could see again. It was a more wonderful and beautiful world than I had remembered—the rivers, the trees, the snow. Thanks, Doc."

"I was in prison and you visited me...."

And this group will be very few in number. But Pat Reynolds will be standing next to Bob Irwin who at one time was simply referred to as N 130539 at the state prison in Trenton, New Jersey, where he was serving a sentence for first-degree murder. "Over the years," Bob will say, "Pat must have corresponded with hundreds of prisoners. These letters forged real friendships that helped to combat the loneliness which in prison can turn sanity into insanity. She helped me to see myself as a name, not a number. A person, not a reject. Thank you, dear friend."

Then the king will say to those on his left, "Out of my sight, you condemned!" (Notice the words: "out of my sight.") "I can see nothing of good in you for you saw nothing good in me. For I was hungry and you gave me no food, thirsty and you did not give me a drink...." And those on the left will be heard muttering as they depart: "It's not fair. I never saw you. Anyway, all I needed was one more day. I had already made plans to help out at the soup kitchen—tomorrow."

Those on the left could not see because they did not step away to pray. Not seeing, they did not act, did not become missionaries. Not being missionaries, they did not feed or clothe or visit Jesus, the image of God.

Amen

I will close this chapter, not surprisingly, with a story and a prayer. The story comes from Fred Craddock, a well-known minister and preacher. He tells about an experience he had one day with a man in a restaurant:

> "You a preacher?" the man asked.
>
> Somewhat embarrassed, Fred said, "Yes."
>
> The man pulled a chair up to Fred's table. "Preacher, I'll tell you a story. There was once a little boy who grew up sad. Life was tough because my mama had me but she had never been married. Do you know how a small Tennessee town treats people like that? Do you know the words they use to name kids that don't have no father?
>
> "Well, we never went to church, nobody asked us. But for some reason or other, we went to church one night when they was having a revival. They had a big, tall preacher visiting to do the revival, and he was all dressed in black. He had a thunderous voice that shook the little church.
>
> "We sat toward the back, Mama and me. Well, that preacher got to preaching, about what I don't know, stalking up and down the aisle of that little church preaching. It was something. After the service, we were slipping out the back door when I felt that big preacher's hand on my shoulder. I was scared. He looked way down at me, looked me in the eye and says, 'Boy, who's your Daddy?'

"I didn't have no Daddy. That's what I told him in a trembling voice, 'I ain't got no Daddy.'

"'Oh yes, you do,' boomed that big preacher. "You're a child of the Kingdom, you have been bought with a price, you are a child of the King!'

"I was never the same after that. Preacher, for God's sake, preach that." The man pulled his chair away from the table. He extended his hand and introduced himself. Craddock said the name rang a bell. He was a legendary former governor of the state of Tennessee.

So, child of the king, pray this prayer from the great Cardinal Newman:

> God has created me to do him some definite service.
> He has committed some work to me
> which he has not committed to another.
> I have my mission.
> I may never know it in this life,
> but I shall be told it in the next.
> I am a link in a chain,
> a bond of connection between persons.
> He has not created me for naught;
> I shall do good—I shall do his work;
> I shall be an angel of peace,
> a preacher of truth in my own place while not intending it
> if I do but keep his commandments.
> Therefore I will trust him.
> Whatever I am, I can never be thrown away.
> If I am in sickness, my sickness may serve him;
> in perplexity, my perplexity may serve him.
> If I am in sorrow, my sorrow may serve him.
> He does nothing in vain.
> He knows what he is about.
> He may take away my friends,
> He may throw me among strangers,
> He may make me feel desolate,

make my spirits sink,
hide my future from me—still
He knows what he is about.

Questions for reflection

1. "Christianity is a way of seeing." Do I see with the eyes of Christ? Or, like Bartimaeus, am I too caught up in my pain to see Jesus standing nearby?

2. What is the cloak which I hold on to, my security blanket? What would it take for me to learn to let go?

3. What would I like to see the second time around?

4. Who are the overlooked in our society who have not escaped my vision? How do I minister to them?

5. Where do I most see hints of the divine in my life? this world?

6. According to Jesus, the spiritual and corporal works of mercy are still sound criteria for salvation. How do they fit into my life? Do I see them as viable today?

SIXTEEN

DIRECTOR! DIRECTOR!

Ecology & the Spirit

In 1939, Victor Fleming, the director of such famed movies such as *Treasure Island, Captains Courageous, Red Dust,* and *Dr. Jekyll and Mr. Hyde* released two of America's all time best-loved movies, *Gone With the Wind* and *The Wizard of Oz.* The former was an instant box office hit, while the latter was a box office disappointment that failed to recoup its costs until 1956, when it was shown on television.

Curiously, Fleming, who died in 1949, has never received the honor he deserved although such a luminary as producer Arthur Freed said of him that he "was a poet, probably one of the great unsung men of this business." What makes a director like Victor Fleming great is his poetic sense of the large view, the sense of the wide vision, of pulling together the various elements into a harmonious whole. We might call it a sense of poetic ecology, a sensitivity to the connectedness of everything. You can't have a good scene with bad lighting. You can't have clear dialogue with overhead noise. You can't have a good storyline with too many unrelated subplots. And you can't have a good movie with actors who are interested only in their own parts and have no sense of the wider conversation.

The same truth applies to spirituality: you cannot have a sound spirituality apart from the whole of creation. Spiritual ecology, a sense of interconnectedness with the planet, is vital to the inner life. Yet unfortunately, it has, in large part, been lost in our society today.

People have been disconnected from nature, the universe, the larger picture. As a result, we suffer a terrible unease because we are so cut off from nature. We have lost the intimate connection with the mysterious movements of life, with the sacred world. Immersed as we are in an artificial world, with its fast pace and unrelenting rape of the planet, we feel a sense of loss, the sense that a real spiritual life is hard to come by.

A group of scientists from the world over met in Buenos Aires in November of 1998, to soberly contemplate the reality that this planet is being threatened by severe climate changes. They know the cause: it's no mystery. These climate changes are caused by the effects of industrialization as well as by the proliferation of internal combustion engines (such as those in cars), which release gases into the atmosphere that raise global temperatures and reduce moisture. The consequences are the extreme weather patterns we are experiencing all over the world. Think of the severe storms in Central America, where thousands of lives are lost and property damage runs into the billions. Note the multiplication of monsoons, the rising sea levels which threaten the seventy percent of the world's population who live near water. These conditions, perhaps alarming to us now, will become quite intolerable by the time our grandchildren are grown.

This wanton abuse of the planet is not only self-destructive but it also reveals a market view of the universe: that the universe is there to be exploited. We take. It gives. Except, as the old saw goes, mother nature never forgets. Only a sense of respect rooted in mystery can change our attitude toward our planet from one of exploitation to one of cooperative reverence. And this, basically, is a spiritual stance.

Awash in deafening soundtracks and blinking lights, seduced by lottery tickets that promise instant wealth without work, daily distracted by an array of treasures from shiny cars to lavish cruises in the Caribbean, we can in fact manage to gloss over the damage we do to the planet and to our lives. All of our modern day "toys" are supposed to enrich our lives, make us feel good about ourselves. But in the end, all that we really feel is spiritual emptiness. All our stuff is a barrier to true happiness; every toy has been bought at the expense of the planet and at the expense of a genuine spiritual journey. Rich Heffern puts it well in his book, *Daybreak Within*:

> What surely will be judged the great sin of our age—the systematic destruction of the natural world—is also the step-by-step obliteration of the cradle that births our sense of wonder and ultimately the thoughtless massacre of our religious imagination and sensibility. Abysmally disconnected from the sacredness that is in the world, we make poor decisions, we blunder into irreversible mistakes. The current alarm and debate over the drastic climate change predicted as a result of global warming or the destructive hole in the protective ozone layer of our upper atmosphere are good examples. We overheat the planet and lacerate its skin. The rain forests, the very lungs of the world, disappear in a huge holocaust of greed. In our discontinuum kitchen, we squander the heritage that should be passed on intact to our young. Is it any wonder our young are deeply troubled?

Heffern continues:

> "Because we are stuck in this view of the universe as a lifeless machine," said Fr. Diarmuid O'Murchu in a *Praying* interview, "we feel a deep sense of cosmic homelessness. The tragedy and scandal here are that this homelessness alienates us not only from the vibrant, creative universe we live in, but even from our own most intimate inner life, from our true self."
>
> Fr. O'Murchu points out that "the only discipline now that recognizes and explores this connection between cosmic homelessness and our inner desolation is one that is quite new.... A lot of mental illness and the huge amount of stresses we suffer as humans are because of what we are doing to the planet, because of the ongoing destruction of the environment. Until we begin a new relationship with the cosmos around us, we can't know how to relate meaningfully to anything, especially to our own innermost being. Without this meaningful relationship between humans and the earth, the planet suffers profoundly and so do we suffer grievously, both physically and in

our psyches as well."

The spiritual journey encompasses all of creation. It is no accident that the Yellow Brick Road traverses gardens, forests, glens, and meadows. The journey simply would not work taken down an asphalt pavement lined by concrete canyons and belching cars. That is why, when Fr. Thomas Berry was once asked about the most important quality in the spiritual life, he shot back with one word: "Enchantment." (This recalls Thomas Moore's comment in chapter six, page 84.) In the remarks that follow, therefore, which are more didactic and pedantic than those in the previous chapters (but hang in there, dear reader), let us explore some ways that enchantment has been subverted, thereby affecting our spiritual journey.

The mechanical body

First, some heavy stuff. As you may be aware, it is commonplace today for genetic engineering to rearrange the genes of vegetables and plants, such as the potato. These "biotech foods" have come about as cultivated lands surrender to housing developments, and the growing food industry comes more and more into the hands of chemical corporations. Due to genetic manipulation, food production has increased dramatically to feed a growing population.

We are still not sure of what all this will mean to the planet as the mutant plants and mutant insects of genetic engineering escape into the atmosphere and into our body systems. As a result of genetic manipulation, we have already inadvertently produced dangerous microbes that are totally resistant to any antibiotic we have. But it is the direct manipulation of the human person that is our concern here.

Recently, scientists have combined human and animal (a cow) genes: where is this research going? Other scientists are hot in pursuit of human cloning, which raises a host of legal, moral, and ethical questions. Cosmetic surgery, increasingly popular not only with adults but with teenagers, routinely rearranges the body. Body parts are for sale as are human embryos. This unprecedented advance in human genetic engineering will be the defining issue of the next century. For such engineering is giving us the power to literally remake ourselves, to retool our bodies and minds as we more and more uncover the blueprints of our biology.

In his book, *The Biotech Century*, author Jeremy Rifkin reminds us that the highly sophisticated computer has now fused with genetics. The result of the merging of this technology is that genes are fast becoming a "commodity," a genuine raw resource which will be bartered very much as an earlier age bought and sold soy beans, precious metals, and oil. Many of the giant corporations, such as Monsanto, DuPont, Novatis, and First Chemical, have sold off their chemical divisions in order to concentrate solely on the manufacture and sale of genetic material.

Rifkin reports another shocking development, unknown to most people: the U.S. Patent Office now allows genes to be patented. It must be noted that this policy is in sharp contrast to the Patent Office's heretofore sensible policy that no one could patent a discovery of nature; for example, one can patent a process for obtaining, say, oxygen, but one cannot patent the isolated oxygen itself because it is a natural form of nature. Yet, as Rifkin reveals to us, the Patent Office has allowed these major chemical companies to patent genes and chromosomes. And this includes human genes. All hundred thousand genes of the human person will soon be identified—in another five years, at most—through the efforts of the Genome Project. Then, almost every one of these human genes will be the "property" of one of these companies. Major corporate companies are already scouting the planet for rare and desirable genes in animals and human beings, and applying for patents on them.

It is not hard to see that all this patenting gives them, ultimately, control over the blueprints for human life. For example, there is a company called PPL which has actually applied for a patent on the process of cloning and for the intellectual property rights to all cloned animals. But the patent request does not stop there. The company has also applied for a patent on all human cloned embryos as the invention of Dr. Wilmont, a principal in PPL, who is also the man who first cloned a sheep and is now involved in human embryo cloning. Actually, you can't patent a full human being since the Constitution forbids that as a form of slavery; but you can obtain a patent on all the individual parts of a human being—the genes, the chromosomes, the cell life, the organs, the tissue, and even embryos, since the law does not consider them human beings until birth.

It is easy to see that all this eventually undermines the intrinsic value of human life and reduces it to a utility, a commodity to be bought and sold in the marketplace. It is also easy to see that eugenics cannot be far behind, since in today's climate the motto is "you are your genes." Therefore, to readjust deviance, bad behavior, and so on, readjust the genes.

It won't be long before prospective parents can preview the genes of a desired baby. They will literally be able to look into their child's biological future and screen out any terrible disease or disability they see there. And there is a powerful argument for rearranging the genes that cause horrible and crippling mental and physical disease. This is called therapeutic correction. Most people would understandably redo the genetic makeup of their babies if they could pre-empt such problems. But the issue becomes more problematic in a heavily conditioned and compulsive consumer society.

In a market society such as ours, therapeutic correction may give way to enhancement correction, or "enhancement somatic engineering." This process would enable those who so desire to request a child be "corrected" to match the parents' ideal: perhaps male, or blue eyes, or blond hair, or an IQ of 175, or some other "perfect" combination. Yet once we see our children as the ultimate shopping experience, once we become consumers with the ability to design our own children, where will it stop? What will become of the "mistakes," the little boy or girl who did not quite come out as anticipated?

Power over life

All this reflects a basically manipulative philosophy of the world. In an article titled "Playing God," James J. Walter tells us:

> Daniel Callahan has argued that one of the most influential models of nature that operates in contemporary society is the power-plasticity model. In this view, material nature possesses no inherent value, and it is viewed as independent of and even

alien to humans and their purposes. All material reality is simply plastic to be used, dominated, and ultimately shaped by human freedom. Thus, the fundamental purpose of the entire physical universe, including human biological nature, is to serve human purposes. What is truly human and valuable are self-mastery, self-development, and self-expression through the exercise of freedom. The body is subordinated to the spiritual aspect of humanity, and humans view themselves as possessing an unrestricted right to dominate and shape not only the body but also its future genetic heritage.

The view of nature at the opposite extreme is the sacral-symbiotic model in which material nature is viewed as created by God and thus considered as sacred. As created and originally ordered by God, human biological nature is static and normative in this understanding, and the laws inherent in it must be respected. We are not masters over nature but stewards who must live in harmony and balance with our material nature. Biological nature remains our teacher that shows us how to live within the boundaries established by God at creation. Since physical nature is considered sacrosanct and inviolate, any permanent alteration of the human genetic code, even to cure a serious genetic disease, would probably be morally prohibited.

Sorry to take this quick academic trip into "the brave new world," as Aldous Huxley might put it; but these words serve our purpose here. Much to the harm of a spiritual outlook, we are constantly conditioned to view ourselves and nature as manipulative, exploitative, and salable commodities. As corporations, driven by a profit motive, gain ownership of life's blueprints, we become more and more detached from any sense of mystery. If all is ultimately manipulatable and all is marketable, we become more and more detached from any sense of the sacred, more deaf to the "rumors of angels" behind what we perceive. Our spiritual journey is dead-ended.

Sometimes I suspect that some parents feel like aliens, people in exile, strangers in a strange land—all old motifs in Israel's history as they struggled for identity during the Babylonian captivity or the Roman occupation. Immigrants to our country often lament the loss of cultural heritage in their children. As one lady from Pakistan said, "You try to teach your children the language of the old country, but they refuse to learn. They adopt the slang, the dress, the customs of the dominant culture and, sadly, you see you have lost them." It's an old story for parents with strong religious values. Try as they may, they can't save their children from an all-pervasive secular culture.

We see children being manipulated into consuming units at earlier and earlier ages. Television, web sites, and adult themes in movies and music, coupled with dual-career parents who have given their children more choices than ever, have moved high consumption downward into young lives. This trend, along with the rising affluence of Americans, appeals to the marketers who routinely speak of the rich, lucrative market of eight and nine year olds.

Currently, chain stores are rapidly expanding to accommodate the six- to twelve-year-old market. And why not? The *Wall Street Journal* reported on a study which found that the "aggregate spending by or on behalf of children ages four to twelve has roughly doubled every decade in the 1960s, 1970s, and 1980s. It has tripled so far in the 1990s to more than $24 billion last year." The six to twelve year olds are not people anymore: they are $24 billion.

The point in citing these statistics is that more and more, the marketplace sees the child as a commodity, a consuming unit with tremendous disposable income to be tapped. The result is that, through the efforts of a highly sophisticated media, children are taught to value themselves by their possessions, their clothes, their looks, and their personality (as opposed to character).

Worse, the ongoing, never-ending consumption and one-upmanship present in our world leaves little time to acquire a sense of the sacred, little time to develop an interior life. Mystery is swallowed up by materialism, which is fed at the expense of the earth's resources and the cheap labor of foreign sweatshops that employ underpaid women and children in squalid conditions. The immediate legacy of the cult of consumption promoted to the children is short-term satisfaction and a long-term damaged planet. As Fr. Richard Rohr puts it:

"What sense does it make to be a healthy person living on a damaged Earth?"

We have succeeded in trivializing everything. We suck the mystery out of everything and are therefore no longer able to sense the mystery all around us. In a society where everything is for sale, from wombs to politicians; where we pay ballplayers one hundred million dollars while our schools deteriorate and we underpay our teachers; it is hard to come by a sense of the sacred and to perceive the mystery in everyday life and in nature. In this atmosphere of consumerism, it is hard to travel the spiritual journey with perseverance. What can we do? Fr. Ed Hayes puts it succinctly: "The challenge of the saints of the twenty-first century is to begin to comprehend the sacred in the ten thousand things of our world."

So how do we begin?

First, we begin by celebrating the liturgy and bringing our children to church. We show them the statues, the holy water font, the windows. We help them trace the sign of the cross on themselves. We introduce them to the Christmas crib and the cross draped with purple fabric during Lent. As distracted as children may be at Mass, we take them nonetheless for the sense of community, to see significant people in their lives praying together, to catch the rhythms of song and worship. We let them bring up the gifts with the family. Simply put, we introduce them to mystery and a faith community that exists beyond themselves.

Next, we honor the domestic church within our homes. This is done with rituals, celebrations, and festivities, and by regularly using the symbols of the liturgical seasons, such as the Advent wreath, Christmas crèche, and Easter lilies. Encourage Catholic reading in the home, from the Bible through the lives of the saints. Help the children sense the divine in the daily exchanges of human life, to know that there is really no separation between the secular and the sacred but that, if you look hard enough, there is mystery all around.

Teach them a concern for others. For example, place an empty coffee can on the kitchen table so the family can put its loose change there to be given to the poor. And here's a real challenge: learn and practice the "hi five" in your family. This means that every fifth object

someone might buy—whether a CD or videotape or pair of jeans—
or every fifth time you would go out to the movies or to dinner, you
take the money that would be used for that fifth object or excursion
and give it to charity.

As a family, go to a poor section of your town or a town nearby. Let
the children see that not everyone has their lifestyle. Encourage vol-
unteerism and going on retreats, especially to places of beauty and
peace where everyone can get in touch with nature once more. Give
your family an appreciation for sacred ecology.

Moments of beauty and wonder

Let's return to this theme of sacred ecology as a necessity for the success of the spiritual journey. Here is a longish but good-to-contem-
plate quote from Daniel O'Leary's book, *Passion for the Possible*:

> You and I are growing into God, as the mystics put it. In fact all
> of creation is already sacred, and reveals something of the glory
> and splendor of God. That is why we say that the event of incar-
> nation has ended all dualism. Heaven and earth are forever
> mysteriously intertwined since the Word became flesh. And
> deep in our own inner being the kingdom of God forms an
> intrinsic part of our true nature.
>
> The poets and artists are never tired of playing with this fas-
> cinating theme. Unlike many of the official teachers of religion,
> they have never lost the sense of wonder at the mystery of the
> indwelling of God in creation. For them, the smallest particle of
> creation becomes a window on God's beauty. Their intense
> energy is spent on revealing "the dearest freshness that lives
> deep down in things." They see "his blood upon the rose and in
> the stars the glory of his eyes." Like "flaming from shook foil,"
> God's splendor radiates from all creatures for those who stay
> blessed with the original vision of childhood. The artist and the
> mystic use images and symbols to catch the firefly Wonder
> beneath the seemingly superficial and ordinary. Once we
> become sensitive to the meaning of the birth, life, death, and
> resurrection of Jesus, then everything is changed. We see the

world differently. We finally get the message. The human holds
the key to God. "Salvation," as the Church Father said, "hinges
on the flesh." All things are made new. From now on, our vision
and our focus will be trained on discovering the God of sur-
prises hiding and playing at the heart of life.

[Teilhard de Chardin writes]: "Through every cleft, the
world we perceive floods us with riches—food for the body,
nourishment for the eyes, the harmony of sounds and fullness
of the heart, unknown phenomena and new truths—all these
treasures, all these stimuli, all these calls coming to us from the
four corners of the world, cross our consciousness at every
moment. What is their role within us? They will merge into the
most intimate life of our soul, and either develop it or poison
it." There is no dualism here. God is so intimately one with the
world. We are not healed from outside in. Grace is not something on top of, or part of, or added to nature. Unbelievably,
what we keep forgetting, or denying, or failing to understand is
that *nature itself is intrinsically graced from the beginning*. Because
of the revelation that happened at the incarnation, we can now
be certain that the kingdom of God is within, that the Holy
Spirit is at work and play in our inmost being, that we look for
God not "out there" anymore, but waiting to be discovered in
our deepest self.

Even a partial awareness of this unbelievable mystery of
divine surrender to our hearts brings a challenging responsibility to the way we live. Our style of life is profoundly affected
by our belief that God somehow needs us to continually keep
co-creating the world with him. We begin to realize that the
kingdom of God is first built by us in each others' hearts. Our
worldview is immediately and radically altered. Our relationship
to ourselves, to each other, to the world, and to God is funda-
mentally impacted. In God we live and move and have our
being. Empowered by the Spirit, nothing is impossible anymore.

The Talmud teaches that on Judgment Day we shall be called into
account for all of the beautiful things we should have noticed but

didn't. In Alice Walker's book, *The Color Purple,* the character named Shug says that God must be pretty well fed up when we walk through a field of poppies and fail to notice the color purple. Nor do we have to think of beauty as revealed only in naturalistic settings.

In Ethan Canin's novel, *For Kings and Planets,* a sophisticated native Easterner named Marshall shows Orno, his fellow student who comes from Missouri, the sights of New York from a penthouse suite:

> "Come here," Marshall said. He stepped to the back wall of the greenhouse, where the windows looked onto a courtyard. "Look at that," he said. "The old man had it built this way. He's an old bastard, but he loves the same things I do." He pointed up to where a gap in the cornice let through the view of Central Park and across the dark river of treetops the lighted pinnacles of the Upper West Side. "How can you not love this?" he said. "Look at that. Look at those buildings. The Dakota. The San Remo. The Majestic. Gangsters lived in the Majestic. Meyer Lansky and Lucky Luciano." He took a drink. "They called the Dakota the Dakota because people said it might as well have been in the Dakotas. That's how far up town they thought it was. Now look at it.
>
> "Look at how they built things in those days." He pointed into the clear black night. "In Istanbul there's a huge water cistern below the city, filled with columns and arches that nobody ever sees. It's called Yerebatan Saray, the Sunken Palace. It was hidden for a thousand years and someone realized that the peasants caught fish through holes in their cellar floors. Isn't that exquisite?"
>
> "It is," said Orno. "That human beings would build such monuments. Like climbing Everest, if you ask me. The human urge to build. Sublime. To be close to God."

Orno is unknowingly underscoring what Karl Rahner once said, that if Christianity cannot recover its mystical dimensions, it has nothing to offer. We need a spirituality grounded in real living, grounded in a sense of the sacred here and now. This will take some doing. We were taught at one time to view the world with suspicion if not as a domain both outright dangerous and sinful. Salvation was to be found in fleeing the world. But, on the contrary, if the incarnation has taught us anything, it has taught us that the universe is God's darling; that it is saturated with the divine presence and therefore, God can be experienced in nature.

The Yellow Brick Road is replete with scary forests, wicked witches, and flying monkeys with kidnapping on their minds. Life can be hard and dangerous and terribly unfair. But there are also intimations of God, hints of the divine. Along the way, the Yellow Brick Road has technicolor scenes and landscapes. It also gives us engaging melodies, clever lyrics, and a stunning Emerald City at its end. Anyway, who ever said it was going to be easy?

And so we are at the end of our journey through this book. Perhaps it is well to end with some words from Rich Heffern, whom we have quoted before in this chapter. He writes:

No doubt every child's favorite parable about how enchantment works has been *The Wizard of Oz*. It's chockful with towering tornadoes, witches sporting striped socks, officious munchkins, fanged flying monkeys, and bad puns. With its open-eyed gaze at aspects of nature that don't dance in goody two shoes, some tots watch it stiff with fright. As every kid knows, the larger-than-life figures over the rainbow turn out to be the same people found at home, out in our backyard, in the neighborhood.

When you know down in your joints and up in your straw-filled head that you live in a sacred cosmos, well, the ordinary is always extraordinary. The way to the Emerald City is an adventure-filled enterprise that tests our courage, compassion, steadfastness, and wit—as good a definition of spirituality as any I've heard. Oz the Great and Powerful is revealed to be a bamboozling snake-oil salesman toying with smoke and mirrors. He's a mapmaker, not an explorer. Yet the quest is not in vain, for the real wizardry of Oz turns out to be the plain insight that our feet are shod with the magic of our heart's desire, always have been.

The ruby slippers are in the back of the closet, and the pearl of great price is down tangled in our pocket lint. Unless we become as little children, wide-eyed with healing enchantment, with the mystical dimension of our religious tradition, moving from a fearful life to a bold and generous one, crafting a heart down in the smithy of our soul, all the maps in the world will never get us back home. Unless we become immersed in the enchanting Mystery, we will never really know what humans are about—or for.

Questions for reflection

1. The canticle of St. Francis to Brother Sun and Sister Moon reminds us of our intimate connection to all of creation. Do I respect this relationship, or do I abuse creation for my own needs and purposes?

2. Do I reverence human life to the fullest, or am I caught up in the trend to commercialize and commodify life?

3. Do I celebrate the various feasts of the liturgical year, echoing the joy and love inherent in our Christian faith?

4. The Yellow Brick Road symbolizes the human journey toward God with its many opportunities, detours, and dangers. Using the guidelines in this book, where am I now on the journey?

5. Which areas in my spiritual life need the most help and attention at this time? What do I plan to do about this?

Also by William J. Bausch...

Breaking Trust
A Priest Looks at the Scandal of Sexual Abuse
In this searing and soul-searching book, Bill Bausch considers the current crisis of sexual abuse in the Catholic Church. He seeks out the facts, analyzes the current climate, and gauges the reactions of ordinary people in parishes. He is open and unbiased in his evaluations, respecting both the position of the Church and the feelings of Catholic people. A "question and answer" section considers some common questions that Catholics are asking today. 112 pp, $10.95 (X-68)

A World of Stories for Preachers and Teachers*
*and all who love stories that move and challenge
These 350+ tales from Fr. Bausch aim to nudge, provoke, and stimulate the reader and listener, to resonate with the human condition, as did the stories of Jesus. Includes such tales as "The Tin Box," a gentle parable about memories; "St. Alexander," the story about the charcoal burner who was made a bishop; and the "Ragman," a moving allegory of redemption. 544 pages, $29.95 (order B-92)

Brave New Church
From Turmoil to Trust
Fr. Bausch focuses on twelve challenges facing the Church today and offers responses that can move the Church to minister to parishioners of the twenty-first century. 312 pp, $16.95 (J-85)

Catholics in Crisis?
The Church Confronts Contemporary Challenges
In this book, Fr. Bausch addresses such movements as new age, fundamentalism, and "end-of-the-world mania." Here he examines both the negative and positive aspects of these movements and then goes on to show how a weakened church has difficulty meeting these challenges. In the last chapter Bausch makes practical suggestions on how to overcome these difficulties. 240 pages, $14.95 (order J-13)

Available at religious bookstores or from:

TWENTY-THIRD PUBLICATIONS
185 WILLOW STREET • PO BOX 180 • MYSTIC, CT 06355
TEL: 1-800-321-0411 • FAX: 1-800-572-0788
Bayard E-MAIL: ttpubs@aol.com • www.twentythirdpublications.com

Call for a free catalog